ASKING AROUND
Background to
the David Hare Trilogy

DAVID HARE

EDITED BY
LYN HAILL

faber and faber

in association with

First published in 1993 by
Faber and Faber Limited
3 Queen Square London WCIN 3AU

Photoset by Parker Typesetting Service, Leicester
Printed and bound in Great Britain by
Mackays of Chatham plc, Chatham, Kent

A CIP record for this book
is available from the British Library

ISBN 0-571-17063-3

4 6 8 10 9 7 5 3

CONTENTS

DAVID HARE was born in Sussex in 1947. In 1970 his first play *Slag* was performed at the Hampstead Theatre Club. In 1993 three of this plays *Racing Demon, Murmuring Judges* and *The Absence of War* were presented together in repertory at the Olivier Theatre in London. Since 1983, nine of his best-known plays, including *Plenty, The Secret Rapture, Skylight, The Judas Kiss, Amy's View* and *Via Dolorosa* have also been presented on Broadway.

We can claim to live under a system inherently more agreeable than any other I can personally think of . . . I do not find anything in the essential structure of our institutions or our law, or our sense of continuity with the past, which I would wish to alter.

Lord Chancellor Hailsham, 1983 Hamlyn Lecture

When everything about a people is for the time growing weak and ineffective, it begins to talk about efficiency. Vigorous organisms talk not about their processes, but about their aims.

G. K. Chesterton (1847–1936)

INTRODUCTION

Like most things, my trilogy of plays about the Church, the Law and the State happened by accident. In the summer of 1987, I set off to drive north towards York University, intending to visit the General Synod of the Church of England, with no other motive but curiosity. I had the vague suspicion that priests pretending to be politicians might present me with an entertaining spectacle. I was not even planning a play. After the first session, I detained a passing bishop and, wanting to be able to remember what he was then telling me about hell, I asked him if he would allow me to take a few notes.

The book you are now reading contains edited excerpts from the five years of interviews which followed. Over that period, I made it my practice to transcribe my notes each evening, while that day's conversations were still fresh in my mind. I have certainly not been tempted to include everyone I spoke to, nor have I set down everything they said. I have tried instead to edit their conversations into some sort of narrative, which, as you will see, takes us from the religious uncertainties of the modern Church of England, via assorted criminal processing plants like Clapham Police Station and Wormwood Scrubs, towards the high-tech, high-pressure hysteria of the 1992 General Election.

My purpose in talking to so many people was ostensibly to provide myself with the background I needed to write the three plays, all of which would be individually presented at the National Theatre, and which would finally be presented together on one day. But inevitably, as I went along, the research began to take on a life of its own, and I was moved to interview people I knew would be of little or no direct use to me as a writer of fiction, and to ask questions which I knew in advance would have no direct relevance to my final plays.

It is, I hope, not necessary to have seen or read *Racing Demon*, *Murmuring Judges* or *The Absence of War* to enjoy or understand the material this present book contains. More by instinct and personal interest than through working to any deliberate or organized plan, I found myself visiting prisons, churches, courts, police stations, television studios and even the Houses of Parliament, becoming a sort of friendly channel for people's own doubts about the work they did, and sometimes giving them the chance to describe the ways in which they feared respect for their various professions had declined. In some cases I have been given their permission to identify them by their real names. In others I have protected their anonymity by giving them a first name only, and a false one at that. Many things which people said to me privately could not, for obvious reasons, be publicly attributed.

I make no particular claims for the result. It is not, in the dreaded phrase, a snapshot of the country we live in. Nor is it systematic enough to be a thorough investigation into the Church, the Law and the State. Much more, *Asking Around* is one person's record of what it is like to listen to a variety of people talk unselfconsciously about their work. The special character of the conversations comes from the fact that, until I encounter the politicians who are the subject of the third section, I am meeting people who are unpractised in the art of giving formal interviews. Even then, the tone most people adopt while talking informally to a playwright is a little different from how they might speak to a professional journalist. That at least is my hope.

I cannot pretend that for me the experience of getting out of my study to travel the country and talk to so many people was anything but the purest pleasure. Anyone of my age who has spent the larger part of their adult life writing, even for the theatre, knows the dangers of spending so much time alone. It is not just that the writer begins to project his or her own misery and isolation on to the world at large and assume that other people suffer from neuroses which in fact are the writer's alone. But also sheer ignorance begins all too easily to take its toll. The world is not as it was when we last had a proper job in it. There is nothing better for a writer than to go out and be rebuked by reality.

That said, it is essential to stress at the very beginning of this book of research that the plays which flowed from it are, in so far as anything is, pure works of fiction. I am not a great fan of works of art whose chief aim is to imitate reality. I think the British cinema is chiefly debilitated by its insistence on stealing its stories from newspapers. I distrust faction, and I cannot see the point of plays and films which seek to reproduce how Christine Keeler and Gandhi once walked and talked. No film aiming to explore the psychology of, say, Richard Nixon can do justice to the boundless complexity of the man himself. A play in which an actor has to walk around pretending to be William Shakespeare is, in my opinion, doomed in advance.

At no point in the trilogy did I seek to put any of the people in this book in my plays. Although I would often spend months each time absorbing the details of the real-life world in which I planned to set my play, I was then never in any doubt that the smart thing for any writer who has done a great deal of research is at once to push that research to the back of their mind the moment they start to invent. However well-informed your preparation, a stage play does or does not work according to the intensity of the imagination you bring to it. Even if, as I hope, my characters were informed and enriched by all the time I had spent with their real-life counterparts, nevertheless I knew perfectly well that if they were to live on the stage, they had to find their own vitality as surely as if I had spoken to no one at all. I hardly need add that the situations into which I then projected them were not taken directly from life.

It is important that I make clear the primacy of this distinction in my mind between art and life, because although this book and my trilogy of plays do not have common characters or actions, it will be perfectly obvious to everyone that they do indeed have common themes. In each of the plays, although I have been writing about a particular institution, I have left it to the audience to draw parallels from their own lives. A specially delicious moment came when one actress in *Racing Demon* invited her bank manager to a performance in the hope that he would like the play enough to allow her a larger overdraft. He came away from this play about the Church asking how it was possible that the author knew so much about the inner workings of the Midland Bank. The Bishop of Southwark, he swore, was his area manager to the life.

4

I hardly need say that this was, for the author, a deeply satisfying reaction. All three plays are, unusually, set mainly in places
of work. In bad novels, people are just their families or their love
affairs. For page after page, the characters are dragged through a
version of the world in which the office or factory provides only a
backcloth to the primary business of their lives. Their more
important concerns – their personal relationships – are acted out
on a narrow strip at the front. But even in this current recession,
most of us still spend a fair deal of our time at work, and a fair
many of us in organizations not unlike those described in this
book.

A friend of mine remarked that it was my special good fortune
to have completed a trilogy about British institutions at precisely
that moment when British institutions were finally admitted to be
in a state of collapse. I, of course, would maintain that it was not
chance. A playwright above all other writers responds unknow-
ingly to the mood of the times. But, more than this, my intention
in the plays was never to theorize about the overall state of my
three institutions. It has been much more to portray the lives of
the people trying to survive in them. At a moment in our history
when Conservative governments have been trying to force dramatic changes on this country, I did feel some special sympathy for
those luckless people who were charged with the enforcement of
those changes, or, perhaps, with dealing with their consequences.

It would be impossible, however, for anyone reading the
material I have collected, whatever their political views, not to be
a little taken aback at how deep professional grievances do now
run in Britain. Very early on in my researches into the Church of
England, I was astonished to find a group of inner-city priests
who had virtually abandoned their aim of bringing souls to
Christ, but who were instead interpreting their religious mission
as social work, pure and simple. Although I myself had been
educated in a devout Christian school and was now moved to
write a play which sought to restore to the stage the ancient
subject of man's relationship with the gods, I found to my surprise that many good priests almost refused to discuss God with
me. They had ceased to believe that the divine could, in any

significant way, be separated from the social. They were quite clear-minded in seeing themselves as part of a society which had, to all intents and purposes, abandoned its responsibility to the poor. Although most of them made glancing references to government policy or to the failure of politicians to understand the conditions in which they worked, their primary interest was not in ideology, nor, even less, in allocating blame. They just wanted to bandage wounds. Into the vacuum created by society's indifference, they were pouring as much love and practical help as they could. To do this, they were working long days, and moreover on salaries considerably below those of social workers or of officials at the DHSS.

It was these unexpected encounters with serious men and women of God who had ceased to have much expectation of their seniors which impressed me early on and no doubt shaped the questions I subsequently asked. None the less, whatever my own preconceptions, it was startling to pass from interviewing priests to interviewing policemen and find that both groups were talking in similar terms.

Although the policemen I met were better paid than my inner-city vicars, and of course by instinct undoubtedly more conservative, nevertheless their disillusion with the irrelevance or antagonism of government was considerably more vocal and certainly more profound. Nothing had quite prepared me for the overt politicization of the police. Of all Thatcher's children, these were the least grateful. By throwing money at them, she had not bought their loyalty. On the contrary. She had only made them more cynical. I already knew from books I had read that policemen had been deeply marked by their experience of being asked to help destroy the miners' strike. Many, especially those from the miners' home towns, were genuinely shocked to find themselves attracting the vociferous hatred of people whom they had known from childhood to be decent and law-abiding. But I did not know until I went out in the squad cars myself that so many policemen, patrolling the hopeless housing estates or trying to keep order on the lawless streets, had developed so clear an analysis of their own role. In their view, they were being used.

The Conservative administrations of the eighties had gone hell for leather for economic policies which were crudely biased towards the rich. They had then turned to the police and blamed them for failing to cope with the huge social problems which government itself had created.

Meeting these two groups – the clergy and the police – made me realize how many people involved in public careers now saw their job as picking up the pieces. There was a common assumption among society's sergeant-majors that they had no chance of influencing policy. Nor had they any expectation that policy would be sane or relevant to their own day-to-day experiences. Their task was to stand in the firing line, mitigating policy's effects.

Everywhere I went I encountered professionals who believed that the government had ceased to listen to them. At one time, not knowing which way my trilogy would go, I flirted briefly with writing about education, and met with teachers who were unfakably hurt and bewildered by the refusal of successive ministers to consult with them or to take their knowledge of the classroom into account. Looking for a moment at the National Health Service, I met doctors and nurses who felt themselves reduced to the status of firefighters, dealing only with emergencies, and in despair at the contempt with which politicians seemed determined to dismiss any of their anxieties and concerns as special pleading.

Even for someone who had never bought in to the fashionable propaganda of the period, these were sobering encounters. Seeking to explain the extraordinary disaffection between people on the ground and those ruling them from above, I realized the country was passing through a distinctive period in its history in which a government hell-bent on action was determined to suspect the motives of anyone who brought news of what life was actually like on the street. It had become an article of faith among the ideologues at Number Ten that professionals were incapable of representing anything but their own interests. What was under attack from above was not just the prosperity of all those whose job it was to help other people, but the idea of professionalism itself.

It is not the place here to go into the history of how this political animus developed, and how devastating its consequences have been for the life of the country. It is enough to say that during the writing of these plays the Conservative Party was forced to dispose of Margaret Thatcher in a national mood which was three parts anger and one part shame. Nothing that has happened since has done much to decorate her legend. The Coriolanuses she attracted have stomped off and, in startling displays of bad temper, have all turned into Thersites. Now it is the Right which has taken to declaring that the country is finished, not, they say, because British people followed Mrs Thatcher, but because they refused to follow her enough.

It is a sour argument, and one with which we shall have to live for a long time. But it is also barren. It is clear we need to move on. Here in this book you may hear the stray voices of individuals, most of them unfashionable, who, in a way which is often humorous or exasperated, have nevertheless tried to go on making institutions work. It is to their efforts that *Asking Around* is dedicated. The one thing I have learnt and understood from five years' study is that British society needs not to abolish its institutions, but to refresh them. For, if not through institutions, how do we express the common good?

David Hare
May 1993

PART ONE

Racing Demon

Why, who makes much of a miracle?
I know of nothing else but miracles.

Walt Whitman (1819–92)

'If it be, give me thine hand.' I do not mean, 'Be of my opinion.'
You need not: I do not expect or desire it. Neither do I mean, 'I
will be of your opinion.' Keep your opinion; I mine; and that as
steadily as ever . . . Let all opinions alone – on one side and the
other: only 'Give me thine hand.'

John Wesley (1703–91)

The Church that is married to the Spirit of the Age will be a
widow in the next.

Dean Inge (1860–1954)

The Establishment of the Church is a bit like the sugar crust on
top of a crème brûlée: once it is cracked there is a great deal of
tacky stuff underneath.

Edward Norman, Dean of Peterhouse, Cambridge

Thursday Oct. 24, 1944. News came of death of Archbishop of
Canterbury. PM delighted.

Diary of Churchill's Cabinet Secretary

'I'm ready to accept Jesus as a great moral teacher, but I don't
accept his claim to be God.' This is the one thing we must not say.
A man who was merely a man and who said the sort of things
Jesus said would not be a great moral teacher. He would either be
a lunatic – on the level with a man who says he is a poached egg –
or else he would be the Devil of Hell.

C. S. Lewis (1898–1963)

Are you afraid of the dark?
Do you or have you at any stage had a bedwetting problem?
Have you lost interest in almost everything?

From *A Question for all Prospective Ordinands in the Church of England*,
quoted by A. N. Wilson in *The Church in Crisis*, 1986

All we have gained by our unbelief
Is a life of doubt diversified by faith
For one of faith diversified by doubt;
We called the chessboard white – we call it black.

Robert Browning (1812–89)

It's no good ceasing to be the world's policeman to become the
world's parson instead.

Denis Healey

THE CHURCH

When, in December 1987, an Oxford don named Gareth Bennett killed himself after having been identified as the anonymous author of a Crockford's preface critical of the liberal hierarchy in the Church of England, there was, for those of us who had been following the Church's affairs, an unpleasant sense of the inevitable. Even as distant and recent an observer as myself had realized that, underneath the polite Christian surface, passionate positions were being taken up in the Church which simply could not be reconciled. The Church could no longer be all things to all men. When Bennett murdered his cat, then climbed into his car and fixed a rubber hosepipe to his exhaust, he was offering the Church a death which would be interpreted by his friends as a kind of martyrdom, and by his enemies as the worst and dirtiest kind of suicide: the kind which is intended to upset everybody.

The time I was to spend researching *Racing Demon* involved me in meeting Christians of all denominations. At one point I made a brief and unsuccessful attempt to understand the basics of Judaism. Yet somehow, perhaps because of my own High Anglican education, it was to the Church of England I found myself constantly returning. I admit I was attracted more by the sympathetic loneliness of its clergy than by its sometimes infuriating theology.

I made my first attempt to get back in touch with the Church by attending its General Synod. I was touched to find a room full of perhaps four or five hundred people, most of whom were dressed in the same grey socks, flannel trousers and herringbone jackets that I remembered from my youth.

THE GENERAL SYNOD

The General Synod is the Church's Parliament. It is largely made up of elected representatives who are in either the House of Laity or the House of Clergy, and who, like MPs, regionally represent the whole country. In addition, bishops are automatically members of the Synod. They form the third House. All over the country there are also smaller synods which meet and debate inside each diocese.

The General Synod usually meets at Church House in London, but once a year it goes to York University. Many delegates prefer the atmosphere in York, since they get to stay on campus, and this encourages what they call 'fellowship' – one of those wonderfully distinctive words which only Christians use.

The actual government of the Church is exceedingly complicated, but the general work of Synod (which, like Labour's 'Conference', usually travels without the definite article) involves debating and voting on papers and resolutions which are submitted to it. Although there are officially no parties in what is either a circular or a semi-circular formation, the spectator quickly spots factions which group together to represent certain views within the Church.

At the risk of caricature, to which devout Christians rightly object, it is possible to isolate three dominant tendencies: the Anglo-Catholics, with their High Church emphasis on ritual and tradition; the Evangelicals, with their strong beliefs in good and evil, and personal salvation; and the Liberals, who, in the demonology of the other two groups, are held to be in a controlling ascendancy over the whole Church. Individual loyalties and alliances are actually quite complex, and votes are satisfyingly difficult to predict.

Members of the public are allowed to attend any debate. When the subject is contentious – homosexuality, say, or the ordination of women – then the national publicity is remarkably intense. For less glamorous issues, the atmosphere can be desultory. But whether the Synod is well or ill attended, the standard of debate is conspicuously higher than in the House of Commons. Although the adoption of secular, political language often gives the proceedings an absurd, even farcical air, nevertheless the courtesy speakers show each other and the respect they profess for each other's views (however viperous their private assessment of each other's personalities) does mean that ideas do get debated, and genuine convictions are allowed to shine.

I went back to Synod many times in the following months, and I never once went without hearing at least one speaker who was articulate and moving.

CHURCH SYNOD, YORK

Monday, 13 July 1987

The Synod takes place in a lecture hall at York University. There is a stage which has been decked in purple material for the occasion and a cross has been suspended from the ceiling. Otherwise there are no special concessions. The Synod opens with a hand-bell being rung by a small Malaysian woman. On the stage is set a bench and table, at which three people sit, one of them in full legal gear and wig. One of them works the electric light bulbs which tell the speaker how long they have to go. And next to them sits a woman who puts up the number of the current speaker on a machine similar to a cricket scoreboard on a village green.

The Synod starts with prayers. But as the Church of England cannot agree a common version of the Lord's Prayer, you are aware of everyone whispering different words. Then the man in charge of procedure makes a speech. His name is Canon Brindley (217).

Brindley: My announcement is that I am not in a position to make an announcement. By four o'clock I will be in a position to make an announcement, but I cannot at the moment predict what that announcement will be. May I ask all those of you who are attending the 'Not Strangers but Pilgrims' Conference to meet, not at one o'clock as announced, but at one-thirty?

The debate on Freemasonry

Today's first debate is to consider a paper submitted by a working party on Freemasonry. This subject presents a fairly typical problem for the Church. There is a considerable body of evidence which suggests that Freemasons acknowledge an unspecified God, who, whatever His alleged character, is plainly not named as the Christian God. Yet to make too much of this, or to insist too clearly that Masons are involved in a possible blasphemy, would have disastrous consequences. There are many Masons inside the Church of England, and they are better than other worshippers at turning up every week. It is pointless to alienate them. The implicit challenge to the working party has been to come up with some ingenious drafting which will lead to some anodyne form of consultation with the Masons, but which will not risk the loyalty of Masons in the Church.

The first speaker is Dr Margaret Hewitt, who has chaired the working party and who is plainly a great Synod favourite. She is one of a number of people here who speak in an impossibly cut-glass accent of the kind favoured by BBC announcers of the mid-fifties. She is extremely large in a bright green dress and, as she begins to present her paper to Synod, she is interrupted a number of times from the floor by people who cannot hear a word she is saying. She makes a difficult speech on the subject of the overlapping area between Christianity and Freemasonry. In her view the Church is not making an attack on Freemasonry. It is simply questioning those areas of Masonic ritual which appear to use Christian symbolism. She points out that it is impossible for Christians to allow the symbols of Christianity to be used in anything but their proper Christian context. She is concerned to explain certain ideas which are plainly familiar to a church audience, but not to anyone else. She waves around concepts like synchrotism, indifferentism, and Pelagianism, as if they were things with which we were all acquainted. These turn out to be the heresies of which the Masons are regularly accused. Her final conclusion is that Christians who belong to a Masonic lodge lend credibility to the lodge rather than gain credibility from it.

The next speaker is a Mason from Exeter, and he is a parody of every bad public speaker you ever heard. He announces in his wretched speech: 'I greatly enjoy the fellowship of men.'

As the debate continues, the words 'broad church' and 'tolerance' are much used. People are frightened to do anything decisive, or say anything contentious, for fear that they will be accused of a religious witch-hunt. Over and again you hear the formulation, 'The last thing we want in our Church is a witch-hunt.'

On the other hand, as the debate develops, there is a definite envy for Masonry. The more people talk, the more I am aware that a lot of speakers feel that the signs and symbols Masons use, and the clannishness they cultivate, somehow fulfil a need which the Church, by contrast, is failing to requite. This self-criticism marks all the proceedings of the Synod. There is not a single debate which I attend at which self-flagellation is not in order. The weakness, disorder, hypocrisy of the Church are constantly referred to. The vitality of any other organization is always taken to be an implied criticism of the weakness of the Church. Even when, at later debates, I hear Muslim fundamentalism being talked of in tones of distress, there is nevertheless an uneasy fear that perhaps such a popular religion must have got something right.

The Archbishop of York speaks, and the scorer puts up number 2. York is Dr John Habgood, and he is generally taken to be the leading spokesman for the liberal Church. He describes Masonry as a harmless eccentricity.

Archbishop: It will be a sad day when there is no eccentricity in the Church of England. Men gain a certain pleasure from doing things they wouldn't do in front of their wives.

He suddenly uses the phrase 'boy scouts in the potting shed'. He gives the impression of a highly intelligent, slightly disdainful man who wishes that the problem would go away, and his speech ends with the firm statement that he is more worried by Christians who want to define their Christianity in a way that excludes other people than he is by Freemasons. This is a sharp warning that the issue is not to be pushed. His speech is a model of patrician lucidity, but flecked with the sort of humour which seeks to suggest the whole subject is fundamentally silly.

He also includes, as most speakers do, a little parable or story in his speech style:

Archbishop: God has a hundred names, man knows only ninety-nine. The camel knows the hundredth. That explains his expression of ineffable superiority.

His gags are expert.

Archbishop: I would have difficulty in worshipping an architect, with or without the Church Commissioners' approval.

His final indictment of Masonry is that 'an air of conspiracy creates the impression that a conspiracy is going on'. But he does not believe that any conspiracy genuinely exists.

Trying to define what a religion is, the Archbishop interests me by insisting on three criteria: a religion must have doctrine, it must have sacraments, and it must have a promise of salvation.

For the defence, Canon Brindley is a rotund player to the gallery who has the manner of a grand but seedy actor-manager of the pre-war touring theatre. He refers to himself as 'a strong prayer-book man'. He points out that the Duke of Kent and George VI were Masons, 'and it is unthinkable that George VI should indulge in blasphemy – or rather not consciously'. He reminds us of the story of Jesus and the woman taken in adultery, that He tells the woman to go on her way and to sin no more, but He also says, 'neither do I condemn you'. Brindley, in another sexually charged phrase, refers to the 'fun and the friendship of Masonry'. But the moment he begins to describe the actual rituals, in which a man is laid blindfold in a grave and re-enacts the resurrection, people begin to giggle as if finally realizing that this serious debate is about rites which are intrinsically absurd and puerile.

The next speaker is a vicar from Brixton in an African shirt. He tells a long and funny story about the bookie's funeral at which his friend the tic-tac man gets confused between the sign of the cross and the sign on a race course for 20–1 against. He is followed by my first sighting of a bearded vicar in jeans. His manner is classic polytechnic. Up till now nearly all the voices we have heard are upper or upper-middle class, and it is noticeable that when we do finally get something approaching a forthright condemnation of Masonry it comes in tones much further down the social scale. But even the bearded vicar understands that conciliation is the order of the day.

The session ends with a vote overwhelmingly in favour of accepting the report. Clergy and laity are asked to go out of separate doors, as in the House of Commons, to vote yes or no. A bitter Mason mutters, as he clambers over the railings to get to the 'no' door, 'If you want to vote contrary to the common flow, it makes for great difficulty.'

The Debate on Mission

The afternoon's debate is considerably less well attended than that on Masonry. There is not the same atmosphere of political excitement. The television cameras have departed. A document is presented on Mission, which is so wide-ranging and all-embracing that to have condemned it would have been the same as announcing yourself in favour of sin. At the end I am still rather confused about what Mission is. I knew before the debate started that it involved the taking of the Word to the world at large, but at the end it still didn't seem to me significantly different from Ministry. Again, in any discussion of how things are in Third World countries, there is a palpable yearning for the simplicities of faith the speakers thought they found there, combined with an exhilaration that the moral issues in those countries are so comparatively simple. Although such a wide-ranging and ill-defined debate seems fundamentally pointless, it leads to a number of better speeches than you might have expected.

It is introduced by Daphne Wells, who has a fruitcake voice, even plummier than Margaret Hewitt's. Bloodless, thin, grey-haired, precise. One of the points she makes in her speech is that, in what she calls the 'house' churches, each member of the congregation is a missionary, whereas in the Church of England, only the priest sees it as his responsibility to do crisis work in the parish.

A later speaker quotes a saying, 'When I give bread to the hungry they call me a saint, when I ask why the hungry are hungry, they call me a communist.' He also quotes Desmond Tutu: 'We must love the whites, whether they want us to or not.'

The Archdeacon of Northolt refers to 'our total inability to talk about our faith or be inspired by it, or to have any interest in the deprived'. This is the most forthright example of all the persistent self-deprecation that goes on at Synod.

A later speaker tells the story of an early Cory Aquino supporter – she came to power mainly thanks to Christians – who went round knocking on doors and asking, 'Do you believe in the resurrection? Well then, let's rise up and rebuild our town.'

Throughout the debate on Mission it is clear that the Church of England is very much influenced by both the old Commonwealth and the emergent countries, where the clergy have a much more direct relationship with their parishes than in England. There is a generally satisfying feeling that it is much more fun, and much more rewarding, to spread the gospel abroad than it is in your own country. Someone testifies that in Nepal and Kashmir people were immediately attracted by the Sermon on the Mount and by the idea of 'a God with wounds'.

A speaker points out that although church attendances are steadily declining, birth, marriage and death offer access points for the Holy Spirit. There are 50,000 visitors a day in Canterbury Cathedral, probably more than those attending worship in a week in the whole diocese. This is one of a number of statistics which I distrust.

Next speaker: I was voted in on a Mission-Not-Maintenance ticket in a by-election for the General Synod.
Next speaker: God is prodding us to join in his initiatives.

Personal anecdote is essential to all Synod speeches: 'I want to tell you a short personal story.' Mrs Page of Norwich tells an excruciating story about the whole family doing a jigsaw, in which she points out that everybody contributed something different, including one person who brought 'the gift of humour, funny puns and quips'.

Mrs Page: In doing the jigsaw I was being shown how we work in the Church. Each of us had something different to contribute, but we could only contribute it if we had the top of the jigsaw box in front of us so we knew what picture we were trying to make. We needed a common picture, we needed a vision, we needed the picture on the jigsaw box.

I notice how many people put their hands on each other, guiding them through the Synod. It is a priestly thing constantly to put your hand on someone's back, even on their bottoms. As they walk along the rows, hands are put on arms and wrists.

A speaker is shocked by having listened to Robert Robinson's *Brain of Britain*. None of the contestants knew the answers to these two questions: What is the name given to the feast of the coming of the Holy Spirit? What are the three Christian virtues?

There is a great deal of reference to England being a multi-racial community and how the Church is to respond to that. Statistics are quoted about there being more Indians in Southall than anywhere outside India, except Durban. Similarly, there were said to be more Jews in somewhere (I think Redbridge, but it seems unlikely) than in Israel.

The Debate on Housing

In the early evening, another fairly aimless debate, in which everybody is against homelessness. Not particularly well attended, but remarkable for the fact that one of the speakers is a delegate who carries out evictions for his local council. This is not seen as any contradiction. Nobody would suggest that he was in an un-Christian profession. He describes what it is like to arrive at six o'clock in the morning and evict people from their houses. He claims that they arrive early, not to catch people unawares, but in order to make sure that 'the man of the house has not yet gone out to work'. This speaker's presence, and the absence of any challenge to it, seems to me to raise another fundamental problem. Any church worth the name would take him aside and ask him if he isn't ashamed of himself. But the Church now has a terror of finding sin anywhere, least of all among its own members.

The Dean of St Paul's, in an excellent speech, tries to turn Synod's attention from homelessness in the UK to homelessness internationally. He refers to the poisonous philosophy of the government in San Salvador: 'Drain the reservoir and the fish will die.' He also speaks of some squatters who were living in his house when he arrived to be Dean of St Paul's, and who, before they were evicted, left a crayoned message on his floor: 'This house is full of beautiful vibes.' He uses a striking phrase about the impossibility of an understanding between 'the people who keep order and the people who are kept in order'.

The Archbishop of Canterbury – and number 1 comes up on the scoreboard. It is an odd decision for Robert Runcie to choose to speak now. He has said nothing all day. Now, like a star batsman, he drops himself down the order and comes in when rain threatens and most of the crowd have gone home. He makes an entirely bland speech saying homelessness is a bad thing. He says he is particularly concerned about it because the last action of Terry Waite, before he was kidnapped in the Lebanon, was to attend a function for the International Year of the Homeless. I am very interested in his use of Terry Waite, as if it were taken for granted that Waite were more saintly than he. Canterbury exploits Waite, using him as a way of corroborating and lending dignity to his own ideas. It is assumed that anything which Terry Waite is in favour of must automatically be holy and worthwhile. Understandably, an instantly serious and attentive air comes down the moment Waite's name is mentioned.

The debate on homelessness drifts on until there is some reference to the question of mortgage tax relief. It is quite clear that everyone believes that this is a middle-class perk and flagrantly inequitable. But, again, the Church stops short of recommending a repeal because it doesn't want to offend home owners.

Somebody quotes Charles Lamb: 'There is nothing more satisfying than to do a good turn in secret and have it discovered by accident.'

Evening – the tea-room

Although I have been sitting by myself during debates in the public gallery, I am lucky enough in the tea-room afterwards to be introduced to a bishop on the evangelical wing of the Church. I am fascinated to find out if he still has fundamentalist views about heaven and hell.

Bishop: Oh, yes. I mean, I do believe that people will be separated out at Judgement Day. But I don't necessarily believe they will be separated out for ever.

DH: *I was very surprised by the references in the debate to 'God's initiatives'. Does that mean God does make active interventions in the world?*

Bishop: Most certainly.

DH: *What about the devil? Does he make initiatives also?*

Bishop: No, I think he just tries to mess God's initiatives up. To be honest, we don't talk much about the devil. We are trying to get away from that figure with the forked tail. So I just use the adjective 'demonic' and that way try to avoid the problem.

DH: *So you do believe in Heaven and Hell?*

Bishop: I do. But I have learnt that it's pointless to talk about them. It's part of being a bishop. I mean, actually it's the same with Freemasonry today. The fact is, privately I think the Masons are just bloody stupid. But I'm not sure it would do any good to say so. On the contrary, I was actually worried today's debate was far too condemnatory, and I spent most of it thinking about the diocesan letter I'm going to have to send round explaining that the vote wasn't anti-Masonic, it just looks that way.

DH: *What's the Bishops' Bench like? When you have your debates, is the atmosphere friendly?*

Bishop: Extremely. A lot of us believe different things, yet we manage to discuss them in a way which is always fair and pleasant. There has to be balance in the bishopric – you need one chap who knows about Buddhism, for instance, so that whatever theological problem comes up, there's someone to deal with it. The only real tension recently was when the Bishop of London came back from the United States after deliberately celebrating communion with a priest who had been un-Churched for his opposition to women priests. He got a real bollocking. It's quite a well-known scandal. Things really did turn nasty.

DH: *One of the things which most interests me about the Church is the parallel with the Labour Party. They both seem to me organizations which can't decide whether to have rules of membership or not. Anglicanism seems to have become a party at which everyone's welcome.*

Bishop: I think that is true, at least at the beginning. I think it's important not to alienate anyone straight away. Once they get in, they will learn that the Christian way is hard. It's very, very hard. But don't tell them that in advance, because it will just put them off.

Tuesday 14 July 1987

I am slightly thrown at breakfast by somebody showing me a copy of *The Times*, in which there is a diary-piece noting that the playwright David Hare is attending Synod. Later in the day, I ask the Church's press officer, a genial ex-naval officer who is unfailingly helpful to me, how on earth *The Times* knew I was there. 'Because I told them,' he replies cheerfully. When I ask him why, he looks at me without apology and says, 'Because the Church needs all the publicity it can get.'

The debate on rates

The morning debate, on the revision of the rates system and introduction of the poll tax, is extremely well attended. The press officer says to me that Synod is always very tough about money. It is quite clear from the printed correspondence between the Archbishop of York and Margaret Thatcher that her way of getting back at the Church for its attacks on her government is to make sure that the Church is not exempted from the new poll tax, which will cost the Church approximately £4 or £5 million a year. There are two schools of thought. The great majority of delegates consider that the Church of England should be exempted from this tax, but there is a tiny minority, among whom I notice the Bishop of Durham, who vote against the motion on the grounds that the Church should identify with the people, and that if the people have to suffer this poll tax, the Church has no right to ask to be exempted from it.

The Archbishop of York opens with a prayer that 'having had to concentrate on things temporal we do not lose sight of things eternal'.

The first speaker is the Bishop of London (3), in gaiters, and looking as lanky and forbidding as a Ronald Searle cartoon. He is the famous High Anglican whose passionate opposition to women priests is matched only by his enthusiasm for the current government. A religious journalist tells me, 'London is very much a Maggie man but he doesn't mind knocking her.' London starts by bidding goodbye to the retiring Dean of Carlisle, who is a hugely humorous figure as far as Synod is concerned. The Dean is given a special vote of thanks, and then falls fast asleep during the subsequent speeches.

Wakefield (64) talks about how odd it will be if the people exempted from the tax are 'the pensioner, the unemployed, the disabled, the mad, and the Minister of Religion'. He finishes up, 'The world will listen to us in inverse proportion to our vested interest.' He refers to an 'eternal dimension to our work'. But London counters by saying, 'Faith does not exonerate us from doing what has to be done in a concrete situation. We must have a deeply spiritual concern and also be intensely practical.' He goes on to call the clergy the only professionals who are still giving expert care twenty-four hours a day, seven days a week.

The final vote is 219:28. There is then a procedural flurry which is completely incomprehensible to outsiders. The Dean of Carlisle stands up, and my notes have him saying, 'My point of order came before the point that the question be not put. There is some unclarity in standing orders and I am not sure if under 43(b) I can refer to the standing committee. If the procedural motion is put, then in my view part (b) of 36 will lapse.' Various people at once raise their hands and start shouting, 'On a point of order!' but the chairman counters by insisting, 'Under 41(b) I cannot take a point of order.'

The most referred-to figure in all the speeches, besides God, is Oscar Wilde.

The debate on women

The general feeling here is that whereas homelessness was a bad thing, women are a good thing. However, the ostensible subject of the afternoon's debate – how can women do more? – does not stop the knee-jerk self-criticism.

Speaker: My first point is that we are well on the way to spiritual ruination. My second point . . .

The Bishop of Durham (4) makes an unruly and barely comprehensible speech, gabbling phrases: 'social investment', 'human resources', 'God's dream of love, joy, peace', 'deeply divided society', 'very difficult world', etc.

The next speaker is again Mrs Page from Norwich. I have noticed she misses no opportunity to make a personal contribution. She makes a rather embarrassing speech about how she expects to be 'fulfilled in her job, fulfilled as a wife and fulfilled as a mother to my children'. She then adds, with unnecessary candour, 'I want to be fulfilled as a lover.' There is a moment's uneasy silence as collectively the Synod stops to imagine the sight and sounds of Mrs Page fulfilled as a lover.

Mrs J. Kidd of Christchurch Vicarage, Virginia Water, Surrey (400), is plainly the hard-line keeper of Christian morals – white-haired, very suntanned, in the kind of dress usually seen only in Majorca. In the whole Synod there is not a single woman in trousers. All are in skirts or dresses. Mrs Kidd has the true rabble-rouser's gift of seeming only by the utmost self-control to be keeping far stronger feelings at bay.

Mrs Kidd: We have had a report written by women. Can we now have one written by the children? It's the children who suffer when a woman goes out to work. I'm being emotional, but, sorry, I'm a woman.

Barrie Etherington is a bearded vicar, in his 40s. He is one of the many people at Synod who tell us their life stories. He is a priest who has remarried. Nobody outside the Church, I think, appreciates just how contentious this issue is. Etherington's first marriage, he tells us, broke down in spite of 'guidance by a Christian psychotherapist. Two years ago, I met a woman to whom I am now married. With due respect to Mrs Kidd and Mr John Selwyn Gummer, she is my wife.' This ringing declaration is a reference to certain well-known people's opposition to the remarriage of divorced clergy.

Someone says clergy should reflect the 'is-ness' of God not the 'ought-ness' of the moralizers. But the debate's tone is best caught by one speaker who refers to 'theological undergirding' and who notes: 'My wife tells me that I have a growing reputation as a pedant, and anyone who claims, as I do, that Easter Eve is different from Easter Saturday, must plead guilty.'

TEAM MINISTRY

Some months later I was to attend a session of Synod at which the Archbishop of Canterbury had to endure the humiliating ordeal of sitting silent while 400 delegates discussed the degree to which he was or wasn't personally responsible for Gareth Bennett's death. But by then it had already become clear to me that my true interests lay not with the bishops, nor indeed with the kind of priest who relishes the politics of Synod, but with those people who give up their lives to minister in the inner cities. I was interested to discover the attitudes sustaining them in what might appear to be the thankless task of interesting the local population in Jesus Christ.

To this end I started by interviewing a number of clergymen who were experienced in working in teams. Team ministry was an idea which had grown up and become popular in the seventies and eighties. Clergy came to believe they could be more responsive to the needs of their local areas if they pooled their collective efforts and began to specialize in those aspects of ministry at which each one of them was best. The hope was that they might play to their strengths. Although churches still had individual vicars, nevertheless team leaders or rectors were appointed to manage the newly created larger areas. The single parish was no longer autonomous.

Although the idea was initially popular, it had one major drawback – one which struck at the heart of the clergy's own livelihood. Claiming to be worried about the possibility of personality clashes, bishops demanded the right to make sure they could control the balance of each team. This meant taking away from individual priests what had been until then their most precious right: the gift of freehold. Through the centuries, this had been the essential democratic instrument which characterized the structure of the Church, and which also, to some extent, compensated the clergyman for his low pay. However poor his livelihood, he had a job for life. With the arrival of team ministries, clergy were being told they had to go over to five-year contracts. Unsurprisingly, there had been conflicts. The more I interviewed priests and parishioners in that amorphous area of South London which runs between Elephant and Castle and Streatham High Road, the more aware I was of the anxieties the team principle had created. But at the same time I never lost my conviction that on £8,000 p.a., loving God and trying to clear up society's worst problems, here were some heroes for our age.

Walter

Walter was a priest in his late 50s, who had been a vicar in South London and the leader of the local team. After a disastrous row, when his bishop had managed to unseat him, he was now working in an industrial mission. White-haired, liberal and intelligent, he came from a family in which almost everyone had served in the Church of England in some capacity. He was the first vicar I met who had little interest in spreading the Gospel. As far as he was concerned, people would be drawn to God by the example of a priest's actions, not by his words.

Walter: The system of patronage, of how people are appointed to churches, is extremely complicated – a system of Crown Commissioners and Patronage Boards. It's rather like pubs: the manager goes and the congregation punishes the brewery by going to the pub down the road. This is an Anglican phenomenon. In the Roman Catholic Church the particular priest is much less important. The priest goes but the Church remains. I have to admit I do like the Catholics and I enjoy their company most of all. I've just spent the weekend sailing with the Catholic mafia.
DH: *South London seems to have all sorts. I gather St Anne's, Kennington, is now full of charismatics. What do you feel about them?*
Walter: I'm not going to condemn them. It's too easy to poke Charlie at one's neighbour.
DH: *I gather there's someone called the Patronage Secretary whom you have to go and see when you want a Crown Parish.*
Walter: Yes, that's right. When I was appointed to my South

London parish, I had to go and see him. He works in Ten Downing Street. It is hilarious getting into a taxi and saying, 'Ten Downing Street, please.' During my period we formed a team ministry with four vicars servicing four parishes. To do this, we had to appoint a team rector, and because we were all into leaderless things in those days, nobody wanted to be leader. I went to Biafra for six months and was elected in my absence.

DH: *Obviously to an outsider it looks like a very depressing job. I mean, such a huge number of people in your area, and so few of them regularly attending Church.*

Walter: It's very difficult to know what impact a Church is having on a community. You think nobody cares, and yet one day we were throwing out some pews and there was great consternation. A crowd gathered in the street because they feared that the church was being closed down, in spite of the fact that very few of them actually attended church themselves.

As to numbers, well, it's such tiny figures, it's all silly. I have sixty communicants. If it were thirty I'd be very worried. If it were ninety I'd be delighted. But really it's the quality of worship. There's a church where I take communion with seven others on Sunday, but it's real. People who attend are just the tip of the iceberg. Everyone is part of the church, in a funny way, including the dossers who come and sit on the ledge outside. I asked a window cleaner if he'd mind if the church went. He said, 'You mean so we wouldn't see the vicar walking down the street? That would be a disaster.' Some people would say I was fooling myself, but I believe you must accept people as they are.

I'm trying to enable people to develop their relationship with God. A boy came to me and said he was going to become a Muslim, and I was obscurely pleased because it meant he had a relationship with God now, even if it was, from my point of view, a wrong direction. I met a black woman who talked to bus queues about the joy of the Lord. It wouldn't be authentic for me. I wouldn't expect God to want me to do that. It's got to be in a right and meaningful context. I hate it when I hear priests saying they're screwing themselves up to talk to someone about God. If you're screwing yourself up to talk about Jesus, you must be doing something wrong.

I couldn't work with someone who imposed their own insecurities and pressured in the wrong way, imposing their own cultural baggage instead of working from the individual's relationship with God. It is pointless talking to people about God. The Jesuits understood years ago that you've got to go native and see things through other people's eyes. Only then can you begin to make tentative connections. I personally think it's a helluva help to believe in God, but it's not a *sine qua non*. I admire anyone who is genuinely wrestling with the problem of evil.

DH: *Yes. I mean evil is a very difficult one for the Christian, isn't it?*

Walter: Yes. Earthquakes do seem a bit mindless.

DH: *I can see that your whole effort is not to force God on people. But isn't there a danger in going too much the other way?*

Walter: I met a man at a party who was on the board of a hospice. There had been some discontent at this hospice because the dying felt that Christianity was being rammed down their throats as they died. The man at the party said, 'But it's a Christian hospice. They must expect to have Christianity given them as they die.' In my view this man is a danger to humanity.

I went to a secular funeral recently, where a non-believer was cremated – a woman who had specifically rejected Christianity – and I attended in spite of the family's wishes. During the ceremony a piece of her sculpture was passed round and there was a period of quiet reminiscence. I was so moved that I was absolutely sure that I was in the presence of God but felt it was arrogant to say so to them, so I said nothing. Then somebody holding the sculpture said, 'It's as if someone has to die in order to become more universally acceptable.' This remark hit me with astonishing force because it was of course an exact statement of Christ's life and death on the cross.

DH: *Tell me a bit about how you lost your parish.*

Walter: At the end of my five-year tenure as a parish priest in South London, I was aware that my bishop disapproved of team ministries. He described them as 'a refuge for the inadequate'. The bishop was determined to appoint one of his protégés to the team rectorship, and when I went to see him and told him another, more junior, bishop had implied my tenure would be renewed, he lost his temper. He said, 'He has no right. I make the appointments. I have taken legal advice and you have no security of tenure.' He then offered me a job in Thamesmead. I went back to the junior bishop, the one who had told me I was secure, and said I was thinking of taking legal advice. I asked what would happen if I did. He said, 'I can tell you what will happen. You will never get a job in the Church of England again.'

DH: *What was your reaction to that?*

Walter: I suppose until then I'd always thought the Church as an institution was a vaguely Christian sort of thing. But I got over it. I concluded God was OK, even if the bishop is a shit.

DH: *Isn't there a danger in a Church which seems to be all things to all men? Wouldn't it have a stronger identity if it had stricter conditions of membership?*

Walter: If we are about the search for faith, a few burnings or excommunications would of course sharpen the whole thing up a bit, but I'm not sure you can take that short cut to truth. The Prayer Book says you have to take communion three times a year, one of them Easter, and it demands that you have faith in the Trinity. Dorothy Sayers said of the Athanasian Creed that God the Father is incomprehensible, Jesus Christ is incomprehensible, the Holy Spirit is incomprehensible. In fact, the whole bloody thing is incomprehensible. I think the Trinity means so much to me because it is a mystery, and because of that makes more sense to me than a lot of other concepts such as Heaven, Hell or the resurrection. It is a mystery, so how can you teach it?

Michael

I then wanted to speak to a more junior priest in the area, and chose Michael, who was a curate in a nearby church which had recently had a very unhappy time. Michael was cautious and mature, accepting the limitations of his job, his theology very much in line with Walter's.

Michael: We have had very bad problems at the church because the vicar recently had a nervous breakdown. It had two causes. He was suffering from terrible doubts about his own identity, but also – this is just my view – he paid the price for taking a wrong attitude to his work. He was quite simply trying to do too much. We're talking about one of the most deprived and difficult areas of South London, and there isn't any way a single Christian priest is going to be able to solve all its problems. Yet he saw his own appointment as being so central to the life of the area that he fretted himself to the point of collapse.

DH: *You yourself entered the Church quite late.*

Michael: Yes. I was a solicitor in Putney when, in my 30s, I went to see my own vicar and told him I wanted to be a priest. I saw the Director of Ordinands for the diocese, and was sent to the Advisory Council for the Church's Ministry, which has people resident together for two and a half days. It's nice to be able to talk about yourself without people glazing over with boredom. You play various games like the Ten Minute Topic. You talk on a given topic for one minute, then chair a discussion for nine minutes on that topic. This is a crucial skill for a priest.

The buzzword for the last ten years has been 'facilitating'. The job is not seen as lecturing or addressing people, but facilitating them to bring out qualities in themselves. You have to draw their skills out. If you think of the job as 'doing' you're on the way to a nervous breakdown; if you think of it as social work, there is so much to be done you're overwhelmed. Recent changes in social security rules mean you can't get a loan for a cooker unless you can prove your ability to repay. Maggie says OK, go round to the charity shop and buy a third-hand one, but I try and help people to see if they can work the DHSS rules to their advantage.

You must understand the limits of your role. Help other people to feel *affirmed* to do something. The congregation is a team who will do your work for you, if they're any good. Luckily here they're terrific and have been very supportive through our troubles. My first few weeks here, I just reacted emotionally to people's problems, and another priest criticized me for trying to 'solve' people. You can't do it. And anyway, it's wrong trying to make people like yourself. The priest told me, 'Whap in, do the minimum and get out again.'

DH: *So how did you come to this area?*

Michael: I did a two-year residential course in Oxfordshire, then went to the bishop to see what jobs he had. There was a problem about whether this diocese was entitled to a curate because they hadn't 'paid their quota', meaning the church's money contribution to the diocese. In the old days, a curate wasn't allowed to leave the parish without the vicar's permission. He was simply a skivvy, working to orders. I must say, it has helped me here with the congregation that I happened to marry one of the church wardens shortly after I arrived. It delighted everyone. Now we have a child. Very good for morale.

DH: *How do you see your job, then?*

Michael: Most clergy feel there is a need for the world to be loved. It's the minister's job to do the loving. It's exhausting, emotionally. You think all the time, 'I should have spiritual resources for this.' In a way the front line is in the suburbs, not in the inner cities, because in the inner cities the problems are so chronic it's easy to get the congregation geared up, but the hard job is to convince comfortable suburbanites that things are terrible elsewhere. And we need the whole Church behind us to do our work here.

DH: *Do low numbers depress you?*

Michael: We live in a post-Christian society. That's understood. There are fewer of them, but the quality is better. The main job is preaching the gospel, not getting numbers up, or saving souls.

DH: *Do you think it's important to get people to believe in God?*

Michael: Only in a secondary way. I'm not much concerned with personal salvation. I mean, churches will always be full of nutters, people who need love. I suppose it ought to matter more that the church isn't full. It would be nice if it were full. But what's the point of worship? What happens when they close the doors and sing the hymns? All too easily it's just spiritual masturbation.

DH: *Why does God need to be told He's wonderful all the time?*

Michael: Are you a father? Well, don't you like to be loved by your children? Don't you like to be *told* you're loved?

DH: *What's your view about Hell? Does it exist?*

Michael: How can we know? Better to concentrate on what God is.

DH: *(Smiles) Are you handing down any teaching at all?*

Michael: My wife would say no. To me, the Church is based on three things. Scripture. Tradition. And understanding. My job is to mediate between the three. I do believe blessing arrives through the sacraments.

DH: *Well then, surely you have some obligation to get those sacraments to as many people as possible?*

Michael: Not at all. Of the eight thousand people in the parish, a hundred are regular churchgoers. Five thousand believe in God in some way, and they just need to know we're there. That's enough.

DH: *So really you do see what you're doing primarily as social work. But surely you must get overwhelmed by the sheer volume of problems?*

Michael: Of course. Every time you go into town, you see beggars, prostitutes, male and female. You know you're not helping them. The borough is full of inadequate people let out of mental homes into what's called the community, meaning no one looks after them. Practical help is essential. We recently led the squat at the Belgrave Hospital and turned it into a homeless centre. It's now almost self-supporting.

DH: *Did the bishop approve?*

Michael: Look, Kingston led the service at which people were encouraged to go and daub slogans on the walls of the Ministry of Defence, for which they were all then arrested. So it's hard to imagine him disapproving of anything we do in this parish.

DH: *Do you have any contact with the evangelicals in the next-door parish?*

Michael: There's a new priest nearby who's doing what's called church-planting. It's something evangelicals do. They encourage a whole congregation from the suburbs to move into the inner city and start a thriving church there. It's rather controversial. Needless to say, I don't approve of it. I think you should build on what you've got, not draft believers in. Anyway, we had this bloke round. He talked about Jesus all the time. You probably notice I don't refer to Him much. But anyway, we fell to arguing, and the truth is, my vicar tore this evangelical apart. Limb from limb. Afterwards, it left a bad taste. I didn't like this bloke but . . . I don't know . . . I wish we hadn't been quite so rude.

Bernard

The next vicar I interviewed had resisted letting his parish enter the team system. Bernard had been sixteen years in the same job, living as a bachelor in tiny rooms on a very ordinary housing estate. His voice was gentle, and he had the unmistakable air of a man who has been alone for a very long time.

Bernard: I trained in Surrey. Couldn't be more different from here. The archdeacon still wore gaiters. Actually, he asked me to buttle for him at one of his parties. So I did. But I never spoke to him again. I was happy in Surrey, but when a new rector arrived I knew it was time to move on. I've always been South of the River.

DH: *So how did you find it here when you first arrived?*

Bernard: My first job here was to build up the black side, to get blacks as sidespeople, handing out the books, collecting the money. We reduced the Church Council from thirty to twelve. And we formed an entertainments committee which organizes coach trip outings to the seaside. Many don't have any holidays except a trip back to the West Indies every eight years. The problem is, they won't eat in restaurants, so everything goes into tupperware – the curried goat, the whisky, the rum. And everyone wants to feed the vicar, so I end up eating six dinners on these trips.

DH: *How do you approach the job?*

Bernard: An evangelical would find it very hard here. Direct preaching of the Gospel is a waste of time unless you are also interested in the environment in which people live. You show God's love in the way you behave. We're making little circles in a very large pond. My job is to build a sense of community in a place where there is none. Church is somewhere people can be loved and welcomed, and where I try to make the service as beautiful as possible. To feel the otherness of God so it touches their souls. This actually happened yesterday, Ash Wednesday – we only got half the congregation but there was a quiet, meditative atmosphere, very good.

DH: *But isn't that just theatre?*

Bernard: Well, there's much of the actor in priests.

DH: *Are you interested in doctrine at all?*

Bernard: Not much. I'm not an academic. I believe in the love of God, and it must be communicated by what we do. I have to take a lot of anger and frustration and not hit back. People come here to complain. They come to the vicar to talk to someone they can beat up on, and I have to sit there and take it. I have to accept that. When I get home, I want to kick the dog. Because everyone comes to let off steam at someone they know can't hit back.

DH: *How do you put up with it?*

Bernard: I get out one day a week. It's essential. I go down to Sussex and walk by the sea. Then I come back up and go to the theatre in the evening. I love the theatre, but I feel guilty unless I go on my one day off. Nobody could do this job seven days a week. When I started, it was physically hard. I had a bedsit without water. Those days are gone, but they've been replaced by something mentally much harder.

DH: *Do you take any interest in Synod at all?*

Bernard: Not really. It actually doesn't concern me. I mean, papers are pushed at us all the time, but we don't take any notice of them. The Church has got like Thatcher's government. Market forces are all. That's one of the reasons I don't want to be part of a team. I just saw it as an economic measure. Things were to be decided not on the basis of need, but according to what we can afford. You're asked to discuss propositions but you know full well the eventual decisions will be made on an economic basis. So what we say makes no difference.

DH: *Did you read the Church's report on the inner cities,* Faith in the City?

Bernard: I must say I didn't take it very seriously. There was all this stuff about our commitment to the inner city, and yet when I asked the Archbishop of Canterbury to come and re-open our church school, he refused. We kept changing the date and he still wouldn't come. We're half an hour away from Lambeth Palace. It does make you doubt their conviction.

DH: *Are you doing anything in the parish differently from what humanists or social workers in the area might do?*

Bernard: No. But we have more energy. Because we recognize a power that's helping us to do it.

Trevor

Of all the inner London vicars I went to see, Trevor was in many ways the most unpredictable. A team leader in his late 40s, he was lean and apparently academic, often showing a rather sharp contempt for the people he was meant to be helping. Yet the traces of a disturbing spiritual struggle plainly marked the way he looked and spoke.

Trevor: The trouble with bishops is that after a while they think they're God. They move us around like chess-men. All you hear when you refuse a job is, 'Well, Ronnie won't like it.'

DH: *Presumably it's worse now, with the team system.*

Trevor: Yes. With the team system, you have to give up freehold, or else how do you get rid of a man who's not pulling his weight? Though even on contracts it's actually very hard to get rid of anyone. You can't just turn them out on the street. My own security isn't too bad. When my seven years here are up, then the bishop and I will agree on an outside assessor who will come in and judge if I should go on.

DH: *How does the team work?*

Trevor: The team meets every Tuesday at lunchtime for two hours. There are six parishes, four permanent priests, one deacon, and a deaconess about to join. The Sheffield formula (which is a weighting device to make sure that all clergy don't work in the south) won't allow me any more priests, so I've grabbed a deaconess. My powers as team rector are not defined. I'm also the rural dean. There are monthly meetings of the Deanery Synod Chapter – clergy only – about twelve people. And three or four times a year, the whole Deanery Synod meets to discuss referred papers. It's a soviet system.

DH: *But there is some flexibility?*

Trevor: Of course. Most of the time you're just dealing with anything that turns up. And of course in this area, if you want to minister to black people, it's fairly pointless trying to do it unless you have a strong sense of the supernatural.

DH: *Does that mean you believe in miracles?*

Trevor: I do.

DH: *Can you give me an example?*

Trevor: Well, after the Brixton riots, I had heart surgery. I suffered from terrible hallucinations. I believed that the black nurses were trying to kill me. But, worse, when I looked down the ward I saw this terrible black mob advancing towards me. They were trying to kill me as nastily as they could. When I got home and was meant to be recovering, I started learning to draw. And every time I drew, the hallucinations returned. So then I decided, deliberately decided, to summon up the hallucinations, and I said the Jesus prayer over them, again and again, trying to let God occupy the top of my mind. The hallucinations vanished as if a drop of washing-up liquid had been dropped on grease. If I were an evangelical, I would call this a miracle.

DH: *Have you seen miracles affecting others?*

Trevor: Once when I was a curate I said the Lord's Prayer over a dying child. I came back two days later and the child was well and out of hospital. A miracle.

DH: *But when a child dies, do you then feel the devil has triumphed?*

Trevor: To be honest, I'm so surprised when anything happens that I don't really think about it.

DH: *But do you believe in a supernatural power of bad?*

Trevor: I don't think I do. Ultimately evil is unreal. I once had a South American couple where the woman accused the next-door neighbour of putting a spell on her husband to alienate his affection. They went to the Luiz Paulo mission, and that helped for a bit. But I must admit finally I threw non-directive counselling to the wind and told her no wonder her husband was alienated, she was so stupid.

DH: *Goodness. Do you do that often?*

Trevor: No.

DH: *Does the work oppress you?*

Trevor: No. If they're people you know you're not going to get anywhere with, I send them away. A bloke rang me and said he thought he'd indecently assaulted a 14-year-old boy. I said, well, have you or haven't you? Fourteen-year-old boys are pretty strong, you know. This man's just wasting my time.

DH: *Do you worry about numbers? I mean, wouldn't it be wonderful if more people believed in Christianity?*

Trevor: No, I don't think so actually. I think it would be dreadful if it were a majority religion, like in America. I'd rather have six people in a tent.

DH: *Why?*

Trevor: An over-successful Church can't represent Christ, who conquers through vulnerability and helplessness.

DH: *Then tell me what a perfect Church would be like – one which really was relevant to people's lives.*

Trevor: (*After an agonizingly long pause*) It's difficult to get your mind round that. I'm into individuals and small groups. Large numbers don't turn me on. The problem is, most of us get side-tracked by problems of fabric. The sensible thing would be to close down two-thirds of the churches and get the congregations all together. That way you wouldn't waste all your time getting the palms organized for Palm Sunday. Instead, you'd have groups meeting in people's houses to worship and swap ideas. The trouble is, the congregation wouldn't accept it. All the group pressures are club-oriented.

Look, this is non-attributable, but my problems come from one thing. All the people in our church are second-rate. If they were any good at organizing things, they wouldn't be organizing the church. We've got a bloke who's meant to be good at computers. Well, I know more than he does. Our head warden's meant to be a brilliant organizer, yet she's up till three a.m. the night before the church fair, running off the programme. I don't call that good organizing.

DH: *Do you think it's important that people subscribe to the two central beliefs of Christianity?*

Trevor: I do believe in the empty tomb. It doesn't really matter whether you *believe* in it, more what you understand by it. This man who was abused and scorned turned out to be the Messiah, so his values have eternal significance. As to the virgin birth, well, John and Mark don't mention it. Matthew and Luke have conflicting accounts. I wouldn't be much worried if people didn't believe in it, but you do have to believe in the resurrection.

DH: *So your faith is predominantly a practical matter?*

Trevor: I give sandwiches to the poor. They come to the door. The sandwiches are not from the church, they're from me. The church tried to take this service over from me, but I said, no, it's something *I* do. Sometimes I say, look, actually no, because if I give you bread tonight my children won't have any in the morning. One man came for shoes, so I took mine off and gave them to him. The trouble was, he then came back on an apostolic visit with eleven friends.

ONE STEP BACK

Canon Eric James

Some of my original interest in inner-city churches had come about from my reading the famous Church of England report *Faith in the City*, which seemed to many commentators to offer a more telling and radical indictment of the Conservative governments of the eighties than any document produced by the official opposition parties. On its publication, some idiot in the Tory Party had anonymously condemned the report as 'Marxist', and there had followed one of those insane English rows, stoked up by newspapers whose interest was in making everyone look foolish.

Because I admired the report, and was so intrigued by the section which argued that the physical body could not be separated from the soul, I was keen to meet Canon Eric James, who was one of the people behind its publication. Canon James is well-known on the radio as a regular broadcaster on *Thought for the Day*. He is large, easygoing, in his late 50s. As well as understanding South London very well, he is also an expert on Church reform.

Eric James: In the sixties I worked a lot on the idea of a Synod. That was in the days when I passionately believed the Church should be reformed, if you know what I mean. But, sadly, one evil soon replaces another. There are certain subjects that Synod is ill-suited to handling. Take homosexuality. You've got to balance the scientific, the biblical, the doctrinal, the moral evidence. You can't do that in an adversarial, party-debating kind of way. In 1974 the General Synod Board for Social Responsibility appointed a working party. The working party concluded unanimously in 1978 that no longer could you say it was wrong for all gay men to have genital relationships. Then it had to go to the Board who had set up the party. The Board were divided. There was a year of arguing, followed by two years before it came to Synod. Then silence. No one did anything. Now – a few years on – there's to be a bishop's report which is very hush-hush, because everyone's terrified of the subject.

DH: *What do you think of the opponents of homosexuality in the Church?*

James: Some of them are Protestant nutters, no doubt with sexual problems of their own. Some are Catholic. Religion has a long tradition of stoning prostitutes.

DH: *Tell me what you feel about declining attendances.*

James: I think numbers are not important. 'When all men speak well of you, so did they to the false prophets.' One year no one came to my first Lenten address. I go round trying to tell people in Basingstoke and St Albans about the inner city and meet many people too frightened to find out. It's often fear. It's all in the parable of the Good Samaritan. Why did *he* cross the road and the Levite didn't? One old lady said to me, 'Well, surely because he was a Christian.' Of course he wasn't! He was a Samaritan.

When someone calls me Padre, I always know what's coming. The other day I was asked, 'I don't mind these Bengalis and Pakistanis, Padre, but why can't they adopt our ways?' I said, 'What, you mean like we adopted *their* ways in India?'

DH: *What did you feel about the row over* Faith in the City?

James: Ridiculous! Mrs T. doesn't mind religion and politics being mixed when it's to do with law and order, personal responsibility, charity. But prophecy has always been about the poor, land-ownership and the plight of the immigrant. She's not so keen when you point that out.

DH: *I know I don't understand this doctrine of justification by faith, but doesn't it mean that what you believe is more important than what you do?*

James: No. Not really. Justification by faith is against the heresy that you can earn points by good deeds. You must do good deeds in thankfulness to God, not in the hope of earning redemption. It means you know yourself to be accepted by *God* even if large parts of you seem unacceptable.

DH: *What does that mean?*

James: I'll tell you. The most moving thing I ever saw was Alastair Sim playing Prospero. When he embraced Caliban and said, 'This thing of darkness I acknowledge mine.' That's Christianity. Knowing our potential for sin: knowing the dark side of ourselves – yet experiencing acceptance by God.

DH: *I've always had a problem with this. I mean, the way you all go on about being sinners all the time. The fact is, in the last few months I've met a lot of Christian priests, and I can't help noticing you're all remarkably nice, decent people. In no way do you look like sinners to me. Yet you spend all your time telling yourselves how deeply mired in sin you are. I mean, do you feel you're a sinner?*

James: Well, I don't have great feelings of sinfulness – so I see sin much more clearly in others than in myself! – but I've never been very good at feeling myself 'acceptable', and I have to work at that. When I was a student at King's College, London, my dean said I was going to find myself in all sorts of trouble if I didn't have a high doctrine of corruption. But he said I must have a high doctrine of glory as well – and my doctrine of glory must be an inch higher than my doctrine of corruption.

DH: *Do you believe that Christianity is the only way to God?*

James: How can I? I was in Delhi for some time. It would be absurd to say only Indians who happen to be Christian speak to God. I don't believe in going out of my way to convert people of the other great religions. All that stuff's out of the window. Over-precision is what gets numbers into churches, moral certainties. But actually, faith is that which enables you to live with complexity. 'If any man think that he knoweth anything, he knoweth nothing yet as he ought to know.' There is a famous story of a vicar who marked his sermon, 'Shout loud. Argument weak.' That sums up religious extremists.

DH: *There seems to me a contradiction here. In private matters the Church is very liberal, talking about complexity and balance and understanding. But in public matters, it's become very moral.*

James: Yes, that's fair.

DH: *Is a priest now freer to live as he chooses?*

James: Not really, but the reason there are so many gay clergy in the cities is that you can hide your relationships much more effectively. In the country everyone knows your business.

DH: *I know a vicar whose boyfriend runs a sauna in St Martin's Lane . . .*

James: Do you? Well, he can probably get away with that in the big city.

DH: *The other reason seems to me the hours. It's gay clergy with no families who are willing to work these appalling hours. Their dedication is fantastic.*

James: There's a truth there; but I couldn't say gay clergy worked harder than married clergy – or vice versa.

DH: *But a priest can't, say, live openly with a woman?*

James: No. That's still impossible. There'd be letters to the bishop from jealous spinsters! Rejected lovers are the stuff of episcopal correspondence.

DH: *Isn't a gay priest necessarily a hypocrite?*

James: Of course. If by that you mean they can't 'tell all'. They're in the same position as priests in South Africa. If they tell the truth, they're thrown out. If they don't tell the truth, there's no point in their staying. I used to be very absolutist about things like this, and say the gay clergy should be allowed to be open and do what they like. But actually, I tell you, my greatest hero is the theologian Bonhoeffer. His friend was very shocked when he saw him give a Nazi salute during the war. But he said, 'Why not? It's not worth dying for. You have to decide what your sticking point is, and raising my arm isn't – just now.' Later, of course, Bonhoeffer gave his life.*

DH: *And presumably you mustn't offend the congregation?*

James: Yes, you mustn't offend them – and yes you must! It offends them deeply if they know that after the service, for the priest, it's 'on with the leather and off I go'. Your love must have integrity. But what is integrity in homosexual love? In the Anglican Church, no one ordained in the Church of England is allowed to live that out – as they are heterosexual love.

Tony Higton

I was very aware that in meeting so many liberal priests in the inner city I was getting a one-sided impression of the Church of England. So I decided to visit the Revd Tony Higton, whose name had been mentioned a number of times in the interviews I had so far done. Higton runs a spectacularly successful church in Southend (the town your Access bill comes from). It has an overflow hall with a TV screen for those who cannot get in every week. But the day I wanted to see him he was at the offices of the Christian Mission to Convert the Jews, which, for some reason, is based in St Albans. In a modern building, all around me, trucks were being loaded with pamphlets to go out and spread the word among Jews.

Higton was wearing cavalry twill trousers, suede shoes and no dog collar. He is well known on television and has run high-

---

*Dietrich Bonhoeffer became involved in the German resistance movement and in 1943 was arrested and imprisoned. In 1945 he was hanged at Flossenburg.

profile campaigns against what he sees as the dilution of Church doctrine.

Tony Higton: To me, Christianity is a supernatural religion, first and foremost. The transformation of human beings comes about through God's miraculous intervention. There is healing, and prayer has power to bring about God's intervention. I don't like that way of putting it, because it implies God is outside and sometimes comes along with a screwdriver, as if tampering with the system. In fact, He's present everywhere.

DH: *I'm very interested in this question of intervention, since the claim of intervention – Christ came down and intervened – seems to me at the very heart of Christianity. Can you give me an example of God's direct interventions in the world?*

Higton: God's intervention must involve something unusual such as the virgin birth or resurrection, or when a person is transformed through making a specific commitment to Christ. Then there is healing through prayer. I'll give you an example of the devil's intervention. The abortion rate. There have been three million cases of life being destroyed in the womb since 1967. This is demonic. It's a death-wish. We're not dealing with blobs of jelly.

DH: *Is the idea of judgement very important to you?*

Higton: The primary thing about God is love, not judgement. But judgement is *part* of love. You've got to be a nutter to like the subject of Hell, but if I believe in it, then it is deeply unloving of me not, at an appropriate time, to tell people about it. The absolute division is between those who believe that we all get to Heaven in the end, and those who believe in the alternatives – Heaven and Hell. I believe in the second, and in being honest about it.

Liberals have a vested interest in pretending the scriptures are open to many interpretations. I don't believe in a neurotic allegiance to the Bible – being sound on scripture *can* mean being dead from the neck up – but most of the New Testament is clear. There are certain issues, like infant baptism, on which we are not given direct instruction, but they are quite few. People respond to clear, definite statements. They hate waffle.

God is personal, God is loving. If that is true, then I would expect God to communicate in ways that are clear on all salient things. On the way of salvation, I would expect him to communicate with clarity. And that's why there's a written document, which gives you a permanent record of such vital teaching.

DH: *What do you think of inner-city priests who are not interested in converting souls?*

Higton: I cannot understand any Christian not interested in conversion. 'Make disciples of Christ' is the whole thrust of the New Testament. Of course, what's called 'the language of Zion' may not always communicate, you may have to find a new language, but the substance never changes.

I've learnt never to pontificate about individuals, but if a man dies without faith in Christ, then this will affect his destiny in the afterlife. There are two main commandments: Love the Lord your God with all your heart, mind, soul and strength; and Love your neighbour as yourself. Many Christians tend to make the second more important than the first. Of course your neighbour is important, but first you must be conscious that Jesus said, 'If you love me, keep my commandments.' You are not really loving to your neighbour if you are encouraging him to disobey God.

DH: *What do you think the essential commandments are?*

Higton: In addition to those I've mentioned, they are: sanctity of human life; respect for property; the commandment on coveting; that sex always be seen in a context of total commitment, i.e. marriage.

There is nothing immoral about homosexuality as a tendency. Being attracted is not a sin, it's a temptation. The sin is to gloat over the temptation, or to commit an act. Homosexuals deny it, but the latest research shows that sexuality *can* change, where there's a willingness for change. Nothing makes homosexuals angrier than this claim, but it's true. However, I do regret the finger-pointing that now goes on towards all single clergy, because of the prominence of this issue.

DH: *You've played an important role in Synod. Did you stumble into Church politics by accident?*

Higton: I'm not a political animal. I was sick to death of the Church of England because of its theological and moral confusion. I was thinking of withdrawing my church from the C of E. Then I went on a 24-hour retreat with a friend, and all I can say is, I did get what was clearly a call: to stay put but not to stay quiet. So I eventually stood for election to the Synod.

I was furious with the Archbishop of Canterbury at Diana's wedding when, bless his cotton socks, he spoke to 700 million people and did not proclaim the gospel, did not mention Christ. He missed the opportunity to do something very simple: to relate the act of faith two people make in marriage to the act of faith involved in the gospel. Any priest can do that, it's the simplest thing to do. And he didn't.

The Church should win the nation to Christ. Instead, many are inward-looking. The whole attitude is 'Let's keep this show on the road. Just maintain it.' Such churches deserve to close.

DH: *What provokes you most?*

Higton: Three things. The Bishop of Durham. I wrote to all 11,000 clergy to point out that the man was now denying something he had affirmed in order to become a bishop. Second, sexual immorality. That's adultery and homosexuality. Third, inter-faith compromise. And I have to say the third is much the most important. Christianity is the only true religion. We've lost our nerve if we don't proclaim that Christ is the *only* saviour. This is desperately serious. There's no gospel left if you go down the road of saying all religions are the same. Jesus said, 'No man comes to the Father but by Me.'

DH: *What's your objection to the Bishop of Durham's speech in which he denied the plausibility of the virgin birth and resurrection?*

Higton: I believe there was a literal, physical transformation, both of Mary's genes, and of the corpse in the tomb. Durham said that if you believe in a God who interfered with the chromosomes of Mary and the corpse of Jesus but didn't intervene in Auschwitz, then you are worshipping a cultic idol or even the very devil. Well, that is the God I believe in. His remark was blasphemous.

Why are we so nervous of the supernatural? I have seen evidence that an AIDS patient was cured by the laying on of hands. God is not outside a closed system. If he chooses to work in a different way, then he may. If he decides to do something differently, then he does. Christianity is essentially supernatural, and transformation may be spectacular, or it may be gradual, or unexpected, as when a liberal priest is converted even *after* ordination.

DH: *What do you feel about the bishops?*

Higton: Individually the bishops may be good men, but together they cancel each other out and the result is the lowest common denominator. My problem is, that denominator is too low. 'Don't rock the boat' is the motto. It's an old boys' club. I believe in satanic opposition, and of course the devil influences the House of Bishops. The leadership is always going to be the devil's number one target. I could forgive them failing, as long as they were seen to be trying. But they're so pathetic and over-cautious.

I'll give you an example. In the new catechism of the Church of England, we are all made to assert that we believe in the ministry of healing through the laying on of hands and oil. Why don't we practise it? What did Jesus do? He healed. In public. Not behind doors as some bishops urge on us. A softly-softly approach is codswallop. The bishops are so concerned that we are sensitive and relevant to modern culture. But when a culture undermines what the Church is about, then it is the culture that must change, not the Church. This phrase 'culturally sensitive' has come to mean 'hiding behind the culture' or changing our beliefs according to the culture.

Durham is intellectually dishonest because he made a vow when he became a bishop to uphold the creed, including the virgin birth, and now he denies it, which takes him down a theologically dangerous path towards Adoptionism – an early heresy that God united with an already-formed human being, which makes Christ two persons, not one. Christians have to believe in the resurrection of the body. Immortality of the soul is Hellenistic, not biblical.

DH: *So you're saying Christians have to believe in the resurrection of* *their own bodies. Does that mean we will recognize each other in heaven?*

Higton: We will have a body, yes. But it will be transformed, like that of Jesus on the road to Emmaus – it took the disciples a little time to realize who he was.

DH: *Do you believe in miracles?*

Higton: Belief in miracles is essential to Christianity. Some are just miracles of timing, as when Peter found the fish with the coin in its mouth. Well, I've been to Israel, and fish in the Sea of Galilee do swallow things, so the miracle is not the coin in the mouth, it's that Jesus knew the fish had swallowed it and that was the fish Peter caught. It's a miracle of timing.

DH: *You seem often to be saying the man or woman in the pew can pick or choose what beliefs they like, but that the leaders mustn't.*

Higton: The ordinary individual is, of course, free to choose his or her beliefs. But a teacher in the Church should believe what the Church stands for. Otherwise, you have every right to complain. On the sanctity of life, the Archbishop of York, as a scientist, says that he doesn't know if a new foetus is human or not, yet he will permit experiments for the first fourteen days.* These two statements are mutually contradictory. If it *may* be human, how can you allow experiment? Bishops have got to think harder than this.

DH: *One of the things I've noticed is a class difference, that the liberals tend to be upper-middle class and the evangelicals are lower-middle.*

Higton: If you say so, but I haven't noticed this.

DH: *Do you actually object to the Church being involved in social issues?*

Higton: No. Christianity affects the whole of life, including politics. But everyone likes being prophetic about South Africa and the Thatcher government because you can't get caught out being guilty of their crimes yourself. Whereas we're frightened to condemn private sin, adultery and so on, because we're worried we

---

*The Archbishop of York took part in two debates in the House of Lords on the Human Fertilization and Embryology Bill, on 7 December 1989 and 8 February 1990.

might turn out to be guilty of them ourselves. We're not obviously oppressing the poor. So we don't mind condemning those who are.

DH: *I'm sorry. I realize we've been talking for three hours. I've taken up far too much of your time.*

Higton: It's been very good for me. It's the kind of conversation I most enjoy.

Charles Moore

To find a representative of the Anglo-Catholic tendency, I went next to Charles Moore, who as editor of the *Spectator* had let his magazine become a platform for those who wanted to defend the traditional faiths of the Church. He had become interested in the workings of Synod while writing for the *Daily Telegraph*, and with A. N. Wilson had produced an extremely funny book, *The Church in Crisis* (1986), which guyed some of the absurder aspects of the modern Church.

Still in his early 30s, Moore sat in his Georgian office in Doughty Street, laconic, articulate and absolutely confident, barely needing a question from me to set off perfectly grammatical answers which offered that strange blend of high-power argument and unusual feeling which often marks the most successful journalists.

Charles Moore: My position is that the Synod undermines the nature of the Church of England. I believe that the brilliance of the arrangement in England is that there is a Church which is part of the Catholic Church and yet which also provides a solution to the problem of Church and State. The State can get on with its work without interference from the Church, and the Church can be protected from persecution.

What is also distinctive about the Church of England is that the structure of parishes is preferable to a command hierarchy. Its other virtue is that it's not a sect. Sacramentally you're a member by baptism, but you are not tested on your own beliefs. Just by being an Englishman you can get your religion.

DH: *Then what is your objection to the Synod?*

Moore: I believe the Synod undermines this arrangement by using the cant phrases of freedom, democracy and reform. Its effect is to centralize and to make it like the Church of Rome with God taken out. It's certainly more autocratic and more bureaucratic than it used to be. People think the Church is confused, which it certainly is intellectually and spiritually. But organizationally, it's very ordered.

In the twentieth century, people have been unable to understand what I call the 'genius of institutions'. The genius of the Church of England depended on the parson's freehold. That is to say, the right of a vicar, once appointed, to stay for the rest of his life if he wished. This was appropriate to the parish structure, and it spread power so that the priest did not have to do what the bishop wanted. But of course, this system goes against all the modern tenets of man management. Now, freehold is curtailed. And when parishes are amalgamated, bishops are able to appoint priests in charge who don't enjoy the same tenure.

DH: *But surely the problem of the modern Church is that it is all things to all men? Isn't it a good thing to have a debating chamber in which people decide what things they have in common?*

Moore: The Church has to have uniformity, but only in liturgy. There must be formulae shared by all its members. The Bible must be accepted, and the form of worship and rules of the Church must be apparent. Damage is done when exceptions are made to these rules – for example in the case of the remarriage of divorced people. It's just bloody obvious what the teaching is. Out of a misplaced desire to help, priests will say, 'Some of the most faithful people are divorced.' They want to help by telling a couple it's all right for them to get married again. But this is unfair because other parishioners say, 'Why should one person be allowed to remarry and not another?' Once moral judgements are introduced, dangerous subjectivity appears. Priests shouldn't be in a position to make these decisions, there should be rules and no exceptions.

Although there should be uniformity of liturgy, everyone in the Church may have a different understanding of the words. You can all say the same prayers and mean different things by them, whereas as soon as you force people to make a choice and express what they believe, then conscience enters into things. Everyone has a different understanding of the way in which they are talking to God, and for that reason bishops have to be very careful about what they say in public. Evangelicals believe in one thing: Bible study and personal conversion. Anglo-Catholics believe in something else: the real presence of Christ in the liturgy, purgatory and so on. All this holds together only because people are not forced into splits.

DH: *You seem to me to be arguing for an organized hypocrisy. The Church can't agree on anything, so they all shut up and pretend they do.*

Moore: No. It's not possible for a human being to understand God. If he could understand God he wouldn't be human, he would be in heaven. Enoch Powell is very good on this. He says, 'I wouldn't call myself a Christian, all I know is I am a member of the Church of England.' What I think he means by this is that nobody really knows what a Christian is. So you can't make up religion for yourself. You can't know, so you have to accept there is a tradition and an authority. Therefore in liturgy you can say things that you don't believe at the time or even understand.

DH: *I think your position is very inconsistent. It's you who's arguing that the genius of the Church of England is that it allows all points of view. But at the same time you threaten your Church by saying you'll leave it if they ordain women priests.*

Moore: That's right.

DH: *It seems to me the worst kind of blackmail. Surely if the Church is mutually tolerant, the one unforgivable tactic for any faction is to start making threats about leaving.*

Moore: I would leave the Church if women became priests. There are two overwhelming arguments. One is that women are already members, so they can't say that the Church doesn't exist unless they become priests. It exists without their becoming priests. All that would happen if they became priests would be that an issue would be forced which would divide people unnecessarily. Secondly, I can't accept women priests because it's not Catholic, it's not what Christ intended. If you believe, as I do, that the priest is sacramental, then I cannot see the evidence in scripture or tradition that women can administer the sacraments. I can't receive it of their hands. It would be a blasphemy. Of course, I'm not a theologian. I do not know for a fact that women cannot be priests. If the universal Church decided that women priests could be reconciled with scripture and tradition, then it would be a different matter. But the one thing I *am* sure of is that it is something which the General Synod cannot decide on its own.

The crucial question about the Church is what the true Church is. I have always believed that the Church of England was part of the true Church. But if, by their actions, they now cut themselves off from Catholic Christianity, they will be making the Church of England into a Protestant sect.

DH: *It seems to me that you are happy to tolerate a difference of beliefs, but you won't tolerate a sacramental difference?*

Moore: I don't mind if a priest is a bastard, a shit, as long as he performs his work in the accepted manner.

DH: *Really what you dislike about Synod is that it discusses belief at all.*

Moore: The Synod brings in a false idea of time. It is very improbable that suddenly a proposed change will represent the sum of historic wisdom of the Church. Twenty years in the history of the Church is only the batting of an eyelid. Therefore, to force issues is to turn people into a state of agitation. Religion becomes like politics.

The Synod doesn't command respect. Half of its membership is theologically unlearned, so it's in no position to dictate things theologically. It simply represents the opinions of a group of concerned people, which are of as much interest as that of any other group of people. The Synod is basically foreign to people's view of religion. You arrive at religion via a particular priest, or your friends, or by reading, not by what the Synod says.

DH: *I had a very interesting conversation with a bishop, who is on the evangelical wing of the Church. We were in the tea-room at Synod, having macaroons. He told me he definitely does believe in hell. I asked him why it was now so downplayed in the Anglican Church. He* *said he doesn't like to mention it for fear of putting people off.*

Moore: (*Angrily*) As a strategy, that has constantly failed. It's a counsel of defeat. It bewilders me how people can go on saying that the Church of England is doing the right things. If the Church of England was a cinema and showed Mickey Mouse films and nobody came, and everybody told you to show war films, and you said, 'I don't want to show war films, I want to show Mickey Mouse,' then you would say it was a lousy cinema. In the same way, ours is a lousy Church. People use spurious arguments to defend declining membership. They say that the mink-and-matins set have gone, and that people no longer go to the Church to impress their neighbours, and that there's a better quality of membership, that people now come with a more real faith. This is simply nonsense, an apology for the fact that our attendance goes on declining. The statistics are hard to get, but there are now more practising members of the Roman Church in England than practising members of the Church of England.

The main problem is a lot of sloppy PR. Priests going around saying they've got to do things which appeal to lots of people, particularly the young. They've done it fantastically badly. Bishops throw up their hands in horror at the idea of advertising, but I can't see what's wrong with it. It would be a good thing if the Church used modern PR methods – direct mail shots, advertising on hoardings. It's quite stunning, the Church's refusal to countenance proper religious broadcasting. All religious broadcasting is so bland. If you went on the *Today* programme and said, 'You'll go to hell if you don't come to Church,' it's pretty certain you'd never get asked again.

The Christian religion benefits from a mass following. It prospers when it has a vigorous popular expression as the Catholic Church in Europe does. There has to be a common habit of piety. In the United States, it's there. I don't like everything about religion in the States, but that's a cultural problem, a minor cultural objection. In England there once was widespread religion and it came through respect for the Word. Everybody had read the Bible, *Pilgrim's Progress*, The Book of Common Prayer. That is no longer true.

DH: *What worries me in the US is that in the average small town, yes, there's a religious bookstore and there's also a pornographic bookstore. The problem is, there's nothing in between.*

Moore: I'm not a liberal, so I can't say that's a matter of overwhelming concern to me.

DH: *Can you imagine a revival in the Church of England's fortunes?*

Moore: Not really, no. But at least atheism has ceased to advance. A Christian is no longer thought to be a contemptible backwoodsman. You don't lose points among intellectuals now if you say you are a Christian. My feeling is that the age of atheism is over. Other religions are going through a revival and the Church of England ought to be in on this but isn't, because bishops are wrong about what is the right way in for people. Television is absolutely crucial. So is education – more Church schools. The point about Christianity is that you need to know quite a lot in order to understand it. You and I take it for granted because we were taught it at school. The most important thing is to make sure that it goes on being taught in school.

DH: *It really depends how it's taught. I rather sympathize with T. S. Eliot, who said once you start reading the Bible as literature, you're no longer reading the Bible.*

Moore: You may well be right, but nothing can be worse than the present situation where no one in England reads it at all.

PART TWO

Murmuring
Judges

Out of the crooked timber of humanity no straight thing was ever made.

Immanuel Kant (1724–1804)

Her Majesty's judges are well pleased with the almost universal esteem in which they are held.

Lord Hewart (1870–1943)

So long as a judge keeps silent, his reputation for wisdom and impartiality remains unassailable.

Lord Chancellor Kilmuir, 1955

Someone must be trusted; let it be the judges.

Lord Denning

The hottest places in hell are reserved for those who, in times of great moral crisis, maintain their neutrality.

Dante (1265–1321)

The only reason that cocaine is all the rage today is that people are too dumb and lazy to get themselves together to roll a joint.

Jack Nicholson

You don't blame firemen for an increase in fires. Why blame us for an increase in crimes?

Policeman quoted in Robert Chesshyre's *The Force* (1988)

The first duty is to ensure that a man emerging from prison is not more depraved than when he entered it.

Lionel Fox

Being a thief is a terrific life, but the trouble is they do put you in the nick for it.

Bobby King

Society needs to condemn a little more and understand a little less.

John Major, 1993

British justice isn't interested in getting at the truth, only in obtaining a conviction.

Lord Hailsham

THE LAW

By the time rehearsals began for *Racing Demon*, it was already clear to me that my second play would have to be about the law. It was my original, rather lazy, intention to move the focus of my interests from priests to lawyers. But as soon as I began work I saw the comparison was not going to wash. Whereas priests tried, however indecisively, to minister to the real needs of the people among whom they lived, lawyers were, on the other hand, only the highly paid bit-part players in a much more complicated process. If you ask me the simple question, 'What do lawyers *do*?' then I think, in criminal law at least, the essential answer is: 'They hand people on.'

It was the judges' own refusal to recognize that they were only part of a long and fallible process, and not in any sense separate from or superior to it, which had begun to make them so controversial throughout the eighties. I am sure they had good, legal reasons in their own minds why, as representatives of a State which had wrongfully imprisoned the Birmingham Six, the Guildford Four, and the Maguires, they felt they could not make full and proper apology for the failings of that State's judicial system.* But the impression they created at home and abroad by their obvious surliness did their reputation no favours.

Throughout my researches in the Inns of Court, I met lawyers who would not acknowledge that there had been miscarriages of

---

*The Guildford Four were jailed for life in 1975 after being convicted over the 1974 pub bombings which killed five in Guildford. They were released in October 1989 after discovery of irregularities in police evidence.

The Birmingham Six were convicted in 1975 of the murder of twenty-one people in two pub bombings in Birmingham in 1974. They were released in March 1991 when some of the forensic evidence was discredited.

The Maguire Seven were convicted in 1976 on explosives charges arising out of the Guildford and Woolwich pub bombings. Their sentences ranged from five to fourteen years. Their convictions were quashed in June 1991 after doubts arose over forensic evidence.

justice, but who rather sought to assure me that the full facts of these Irish cases had not been disclosed; that there was more to them than had met the eye; that it was not the prisoners' innocence which had been established, but only their guilt which had not been unarguably proved; and that if only certain other kinds of evidence had been admissible at these appeals, the eventual verdicts might have been very different. It is one of the most illuminating ironies of the Bar that men and women trained in the hard crafts of sifting and examining evidence should, outside their own working arena, have less resistance to the virus of gossip than any other professional body I know. Forensic in court, lawyers are credulous outside. The house magazine of the law is not the *Bar Council Journal*. It is *Private Eye*. Every time a barrister lowered his voice or put his hand on my arm, then I knew what was coming: yet another unattributable briefing on what was always called 'the full picture'.

It did not need a qualified Freudian to see that, during the time I spent in it, the legal system had, with honourable exceptions, gone into an off-the-record state of denial, smarting at its own mistakes and turning round to blame everyone but itself. The Birmingham Six were asked by the Court to leave through the back door. When they refused and, at their own insistence, marched out through the front to greet the waiting crowds in the street, arms held high above their heads, then I admit I cried. It was partly, of course, because I now knew something of the conditions in which the Six had wasted so many years of their lives. But also, frankly, I was jealous. Their case was essentially simple. They had been wrongly imprisoned, and now they were free. The emotion flowed easily because the case was black and white. But I had realized already that if I wished to write a truthful play about the law's more typical processes, then I would be working in more attritional shades of grey.

Most criminal cases are not simple. A large proportion involve habituated criminals doing things which are genuinely damaging and dangerous but for which no available punishment seems to work. Many more involve people who are simply not adequate to cope with life's daily demands, and for whom all the usual processes seem laborious at best.

The people trying to keep their sense of humour in the face of these massive contradictions are the police.

CLAPHAM POLICE STATION

The Metropolitan Police offered me a selection of London police stations to visit. They discouraged me from visiting the more controversial ones, like Brixton or Notting Hill, on the grounds that they were 'untypical'. It was a suggestion I was happy to go along with, since I, too, wanted to find a police station which had not been written about too much in the press. However, the truth is that all policemen are well used to being watched. A constant complaint is that they are never allowed to get on with their work unsupervised. They are always being told from above how to adjust their behaviour. They are accustomed to wearing what they, in their own striking phrase, call 'an overcoat of values'. For that reason, one playwright more or less made no difference to them. But by great good fortune, one of the nicks suggested to me was close to the parish in which I was setting the first part of the trilogy, *Racing Demon*.

Clapham Police Station is known as 'The Alamo'. It is a lone Victorian building entirely surrounded by high blocks on one of the borough's grimmer housing estates. Although crime on the estate is said to have gone down considerably over the years, the little red-brick police station still does have an embattled air. Police at Clapham say that the building is absurdly inefficient and old-fashioned, but its smallness actually creates a markedly happy atmosphere. Everywhere you go is the smell of hearty cooking from the canteen.

Throughout the writing of *Murmuring Judges*, I liked to return to Clapham Police Station whenever I could, just to hang out. It occurred to me that perhaps what I was enjoying was a rather dishonourable feeling of safety. For once in my life, I was on the right side. Whatever poor wretch they brought in through the door, it was not going to be me. But stronger still was the enjoyment of a developing soap opera in which Authority and Fear are the central characters.

First Visit: Thursday, 8 November 1990

I go to meet the man who has allowed me into his police station, Chief Superintendent Bill Wilson. He has an upstairs office which has the mandatory shelf of sporting silverware which most senior officers seem to boast. Wilson is an amiable Scot in his 50s, baldheaded and genial. He is married to the thriller writer Jacqueline Wilson.

Bill Wilson: We have 152 constables and fifty civilian staff working here. We also have CID, Crime Squad and the appropriate number of supervisors. At any one time there are about twenty on the street, usually on reliefs which rotate at seven a.m., three p.m. and eleven p.m. I also employ a Divisional Support Team which is available as an aid unit for demonstrations or public order operations. When not so engaged they provide support on this Division to tackle crime problems. On the mainset radio we have access to a quarter of the whole Metropolitan area, so it's not hard to rustle up officers.

DH: *All your emphasis now seems to be on prevention of crime rather than prosecution.*

Wilson: We are trying to change the attitude of some of our community towards crime. At the moment there are members of the public who do not report crime to us because they fear reprisals. They are genuinely frightened. We are trying to convince them that if they band together against crime then they could transfer their fear on to the shoulders of the criminal – make the villains fear detection. At present, some people sell drugs openly in the street because they believe they are safe. They are confident it won't be reported.

Recently we had a prostitute; she was gang-raped, she reported it to us. But then, when we were going to get the men, she

64

withdrew. Fear. She didn't dare go through with it. Then they attacked and raped her again. This time she did come back to us, and stayed with us, and we sent them down for twelve years this week.

DH: *Does she feel safe now?*

Wilson: She's had post-trauma counselling, victim support and so on. We're much better at all that nowadays.

DH: *I know the crime figures go up and up, but is it true that most of the crime in an area like this is committed by the same people all the time?*

Wilson: That's right. There are 200 people out there committing most of our crime. We rarely arrest anyone for burglary who hasn't got a criminal record. It's very frustrating, but what of course you mustn't do is just round up the usual suspects.

DH: *Are you also frustrated by the mistrust juries now have for police evidence?*

Wilson: We're living with all the mistakes of fifteen years ago. The mistrust comes from then, it's historical. And it's unfair, because we have now accepted the right of the prisoner to have their solicitor present. And we accept the fact that the solicitor is almost bound to advise silence. I can't pretend it isn't frustrating. It is. There's a lot of frustration. I think people should realize that there are a great many safeguards now entrenched in law which give suspects a lot of protection.* These mean that there is now far less chance of a serious miscarriage of justice than there used to be. Another thing that is frustrating is that the Guildford Four, Birmingham Six and other cases had nothing to do with the Met. We tend all to get tarred with the same brush, which is unfair. The irony is that the police are often accused of stereotyping, and yet more often than not we are the victims of it.

*The Police and Criminal Evidence Act, introduced by Leon Brittan in 1984, replaced the old Judges' Rules. Although in some instances it gave the police extra powers, it laid out very precisely what was and was not permissible in the course of an investigation. Certain rights – such as that of the arrested person not to speak before his solicitor arrives – were made absolute. A suspect is entitled to ask for the PACE Codes of Practice, and the custody officer is, in theory, independent of the arresting officer.

DH: *Do you think the so-called canteen culture is still prevalent in the police? The paranoia, the secretiveness, the contempt for the senior officers?*

Wilson: Of course, there are some who sit in the canteen spreading alarm and despondency and lowering morale. You have to remember they are involved in a difficult and often thankless task which can interfere with their home life. There is far less downright cynicism and subversion now because we encourage open, honest and frank discussion which tends to make any criticism constructive. I don't understand what you mean about paranoia and I do not believe there is contempt for senior officers. I trust and respect my colleagues, and as far as possible I let them get on with the job in hand with minimal interference. I believe some think they succeed in spite of management and others feel they do not get the support they deserve. This is particularly true in public order situations. The Force is changing, it's healthier and fitter. Less canteen culture and less canteen stodge. It used to be beer and chips with everything in the service long ago, now it's diet Coke and yoghurt.

DH: *Are they happy to have me here?*

Wilson: They're suspicious of you, of course. You're the media. You must remember, they have put up with an awful lot of misrepresentation. They're used to doing a great deal of good in the community, and they're used to having it thrown back in their face.

Second Visit

6.30 a.m. When I arrive, the constable at the desk says, 'I thought policemen were meant to be easily recognizable, but I could tell you were a playwright the moment I saw you.' The night turn is going off, early turn is coming on. There is parade at seven with the duty inspector.

I go into the charge room. This room is at the centre of all low-grade police work, for it is here that anyone who is brought in off the street is processed. At Clapham, it is still markedly old-fashioned. There is a long desk at which the custody officer sits, surrounded by his paperwork. Opposite him is the door to the outside world. Through it come all the officers, bringing in the trivial offenders who provide the station with most of its work. Off in one direction, to the officer's right, are the CID offices. To his left are six police cells which are supervised by the custody officer and his immediate superior, the inspector. On a board behind him, to make sure he conforms with the rules of the Police and Criminal Evidence Act (PACE), the sergeant pentels the state of play on each of the people in his keeping.

Currently in the cells are two Jamaicans, being held on behalf of Immigration before being flown home. Immigration uses police stations as a dumping ground. An armed robber should be taken in a special van to court, but twenty out of thirty-one drivers have reported sick, so he goes in a police car, handcuffed to a constable named Clive. The robber has apparently kept up a stream of sexual abuse against Liz, who has just done the night shift as custody officer.

Clive: Well, you do get people who hate the police, but I don't take any notice, because I have the last laugh. You lock 'em up and you walk away. So what? It's us who have the key.

About half the local officers live in what they call the blue belt – Sutton, Cheam, Carshalton. The pay is much better than it was, but 'worse than a long-distance lorry driver'. I am talking to the inspector about a 'well-known public figure who's just been acquitted. They took his fingerprints and they've found he's guilty of an armed robbery. But they've been told it's not in the public interest to prosecute him.' Meanwhile, Liz is playing a game with Martin, the sergeant who is today's custody officer. They are testing each other on the PACE Act.

Martin: What power were they using?
Liz: Section 18.
Martin: Think about it! THINK ABOUT IT!!

A 14-year-old Syrian boy comes in, accused of putting his hand up a woman's skirt on Clapham Common. He is very backward, resentful. At first he won't speak at all.

Martin: You have a right to a solicitor.
Boy: What's a socilitor?
Martin: Sign there. Just your normal signature.
Boy: It's small. (*He signs*) Signing's creepy.

They put him in a cell. He starts banging on the door, very loudly and with no rhythm. When they move him for interview, he swings a pathetic punch at Martin, who is six feet tall and very broad. The boy's father arrives, an ex-sergeant major in the Syrian army, whose wife died when the boy was 3. His eyes are full of tears.

Father: In Syria they would shoot you for this.

They are led off. Martin turns to talk to me.

Martin: I don't mind them being rude to me, all the lip we get, it means nothing to me, but I hate it when it's in front of their parents. If they don't know how to behave in front of their parents, then it really gets me. Because that's where the law starts. The family *is* the law, isn't it?

The CID find five similar offences which they want to ascribe to the boy – they have good descriptions. But his attention span is so poor and his mind so confused that they can only interview him for five minutes at a time, then leave him for half an hour with his father.

Martin: The problem is, his father is leading him, turning prosecutor, so we have to stop the interview, because you have to say, well, thanks very much, but that's not on.

Later they apply for a duty solicitor, which they are entitled to under PACE, and along comes a florid Scot in his early 60s, unbelievably sleazy and apparently half-pissed.

Martin: He used to be a detective inspector.
DH: *So how can he now be a solicitor?*
Martin: Well, he's not, is he? He's a solicitor's clerk. It's a boom business. Since PACE everyone's entitled to ask for a solicitor. Well, there's no way qualified solicitors could come out to every call, even if they wanted to, so they send clerks. We do have the right to refuse them, but we almost never do. He gets paid really for just turning up.

Meanwhile, they are charging someone who has come in voluntarily to admit a failure to appear in court.

Man: I'm not going into a court on my own. Last time I spoke to a judge on my own he got very stroppy. Related to Judge Jeffreys, I think.

The desk constable looks in.

Constable: Oh, if the playwright's in, we won't give that bloke a kicking now. We'll do it when the playwright's gone.

Round the desk there is a confusion of paperwork about a lost case.

Martin: Do you know where the custody record is?
Constable: I got it, Sarge.
Martin: Do you know what this other offence was?
Constable: Sorry, Sergeant, no. You see, the papers have gone to Brixton, the warrant came up here. We can't find the papers in the crime desk.

The prisoners need meals, for which the sergeant is ripping out forms marked 'LIGHT MEAL VOUCHER' and 'VERY LIGHT MEAL VOUCHER'. A woman and her son have been brought in on suspicion of passing stolen cheques. She is ordered off to a search. Clive falls over with the light meals, spilling them on the floor.

Clive: Someone left a fucking bucket behind that fucking door.

The testing has started up again on PACE.

Liz: All right, what's a 3416?
Martin: Oh, you always ask the easy questions first.

A CID officer passes a blonde policewoman.

CID man: Do you need to do a search? You can search me if you're bored.

Martin is laughing to me about the boy's attack on him.

Martin: He came in with an attitude. He's got an attitude. He's got to do something about his attitude. He hates the police. (*He smiles, spreads his arms open*) Not much point in hating the police, is there?

The cleaner, Sylvia – in her 60s – is complaining about who banned ashtrays in the canteen, with the resulting fag-ends on the floor everywhere.

Sylvia: I know who it is. It's a man with three stripes on his shoulder. I'm not saying who. I didn't sign the Official Secrets Act for nothing.

Clive is complaining to Martin.

Clive: Cell One doesn't want a cup of tea.
Martin: No, well, I didn't tell you. Cell One's been moved to Cell Three.

Meanwhile I am reading the PACE Act, Guidance for Policemen Manual:

ON RECEIPT OF A <u>BAILREP</u> MESSAGE, THE STATION OFFICER WILL COMPLETE FORM 41 CLEARLY MARKING IT TEMPORARY.

THE FORM WILL BE GIVEN A CONSECUTIVE SERIAL NUMBER
AND PLACED IN THE BINDER AND INDEXED. WHEN THE PERSON
REPORTS, THE STATION OFFICER WILL SATISFY HIMSELF AS TO
THE IDENTITY OF THE CALLER, OBTAIN HIS SIGNATURE ON
TEMPORARY FORM 41, INSERT THE DATE AND TIME OF
ATTENDANCE AND SIGN THE ENTRY. ON RECEIVING THE
ORIGINAL FORM 41 FROM THE COURT, HE WILL STAPLE IT TO
THE TEMPORARY FORM. THE SIGNATURES OF THE PERSON CAN
THEN BE CONTINUED ON THE SAME FORM. ON RECEIPT OF A
MESSAGE STATING THAT A PERSON IS RELEASED FROM HIS
UNDERTAKING, THE STATION OFFICER WILL REMOVE THE
FORM 41 FROM THE BINDER AND FORWARD IT TO THE CHAR-
GING STATION WHERE IT WILL BE FILED WITH THE CASE
PAPERS. SHOULD A PERSON FAIL TO REPORT IN ACCORDANCE
WITH THE CONDITIONS A FAILREP MESSAGE IS TO BE SENT
FORTHWITH . . .

I talk to the CID officer about what will happen to the boy.

CID man: Well, he'll go to Juvenile Liaison. He's obviously a
nut'n'gut.

We discuss the days before the Crown Prosecution Service.

CID man: In the old days, you had your body, you were with the
body, you stayed with the body, you saw the body into court, he
was yours. You got the body sent down . . . The other day, I
interviewed an old villain who maintained his right to silence
throughout, then said, 'I don't know why you don't just give me a
good beating and I confess, like in the old days.'

News comes in of an accident.

CID man: Sounds like a job for the police to me.

Somebody is giving statements for filing to the custody officer.

Constable: Don't read the last one. It's *War and Peace*.

I am discussing ID parades.

Martin: A member of the public gets £4 for doing a parade. Outside Brixton police station there's a load of blacks and students hanging around in the hope of getting on one . . .

I talk to another officer about the shock of being posted to the much plusher surroundings of Banstead in Surrey.

Constable: People say things like, 'Hello, officer.' There are trees and squirrels and people don't throw fridges and mattresses from sixty feet on to your head.

An Asian CID man is laughing about a dinner he went to with other officers, and the comedian, who held back on the Paki jokes.

Asian CID man: Yeah, I got off lightly there.

The PACE game has started again. The inspector checks to see if any reviews are due. After six hours' detention, each case has to be reviewed by him to check proper progress is being made. Then after another six, then another nine. Then, after twenty-four hours, application has to be made to the Magistrates Court. A man is brought in on suspicion of having another person's cheque cards in his car. He is in a bad state – a pop promoter who has gone bankrupt, losing £5,000 on a rock concert. His friend later turns up and testifies the cards are his, and he's released. The boy on indecency charges has admitted the lot and is told to come back in January when he will be dealt with.

Martin: Nice result. How long have you been running it?
CID man: Six weeks.
Martin: It's nice when it ties up. I like it when it ties up.

A lively discussion starts up about magistrates.

CID man: Everyone prefers stipendiaries. If you get three JPs, they're known as The Muppets.
Martin: We always get a rise of crime in November because Christmas is coming and there's a lot of money about. But a lot of petty crime goes down because the weather changes and it's too cold to go thieving. Just because Clapham isn't Brixton, people think it's soft and easy here. But it's the same problems. It's tough.
Asian CID man: It's a time-bomb.
DH: *Oh, you mean it'll go off some time?*
Asian CID man: No. Time-bomb, like simmering, under everything.

I look at the drugs cupboard. The popular current way of importing LSD is inside Ninja Turtle stickers. There is a Batman sticker with LSD in it. There is some brown heroin which comes wrapped in exercise paper for £5 an inch square. Martin is very keen to show me the breathalyser machine. He tries to get me to swallow vodka, but when I say it's too early, he drinks it himself. Then he blows in. It doesn't work. The alternative in these circumstances would be a blood test which would take four weeks. The fingerprints done today for a cheque fraud will take six to eight weeks to return.

Now it's three p.m. and Alf comes on, twenty minutes early, to replace Martin. Change of relief. Alf is less outgoing than Martin. He's darker, more serious. A boy comes in for cannabis possession. He's 17, so his parents don't have to be called if he doesn't want. The arresting officer says he's got two previous convictions, won't tell me what for.

Constable: What's annoying is, I've brought this body in, it takes two minutes to arrest him, now I've got to hang around the station for an hour before I can get out there again. If you get a good body, I mean a really good body, you can end up waiting around the station for eight hours or more. The greater part of the job is waiting around. I was originally suspicious of the boy when we came upon him tampering with a car. He ran off, then returned five minutes later. Most criminals are stupid. John McVicar was meant to be this great criminal, but he still got caught. They do, don't they?

I have noticed already that this whole relief has a different character to the last – less ebullient, less fun. People are slipping off down corridors to avoid speaking in front of me. A man has come in, charged with doing criminal damage to a van after an accident with a lorry. But it was his own van he'd damaged. His account does not tally with that of other witnesses, so this one will go to court. As Alf does the paperwork, he talks to me.

Alf: All the pressure is on me, in this job. I'm insulted by the PACE Act because they're not trusting me to get on with my job. Everything has to be written down, as if I'm not trusted. It was left-wing legislation to make us more accountable and quieten the public, which it has. But the problem is, it's filled the law with innuendos, which the villain understands and can use and take advantage of, so he can delay and delay. Whereas the bloke who's never been arrested before doesn't know the ropes, so the safeguards are no use to him.

When the van driver leaves, the CID man looks to Alf.

Alf: In and out in half an hour. Come on, be fair, you can't do better than that. (*He turns to me*) The thing is, we both know, the court appearance is in three weeks, the case will be remanded for another four, then in January the lorry driver, who has to come from Huddersfield, probably won't appear and the case will be dropped.

There is now a rush of new arrests – a man who has beaten up his girlfriend, another who is accused of attacking his friend's sister while mending her washing machine.

Alf: Do you understand the charge?
Man: Yes.
Alf: Good.
Man: All I need is an interpreter.
Alf: Sure. No problem. What is your language?
Man: Portuguese.
Alf: Uh-huh.
(*Pause. Alf looks at the clock.*)
Alf: Ah yes, now can we get an interpreter who speaks Portuguese at ten minutes' notice at five o'clock on a Monday night?

He lets the man go.

Alf: Thank God I had the sense not to start filling out the form. Look, I've just written the number, nothing else. Because I had him spotted. If I'd filled in the charge, then found he couldn't speak English, I'd have been in all sorts of trouble.

Third Visit

Saturday night in the charge room. On the blackboard someone has scribbled:

NOTIFIABLE ARRESTS	UP 19%
CLEAR UPS	UP 21%
MANPOWER	DOWN 11%
OVERTIME	DOWN 52%

The police have had to get their shields out this evening, because a Scotsman has barricaded himself into his house after a row with his wife, smashed his place up, then thrown a chair at a police car. He has taken seven of his wife's tranquillizers and is having trouble standing up and saying his name. He is a kitchen porter, 35. He has children by his first wife, but none by his second, who is mentally ill. When the custody officer says, sorry, he has to put him in a cell till the doctor comes, he says, 'No, no, you're doing your job.' When the doctor comes, he recommends transfer to hospital. The ambulancemen come later and take him away. The inspector and two sergeants discuss what to charge him with. His wife does not want to press charges, so they settle for 'Affray', and then think which forms to fill in for damage to police property.

A young black woman has been caught in Sainsbury's with a listed stolen cheque card and cheque book. The transaction has been recorded on video. Supermarket security officers have handed her a letter banning her from Sainsbury's – which means that if she does it again, the charge will be burglary, not theft. Her boyfriend has seen the police coming and run off. She has already run up £700 on the card today, buying clothes. She is explaining to Taffy, a middle-aged bald Welsh policeman, that she is an artist really. She is crying. She has recently had cancer and is not sure if she has recovered. She is already on probation for theft and deception. The custody officer gets out the forms. She can't understand what he's saying.

Sergeant: It's all right. I talk to myself. Non compos mentis. Where are you from?

Before she can answer, a very loud Irish WPC comes barging in.

Rhona: I'm from Stornoway, if that's what you're asking. Where are the keys?

She can see they're lying on the desk, but she reaches for some other keys on the sergeant's belt.

Rhona: I know the keys are not in your back pocket, but I can't resist feeling your bum.

The sergeant turns to me.

Sergeant: It's a problem here. Over-excited young women.
Constable: They treat you as a sex-object, Sarge. It's degrading.

Another policeman arrives with Kentucky fried nuggets for everyone. A CID officer arrives, while the young woman is strip-searched by Rhona.

CID officer: When Rhona's finished with her, bang her up.

I have been told Saturday nights can get very busy, but it seems no different from the day to me: the steady stream of petty offenders; the constable who has broken his arm playing rugby; a boy accused of kicking a bus conductor, who is claiming the conductor kicked him first; another boy, thought to be breaking into cars; yet another, on suspicion of possession of drugs. A 26-year-old is brought in for shoplifting a packet of cakes and showing aggression to the shopkeeper. He is brought in by two officers from Kennington, who take the custody officer aside to say that, unless he's got drugs on him, this one isn't worth the bother of charging. So the sergeant authorizes a search.

DH: *Why aren't you bothering with a charge?*
Sergeant: Because you are looking at Kennington's entire police force for tonight, and the sooner we get back on the street, the better.

Rhona comes back in, restless, taking it out on the custody officer for not having yet charged the bus-conductor boy.

Rhona: Things are not moving. Nothing's happening. I've been waiting two hours. Why isn't anything happening tonight? Can't we go ahead and charge and get out of here?
Taffy: You're looking good.
Rhona: You're looking good 'n'all.

An angry policeman slams down the phone when he's disconnected from somewhere and says, 'Oh fuck.' This is all he says all evening. A constable comes in.

Constable: Has Rachel talked to you about going skiing?

Rhona: You don't want me. Because I'd be the centre of attention.
Constable: No. Because, you see, we're going to ski.

In come two dog handlers.

Rhona: Christ. Buried beneath policemen.

We all fall into a group discussion about why there are no police on the streets of Kennington on a Saturday night. It turns out that there were only six in the first place; sickness, marches etc. have depleted numbers. The two Kennington officers who delivered the shoplifter were in the Old Kent Road when the call came, in the area car, the Sierra, what they call the 'jam sandwich'. They turned on the blue light and drove like the clappers to Lavender Hill.

Kennington PC: It was unbelievably exciting. I mean, it really is fun, pitting your wits against idiot drivers who slow up when they see your blue light. A Wing Commander who travelled with us once said it was more exciting than low-level jet-fighter flying.

The cars are called Lima One, Lima Three and Whisky One. One of the policemen's wives is in a writing class.

Constable: They were all asked to write about the police, and people produced the usual stuff about how we're sexist, racist and thick. But my wife's essay was brilliant, just about two policemen sitting by traffic lights, and how all the paranoid public think it's because they're trying to catch people jumping them, but in fact it's because they're waiting for their grub break.

Everyone agrees how bad TV shows about the police are.

Constable: Because they miss the humour, that's the main thing. It is very, very funny in the police. They get the CID wrong.

They don't have any authority over us. If they treated us the way they do in the series, we'd tell them to get fucked. They're *our* servants, not the other way round. *The Bill* is the worst – all that people shouting at each other and banging the desk. It just doesn't happen.

Everyone agrees that *Hill Street Blues* is the best.

Constable: Sorry, mate, but it is. They've got the philosophy and the philosophy curve right.

The CID officer comes out with a girl accused of fraud. He is thrilled with a fax from Wimbledon which describes how the credit card was stolen from a car, plus a note saying the constable will help in any way he wants.

CID man: This is practically unheard of. It's brilliant. First, that he answers at once. Second, that he offers help. You're looking at something unique here.

I'm left alone with the custody officer, and he tells me he was reading in *The Economist* that for some reason Africans are drawn to cheque-book thefts.

Sergeant: It's true. And Indians to fraud. They're very clever. And I'm sorry to have to say it, but the Irish are drunks. Seventy per cent of drunks are Irish. What does go on over there?

He warns me not to speed down Whitehall when I've had a drink.

Sergeant: They haven't got anything to do in that area, you see. No crime in Whitehall. So they sit there all night nabbing drunk drivers. Take it slow down Whitehall, whatever you do.

It's now moving towards dawn and I say I'm only holding on to see what he's going to say to the 26-year-old who's been shop-lifting the £1.06 Jaffa Cakes.

Sergeant: Oh, you waiting for that? OK, well, I've got to give him a bollocking. Pretty pointless, but I've got to pretend I care.

The man is brought in. He works in a car wash and is going to be aggressive until he realizes he's going to be let off.

Sergeant: Have you got any children?
Man: I've got a boy.
Sergeant: What would you do if he did what you've done today?
Man: I'd beat him round the face.
Sergeant: Well, exactly. (*Pause*) Perhaps I should get your dad to come and deal with you.
Man: My dad's dead.

When I get home I find, while I've been out, my house has been burgled.

Fourth Visit

As I arrive, first thing in the morning, I overhear two police constables, one male, one female.

Male: Where's the major incident cupboard?
Female: Try the major incident room.

An officer has died on his motorcycle on the way in to work. The inspector says, 'It throws a pall over the nick.' I go out in the van with Taffy and Peter. Taffy used to be in South Wales police, left to start a gymnasium and health club in Swansea, which failed, and, as 'they never take you back in South Wales', joined the Met. He commutes back to Wales on his days off. Peter used to be a teacher in a comprehensive in Croydon, but left because, 'I just got sick of the government intervention in education.' Of course, on the road you realize how much of the job is driving, and a lot of the talk is about driving.

Peter: I'm classified for a van driver.

Taffy: Did you do a reversing test?

Peter: Oh yes, yes. But it varies from area to area. Surrey don't do chases. They don't do any bandit work. The Surrey Advance course isn't the same as the Met. (*Fast corner*)

Peter: Beautiful driving.

Taffy: Your life in their hands.

Peter: I'd prefer my wife in their hands. Shall we go down Dorset Road?

Taffy: There's a report of someone who looks like George Michael hanging about apparently selling drugs.

Peter: Who's George Michael?

DH: *I used to live down here, in Richborne Terrace.*

Peter: Well, somebody has to.

Taffy: (*As we roar through a light*) Easiest red light in Clapham.

We are going to an alarm which is ringing outside a building by the Common. We brake violently as a man on a pedestrian crossing drops his cigarette.

Taffy: Oh, don't worry about getting run over, just pick up your fag.

Peter: Prat!

DH: *It's odd. You've got a blue light on this van, but no siren.*

Peter: If you're wondering why, so are we.

We hunt for a burglar for twenty minutes at the building, then give up. Next we go to where a man has knocked down a traffic light.

Peter: Why didn't he just drive off, like everyone else does?

We take an injured motorcyclist to St Thomas' hospital, then we go back to the canteen to write up the three accidents this morning. Each one involves filling a whole booklet. There are huge, wonderful-looking plates of sausages, chips, eggs and beans in the canteen.

Peter: Yeah, I was up at five-thirty. A health breakfast is all very well, but by the time you've been four hours on the street, it doesn't seem such a good idea.

In the canteen I fall to talking to an older Scot called Jim, who is the Police Federation representative and who has seen changes in police methods over the years. He claims, as everyone in Clapham does, that things are better than five or ten years ago.

Jim: It's our own fault we alienated the blacks. When they first came, their respect for the law was astonishing. If you had to deal with a West Indian, one person would give their side, the other would never interrupt before they gave theirs, then they would expect you to deal justice there and then. And they would accept it. You could walk alone into a room of 200 people and ask them to turn the music down – which they did, for ten minutes anyway – and you'd get a wonderful reception. I once saw a man spitting in the street and I said to him, 'That is absolutely disgusting. Never, ever do that again.' He said to me, 'Where are you from?' I said, 'Dundee.' He said, 'That explains it.' But he *did* say he'd never do it again. Now, if you said that to a black man today, you'd start a riot. But it's because we didn't understand their culture. They had parties they called Birthnight parties, where you went and bought drink on the door, because there were too many people for the host to be able to provide it for everyone. Maybe 200 people at once. Well, of course, the Licensed Victuallers Association made representation, the publicans were furious, and in we went and broke these parties up. We didn't understand. We didn't understand you can't get a wife to testify in court against a husband who's been violent with her when she's spent ten years with him, and intends to spend the next ten with him.

DH: *Were the police racist?*

Jim: I never *saw* how racist some policemen were, but then there were so many stories, finally I had to accept it was true.

DH: *I keep hearing about this astonishing juvenile in Clapham who's distorting your crime figures.*

Jim: That's right. There is one boy on our patch who is single-handedly responsible for 20 per cent of all the crime in our area. Twenty per cent! He's completely crazy, and he's 13. His latest trick is to steal motorcars and drive them down the wrong side of the road at forty miles an hour. He'll steal anything. Motorbikes – he's sometimes seen on a 750cc bike, just so he can have a chase against police cars. If you amputated both his hands he'd steal with his teeth. We brought him in once with his 9-year-old brother. He punched his social worker in the face, then, when we asked him if he had anything to say to the charge, he said to his brother: 'Say nothing. We'll have them for wrongful arrest.'

A group of us go on talking as the canteen clears, and I realize that everyone I talk to has a physical method of dealing with the frustrations of the job. Apart from rugby, the most popular pastimes are rock-climbing and flying. Few here would dream of *living* in Clapham, or indeed in the inner city at all. They regard it simply as a place to commute into.

Downstairs, I go for my usual fix of charge room petty crime: two runaways from Wales and a couple of bail jumpers.

Constable: What are we waiting for? You get so used to waiting you sometimes forget what you're waiting for.

But the atmosphere is so lethargic today – it's cold outside and there's no crime – that he still doesn't move. When I go into the operations room, the telephone operator looks glumly at me.

Operator: I gather it's stress you're interested in. I'm under terrible stress. My headset broke this morning and I had to mend it myself.

Fifth Visit

I arrive at 11 p.m. The atmosphere is notably more relaxed at night. People talk to me much sooner and more freely. It's like a night-shoot. It's been quite a busy evening. For the next two hours an interpreter, a solicitor and a detective will be dealing with a couple of illegal immigrant cases in the background.

PC Bird should have clocked off at ten p.m., but is seeing his cases through (he's made three arrests), so now he's on overtime, which he first has to get approved by the inspector. The talk is of eights and twenty-nines. If you get less than eight days' notice of overtime (say for a court appearance), you are guaranteed six hours' overtime. If less than twenty-nine, then you can work your rest day on overtime. If more than twenty-nine, then you're re-rostered and no overtime. There is a young CID officer who has just transferred from Chiswick ('middle-class, just burglaries, no villains living *in* the area') who gets more overtime on a daily basis – he always has to stay on and see the case through; whereas the uniformed get more court appearances and cancelled rest days. 'So it's swings and roundabouts.'

There aren't any cars because an inspector has crashed one. Much to his embarrassment, he came screaming out of the police car park and smashed the underside of his vehicle as it came off the kerb. He has filled in papers, which have gone to the Crown Prosecution Service, and he may be had up on a charge of dangerous driving.

A man has been brought in for displaying a licence disc whose number is different from his number plates. The sergeant, Alf, addresses him at great speed.

Alf: You have been brought to a police station. Here is a form which sets out your rights. You are entitled at this stage to contact a solicitor, or a reasonable person nominated by you. Do you want a solicitor?
Man: No.
Alf: OK, sign here, please. And sign here to say your rights have been explained to you. Now turn your pockets out, please.

The largest case of the evening is someone who has been stopped for having a defective tail-light; found to have no insurance; has given an address which won't qualify because it's a squat; been taken back to the squat, where PC Bird has found drugs and the toolbox for fixing the electricity meter. So now three people are in cells, all claiming the other owns the toolbox. A man from the LEB will be called in to testify.

I am reading the catering complaints book:

'I paid 22p for a portion of sausage. Rita gave me a sausage so small I thought I must be on Candid Camera. I asked for a second sausage to justify the price of 22p. She insisted on another 22p. Rita said she had been put in this position by the type of sausage that had been supplied to Clapham by the district catering office. I pleaded with her for an extra sausage but she would not change her mind. In desperation I told her how attractive she was looking, and that I thought she was a lovely person. This was a blatant lie but I was hungry at the time.'

The CID officer is not going to charge the illegal immigrant with an offence, because if you are charged with a crime, you then don't get deported.

CID officer: I learnt that the hard way. Just let them go – it's easier – and forget it.

He is now going to drive down to Streatham to get a charcoal burger.

Suddenly there are five policemen all leaning over the desk filling in different pieces of paper. Another policeman is filling in his form by writing against a wall. The immigration cases are continuing. I count fourteen people in the charge room now – only one charged man, the rest officials.

A man has choked on his vomit after going upstairs to lie down at an office party. He has just been found by the security officer, who came upon his corpse while doing a midnight check of the premises. He was 35. This triggers a macabre conversation about how long people lie without being discovered.

Traffic PC: I had one who had been there for four months. It took three undertakers and me to unstick him from the bed. Then his parents said, 'Oh, yes, we missed him.'

Someone else says, 'After six months, it's just a skeleton.' I have noticed that this particular conversation – the one about who has seen the most horrible corpse of all – is a great favourite among policemen, and this is in fact the third time I have heard it in two weeks.

Sixth Visit

Christmas. They've been larking about. A PC has let a stink-bomb off in the charge room. Martin says he is in a 'horribly good mood' today and starts listing the number of Christmas parties he has been to and will go to in the week – at least ten different relief and police station parties. There has been an invisible ink fight.

Martin: (*As he leaves*) This is supposed to be a police station, boys.

There is no duty officer – 'Christmas lunch'. There is no operator for the area car in which I am meant to be going out. 'He hasn't turned up.' The car also has to go to the garage. When I say how few people seem to have come in, the duty sergeant says, 'Yes, there's a problem with floating rest days.' If he needs an inspector for a review, he'll call Kennington to get one.

A man called Winston is being held in the charge room. He is about six foot six.

DH: *What's he charged with?*
CID man: Sexual intercourse with his duck in the bath.
DH: *How are you charging him? Under the Duck Act of 1880?*
CID man: No. Pond Life Protection Act, 1922.

I am getting into the Christmas mood alongside everyone else, but am rather brought down by a young bearded CID man who is telling me motor damage cases are a pain in the bum because they're one man's word against another's and who cares?

DH: *But you say everything's a pain in the bum. Last week you said domestics were a pain in the bum . . .*

CID man: Well, they are. Awful. The wife says she's going to testify. Then overnight she changes her mind. The daughter says she's been sexually abused, then the family get at her. And suddenly she hasn't.

DH: *So what isn't a pain in the bum?*

When Winston is finally charged he asks if he can know what he is being charged with.

CID man: You don't want much, do you?

Sergeant: (*Reads the charge*) . . . under Section 11 of the Criminal Damage Act. No reply at twenty to five.

CID man: (*Turns to me*) See what I mean? Pain in the bum.

There's a call from Streatham which the sergeant takes. They want a man who they believe is in the Clapham cells transferred to them. But the sergeant has to point out that in fact they have already had him in Streatham for several hours. As he puts the phone down, nobody remarks on this, for nobody seems to find it odd that Streatham has no idea who is in their own cells.

Two plain-clothes men have come in, CID officers, incongruously in T-shirts and jeans. One has a tattoo and a shirt saying 'BEAR ALL THIS SUMMER WITH HOFMEISTER LAGER'. I never cease to find undercover policemen hilarious. Is it just because I know them that I find them so easy to spot?

Martin is back at his desk, filling in a form. He asks me if I know how to spell 'varying'. He then asks me to spell 'character'.

Martin: It was bad luck. My year at school were the guinea pigs for this new spelling system called ITA,* and the result is no one in Britain aged 26 can spell.

Meanwhile, I notice on a drug analysis form, the victim's name is

*Initial Teaching Alphabet.

given as Regina. If you take drugs, apparently the Queen is the only victim. I think, from my weeks in the charge room, that the Queen would be extremely surprised if she knew some of the things her subjects do to her.

CRIMINAL EXPERTISE

Mary Tuck

All the time I was visiting Clapham Police Station, I was beginning to realize that our Criminal Justice System was divided quite sharply into three. At the top are the lawyers, the professionals who, in Ogden Nash's famous couplet, 'have no cares/Whatever happens they get theirs'. In the middle are the police, who are constantly aggrieved at the amount of stick they get from both sides. And at the bottom are the prisoners and the prison service, a group who are basically ignored except when, as in the Strangeways riots of 1990, they make trouble.

It became apparent to me very early on that when I spent a day shuffling between lunch at the Inns of Court, an afternoon in the Clapham nick and an evening in Wandsworth gaol, I was, apart from the prisoners themselves, the only person in London that day who was seeing all three parts of the system.

I therefore needed to find someone who had an overview of the whole process. Mary Tuck had been Head of Research at the Home Office. She took a late degree at the London School of Economics, once her children were in their teens, and then answered an ad in *The Times* for a direct entry principal in the civil service. She managed in her period of work there to get good, reliable crime statistics which were independent of police figures.

Mary Tuck: There are two ways of looking at the police, what you might call the Alderson/Anderton split.* Half of them think, 'We're the embattled thin blue line, protecting civilization against criminals.' The other half think, 'We're here to serve the community.' In fact, 'serving the community' can mask activities just as oppressive and doubtful as some of the things the 'thin blue line' thinking leads to. Most police don't know what they're there for.

DH: *But aren't they given an impossible brief?*

Tuck: Of course. I used to have a presentation in which I tried to show the irrelevance of the entire Criminal Justice System. Every year there are 3.8 million reported crimes. Five per cent have a violent or sexual content. A quarter are to do with motorcars. Another quarter are burglary, vandalism and criminal damage. But 70 per cent of burglaries are of under £100. So much crime is just trivial property theft and to do with opportunity. In the fifties there were 7,000 thefts from cars a year; now there are 375,000. The targets are sitting there on the streets. Suburban homes in Golders Green and Wimbledon are sitting there empty all day because wives now go out to work, and they're stuffed with goodies like VCRs. The wonder is, not that there is so much crime, but that boys from Balham don't get on the tube to Golders Green and nick the lot all the time.

DH: *Is the increase in crime figures due to increased reporting?*

Tuck: To an extent. For instance, because of insurance, 98 per cent of car crimes are reported. And the physical violence which used to be taken for granted in domestic situations no longer is. So, quite rightly, more of it gets reported. Of the three categories of rape, rape with strangers has barely increased at all. It's with intimates and acquaintances that it's really gone up.

So now we name everything as crime and ask the police to protect us, all the time fostering a myth that the past was much more peaceable. But in this very street, you couldn't hang laundry out in the thirties for fear of its being stolen, and there was a fight

---

*James Anderton was the Manchester Chief Constable who claimed to be in direct contact with God and who adopted a notably harsh and traditional view of policing. John Alderson was his Devon and Cornwall counterpart who pioneered the principles of community policing.

on the steps outside the pub every Saturday night. But now the magistrates refer everything to the Crown Courts. All the triables-either-way now seem to go up. As a result the prisons are stuffed 50 per cent with petty offenders who nip in the back door, steal a telly, do probation, do it again, get community service, do it a third time and then prison. There's some evidence that when a recession comes burglary goes up, but violence goes down; when prosperity comes burglary goes down, but violence goes up. Burglary is mostly people at the fringes of the labour market, can't get a job and so on. There's some evidence that the peak offending age is one year before compulsory school leaving; you know, you need to go to the pub on Saturday night, you don't have the money because you're still at school, so you go out and nick a telly. The peak age for crime used to be 15, now it's 17.

DH: *Young men are the problem?*

Tuck: *One third* of all men have a conviction for an indictable offence by the time they're 28. Then remember how few people actually get caught, and how many more that would include if it was unconvicted offences as well, and you have the fact that petty crime is completely natural for a certain age group. Add to that the statistical chances of crime on a class basis, on a race basis, on an inner-city basis, and you have the near-certainty that in particular groups *everyone* is a so-called criminal.

DH: *Presumably the figures are always doubtful?*

Tuck: Most foreign criminologists think our figures are unbelievably reliable. So much hysteria about crime is nonsense. The *Daily Mail* once had a headline: 'SEXUAL OFFENCES UP 10 PER CENT'. So I did a breakdown. Ten per cent meant 1,300 extra offences. Of these, 50 per cent were between consenting males. Of these, 30 per cent were in Slough. I thought, what's suddenly happening in Slough? Then I find *all* these extra offences are from one particular public lavatory in Slough, which accounts for the whole bloody lot of them. So you do have to handle figures with care.

Only 1.6 per cent of all crimes get dealt with by the courts. What you have is about 8,187,000 offences per year. Of which 3,341,300 are reported and 2,122,400 are recorded. Of which, only 550,000 are actually cleared up. And 161,000 offenders are actually dealt with. To get a 1 per cent drop in crime, we have estimated you would have to increase the prison population by 38 per cent. Now add that to the fact that 70 per cent of all crimes are committed by 5 per cent of criminals and you have an overall picture of a persistent drizzle of petty crime by a whole lot of people who spontaneously remit at the age of 30, when they decide that going out thieving at night is too much like hard work. And among these you have an absolutely tiny percentage of career criminals.

DH: *Is it possible to target this group?*

Tuck: It's terribly dangerous. They try to do it in America, and guess what? He's black, he's from the inner city and he's into drugs. These are the predictors. But, of course, most black inner-city kids don't turn into career criminals. So if you treat them all as if they will, you risk a terrible class-based injustice. Of course, in America they don't even process crime, they plea-bargain. They're so overwhelmed by it they can't even get it through the courts. That's because they're so stupid about drugs. We once had the perfect system in this country. You went to the doctor for your prescription for nice, cheap, National Health heroin. But this system got a bad reputation so they started the Drug Dependency Units, and there the doctors began to think, Oh, we ought to be curing these people. So they gave them methadone instead, and all your problems start. Coinciding with a lot of cheap stuff from Iran.

When Mellor was at the Home Office, he was very pleased with the campaign against drunken driving, because the ads pointed out it actually killed people. And this had an effect. So he said, 'Let's do the same thing for drugs. How many people die from heroin addiction?' I had to say, 'Sorry, Minister, if it's properly administered, the answer is none.'

DH: *Would you decriminalize drugs?*

Tuck: Oh, without doubt. It's precisely the same question as prohibition in the twenties. Look at America. You create a gang culture in which all exchange is at the point of the gun. The natural pricing mechanism of the market is destroyed. You have prostitution, burglary, housebreaking, all to finance the artificially high price of the commodity. You destroy South American countries, you create an intolerable burden of enforcement costs which no society can afford. In America the inner cities are totally destroyed and handed over to criminals, all to protect the price of crack and heroin.

DH: *What did you conclude about our own Criminal Justice System?*

Tuck: Prison certainly doesn't work. Over 50 per cent of prisoners will re-offend within the next two years. Prison encourages violent crime, it's a university of violence. If you can decrease the prison population, you will decrease crime. It's hugely expensive. So what is the function of Criminal Justice? Like you, it has a dramatist's function. It exists to say: we disapprove. It has a rhetorical power. Prison cannot be practical, so the Criminal Justice System is mainly symbolic. In the old days, the men in wigs marched through the town to the assizes. And that, basically, is what the apparatus of the law does now.

DH: *You said there was some German evidence that the more people you put in gaol, the more violent crime increases . . .** *

Tuck: That's right.

DH: *How did the Home Secretaries react when it was put to them?*

Tuck: Well, one of the more junior ministers – one of the more honest ones, actually – just said, 'Mary, even if what you're saying is right, how can I possibly put these facts to the public?'

DH: *But where does that leave the police?*

Tuck: Well, it's horrible for them, poor dears, because they don't want to be defeatist. They don't want just to sort of say, 'The rain it raineth every day.' But if they were cleverer they would target where crime actually is, and of course in London it's on those terrible housing estates, we all know. If you spent the money you spend on the prison system on improving conditions on those estates, you would have a far more radical effect on reducing crime.

Mostly policemen are bored. They're sitting around waiting for something to happen. Look how they grab the phone when it rings, they're so relieved to have something to do. There are 150

*See p.145.

at Notting Hill but only eight are on the street at any one time. The difference between American and British police is that the Americans have lovely, well-heated big cars and no canteen. So they're in their cars all the time. The English have less good cars but better canteens. The best possible reform of the English police would be to give them better cars and tell them to eat anywhere they like. These policemen in their 30s really frighten me, the keen ones. I mean, I meet a lot of policemen in my work. Of course, with me, with a woman, there's all this very heavy avuncular charm, that's how they treat women. But underneath they're so guarded. The defences are up all the time. I don't know who said it, but dealing with the police is like dealing with an ethnic minority. Of course, it's hard for them. But I don't like some of the things that are happening in the name of community policing. I mean, sure, there ought to be more social cohesion in London, it sounds lovely, but is it really the police's job to bring it about? Are they the best people to do it?

Jeremy

My second expert was working as a civil servant. Identified, like others in this book, by a false first name, he had now spent some years in the Home Office, observing the tensions in the Criminal Justice System. At the time of our meeting, 8 May 1991, the newspapers were full of criticism of Lord Lane, who was reaching the end of his career as Lord Chief Justice. As well as showing notorious ill grace in conceding miscarriages of justice, Lane had also carried the doctrine of judicial separation to ridiculous extremes. In his desire to keep judges apart from the everyday consequences of their own actions, he had succeeded only in reinforcing their ignorance of the system in which they operated.

Jeremy: In the eighties they had some buffet suppers to try and get the judiciary together with the Home Office, but after a couple the Lord Chief told his judges to stop going. His view of the judiciary's independence is much less intellectual than you think it is. It's romantic, I'd say. The judges should be alone, and that's that. He certainly would never want to be seen in the Home Secretary's company. Judges don't read and they don't like going to conferences. The Home Office set up these Judicial Studies Boards, because there simply was no training for being a judge, and there they tried to put across some facts, tried to get the judges to read, but it was mainly middle-level people, circuit judges and recorders. And of course it was these ones who wanted to go.

DH: *Does the Home Office have any dealings with the Lord Chief Justice?*

Jeremy: The Lord Chief himself keeps pretty distant from us. For anything that needs to be done, the Home Office sees his Deputy, Tasker Watkins. There was one big meeting, where Douglas Hurd wanted to get the judges, the police chiefs, the magistrates and so on together to tell them what the Home Office was thinking. The Home Office had to go to Tasker and say, Douglas would like to have a meeting, and in a few weeks we'll ask if you can come. Eventually, he said yes, they would come, but they would only stay for half of it. That was their compromise.

DH: *Do they refer overtly to the constitutional proprieties?*

Jeremy: No, no, never. It's all about dates.

DH: *So it's not the language of ethics, it's the language of diaries.*

Jeremy: Quite. Exactly. Everybody knows what's behind it, but neither side ever, ever refers to it. There's an emphasis on *time* constantly. For instance, as you know, the chief recommendation of the Woolf Report, which came out of the Strangeways riots, was that there should be forums where judges, prison governors and so on would meet.* You can tell the Lord Chief is against it,

*The report, written by Lord Justice Woolf and Judge Stephen Tumim, looked into the reasons for the riots at Strangeways Prison and 25 other penal institutions in April 1990. Published in February 1991, the Woolf Report's other recommendations included a clear date for ending slopping out, the creation of a network of community gaols, stricter limits on numbers of inmates, written contracts for prisoners defining their expectations and duties, and better training and promotion prospects for prison officers. It led to the publication of a White Paper in September 1991 which adopted most of the proposals for reform.

but the way he frames his argument is to say they'll take up too much time.

DH: *How can the judges be persuaded to take part in these forums?*

Jeremy: Oh, somebody has to go along to Tasker and say, look, Strangeways was really embarrassing, the Minister is under terrible pressure to make progress. That kind of thing.

DH: *It must be so exhausting. Are the judges the only group you have to go through this charade with?*

Jeremy: Oh yes.

DH: *The police?*

Jeremy: The police are great. They're great to talk to. Crown Prosecution Service (CPS) can be a bit tricky because they take such a narrow, legalistic view of their work. But it's nothing like the intensity and range of difficulty you have talking to judges.

DH: *Do you think the judges will eventually come round to the forums?*

Jeremy: I think the Home Secretary can make it known that he's disappointed if they don't. I mean, after the Birmingham Six, if the Lord Chief had any sensible or sensitive people around him, they'd be saying, don't get yourself into another public relations disaster by refusing. But I'm not sure he does.

DH: *Is it essential that the Home Secretary is never seen to be in any kind of conflict with the judiciary?*

Jeremy: It's vital. It would need extraordinary political courage. I mean, when I say the Home Secretary might indicate publicly he was disappointed in the judges over the forums, then that would be going further than any Home Secretary ever has. What he must never, never do is comment on how many burglars are or aren't getting sent to prison and for how long. Though, mind you, over rape, junior ministers aren't averse to seeming to take public credit for getting sentences up.

DH: *People tell me that was Thatcher.*

Jeremy: One of Thatcher's great gifts was for making her view on something known without actually telling anyone in person. It was brilliant. For instance, the CPS *always* knew what her view was on any sensitive prosecution. How they knew I have no idea. But it was a factor, and of course it weighed with them.

DH: *But ministers can't talk about sentences for particular crimes.*

Jeremy: No. Now one thing that is known about the Lord Chief is that he thinks all burglars should go to prison. He's very tough on burglary, he still calls it housebreaking. In fact, only one third of burglars go to prison, but he doesn't know that, because he never reads statistics.

DH: *Can the police be administratively reformed?*

Jeremy: Well, the problem is that in the sixties and seventies people thought that you could change everything by changing structures, but that's gone out of fashion, and nobody now tackles administrative structures at all.

DH: *What about the prisons?*

Jeremy: In prisons it's the quality of daily relationships which are at the moment disgraceful. People are treated without respect. It's lack of mutual respect and consent which caused Strangeways. Nobody understands what Woolf calls Justice in Prisons, because ministers think it's to do with legal representation and rights and so forth. But it's not. It's about the relationships between fellow human beings. It's about day to day practices. When the men are out, do officers chat to them, or do they stand in a group together and only intervene with staves when something goes wrong? It's to do with who you recruit to be officers and how you train them and how they speak to the men.

DH: *How many people should be in prison?*

Jeremy: About 10,000 fewer than at the moment. Which you can achieve. Some people do need to be locked up, but it makes no sense to lock them up for seven years rather than four.

David Rangecroft

In order to get permission to go to Clapham Police Station, I had to go to the Scotland Yard press office, which is impressively large. At any one time it is fielding hundreds of inquiries from newspaper and television, and each day's press clippings are the size of a reasonable novel. The press officer I met, David Rangecroft, told me that they are much more sensitive about what is written in newspapers than what appears on television, because politicians don't watch television, whereas a clipping appears on their desk next morning. ('They're reading the same stuff we are.')

He already had a file on me, on top of which was a hostile profile in an extreme right-wing Sunday newspaper. Before I could introduce myself, he smiled and said, 'I know exactly who you are.'

David Rangecroft: This is the busiest hard news operation in Europe. Police press takes you from cardboard boxes to royalty – and beyond, if I may say so, though I'm not claiming we actually commune with God. Our job is to be as accurate as possible – we're more concerned to be accurate than speedy. It's the press that's speedy. Honestly and truly, we're very open. Of course, the first man you're going to disbelieve is the man who says honestly and truly . . . but our reputation for paranoia is historic. The problem is, we are sexy. I mean, in news terms, we fill column inches. All life goes through a copper's hands. We have to be open, whether we want to be or not – nobody willingly puts themselves in the media glare.

DH: *Is confidence in the police less than it was?*

Rangecroft: Of course. We're the politicians' whipping boys. Thatcher pours millions in, with the attitude, 'We've given them the money, now bloody well come up with the results.' The latest idea is to give them a military command structure, meaning fill them with officers from the army because the army's shrinking as the cold war's over and so on. But we don't want a military police. It would be a bloody disaster.

Everything that drops through the sieve, we get. Everything that falls into the sewer. That's the job we do. We have to sweep up – that's the environment we work in. Like all professionals – doctors, teachers – you start off caring, then you don't. We're there for people to point fingers at.

DH: *What are the police good at?*

Rangecroft: Investigating major crime. Making sure people can walk safely down the street. Brilliant at dealing with terrorism. We're better than we were at sexual offences. We're good at domestic disputes, which are a bloody nuisance. There's always a conflict between what we can do, and what we want to do.

What are we bad at? Communication. Not internally. What I

mean is, officers being authoritarian and feeling justified in that approach. The young people who join us now at 19 don't seem to have the gift our generation had of just being able to sit down and talk to people. That is the basic skill. It means a lot. Now young people don't seem to have it.

DH: *What's the worst thing about the police?*

Rangecroft: The rank structure is awful. A good constable is worth a lot to the community, but he gets promoted to sergeant and he's just worrying about running his relief, or, if he's an inspector, just writing reports. We need some way of rewarding people to remain constables. They all say resources are very stretched, but let's face it, the Met. gets one and a quarter billion pounds a year, so just how stretched can it be? One and a quarter billion, but until recently it didn't have a single chartered accountant.

DH: *What do you feel about the CPS?*

Rangecroft: It started badly. No one thinks they can do a job better than a copper. In many ways that attitude is blind bigotry, but in another it's necessary, it's essential to people who are making life-and-death decisions. They have to believe in their own ability. There was a certain pleasure in catching the right man, preparing the case against him, presenting it well, and getting twelve of your peers or a magistrate to agree with you. But now you're deprived of that secondary interest – the job is done for you by a whole lot of solicitors who, frankly, are so low-grade they're happy to get a job. Any copper will have stories of them fumbling cases, papers not turning up, ballsing up the prosecution. It's typical. Politicians panic that something isn't going to happen, so they kick it into life, whether it's thought out or not, for fear that unless they do, it won't happen at all. The CPS has been a major boon to the criminal fraternity.

ON THE STREET

Alan

I was lucky early on in my researches to run into Alan, as I shall call him, a detective constable in West London, who challenged the benign idea of friendly disorder which I found in Clapham. Alan was 40, thick-set, with a Cockney accent. He was trying at the time to get a posting in Richmond, because, he said, the only thing that influences him is how long his journey is in the morning.

Alan: Basically, PACE, which came in about six years ago, allows guilty people to get off. When it was introduced, the quid pro quo was going to be the abolition of the right to silence, to balance things out. But of course, that got dropped. And why? Because who was against it? The lawyers, of course. Because they have a vested interest in it. And who makes up most of the House of Commons? Why, lawyers, of course. I think the whole law should be changed so that you don't have to prove beyond reasonable doubt, but simply the balance of probability. But then, if that were the law you'd have more convictions, and the government doesn't want that, because then you'd have to build more prisons, and it already costs £20,000 a year to keep a man in prison, and we can't afford that. At the moment, we only catch the wallies, the law is toothless, so the clever ones escape.

In my opinion, people aren't bothered by crime unless it crosses class barriers. Working-class people beat each other up and nobody minds, nobody's going to bring a complaint, but if it's little Jimmy and Jimmy's got an uncle who's a barrister, then suddenly you get all that middle-class stuff about the majesty of the law.

DH: *Things have got worse for the police?*
Alan: The disastrous combination of things was the introduction of PACE and the arrival of the Crown Prosecution Service. The CPS took away the police's right to prosecute, to see a case

through, to present the case even in court yourself. But, more important, it took away your ability to negotiate and do deals. You can't trade with the criminal any longer. You used to be able to say, look, I'll overlook this and only bring you up on this, if in return you do such-and-such. But now the accused takes one look at you and doesn't bother to talk, he just says, 'I'll talk to the engine driver, not to the oily rag.' You used to be able to tell them how to plead. Now they all ask for solicitors, and the stupid solicitor tells them to plead not guilty, and suddenly we're all going to the Crown Court, at a huge cost to the tax-payer, and the guy's getting legal aid as well. It's all costing thousands because the bloke's taking a gamble on getting off; whereas before I'd have taken him aside and said, if you co-operate, I'll present your case favourably, downplay the bad things, and you'll get a lighter sentence. The mistake everyone makes is thinking the law has anything to do with justice. It's nothing to do with justice. It's to do with administering the law.

DH: *Is this very demoralizing?*

Alan: The thing that's gone is the CID's group identity. You used to work as a team. You saw it today – it's deserted. A few years back we would all have been in there on a Friday afternoon, just chatting, kicking things around, but now we get no support from the law, so everyone's given up. Friday's what we call POETS day – Piss Off Early Tomorrow's Saturday. There used to be team identity, team spirit, but it went, partly for financial reasons. I used to do 120 hours overtime a month, but now, because of the budget cuts, I'm not allowed to do overtime. I used to come in at six and get organized before the day began, but there's no money now. The real problem is that the new law enshrines the idea that it's more important that one innocent man gets off than that ninety-nine guilty ones are convicted.* Well, I'm sorry, but that's bollocks. Justice isn't about the absolute rights of every individual, it's about percentages.

DH: *Have you always been CID?*

*This refers to a remark of Lord Gerald Gardiner, Lord Chancellor from 1964 to 1970.

Alan: For a while I was in the anti-terrorist squad, but I hated it. It was all politics. Most Scotland Yard squads are. Backstabbing. Like I imagine big business or the City – don't go on holiday or you'll find your job gone when you get back. Of course, it's very rich – whatever you ask for you get because it's terrorism – but the management don't actually have much to do. There isn't much casework to prepare, because all the evidence is scientific, so there's very little actual policing. So everyone's got lots of time to sit around and backstab. I earned £26,000; now I'm making £30,000. I don't want promotion. If I do the sergeant's exam then almost certainly I'll have to go back into uniform, and I'm never going to do that. I'm fine where I am. I just have to keep up a certain work-rate or people do begin to notice. But the truth is, if you're any good, there isn't actually eight hours' work in a day here. I mean, you develop an ability to read a crime sheet, you actually know the moment you look whether it's worth pursuing and what the percentage chances of its solvability are. Maybe you take a cursory look round the crime – burglary, say. But you know how impossible or likely it is to solve.

And anyway, what's the point of catching them? The sentencing is all nonsense. I'd reintroduce an element of public odium. Paint the car thief's hands red with a dye that won't come off for six months, then we all know who he is. Be very good for crime prevention, he'd have to walk down the street with red hands.

DH: *Hmm.*

Alan: What PACE has destroyed is the crucial idea that every-one charged with a crime is a potential informant. Each arrest should precipitate another. You don't do that by being a sales-man, you do it by bringing them in and frightening the living daylights out of them. To frighten people, you have to have power. If you don't have power, you can't frighten them. Not necessarily by kicking the lights out of them. But now we don't have any power. You can't use informants in the way you used to, you have to be very careful. Never tell the bosses much, that's always a big mistake. If you've got an informant, never give anyone his real name.

DH: *What are the other essential techniques?*

Alan: You have to be sure you're with good performers in the witness box, they're not suddenly going to become honest in a blinding flash, or see God or something. It's important everyone lies together and that we all lie well. That's, of course, why reputation's so important in the police. You have to trust the blokes you're with. You can't trust the people upstairs, God knows.

The best bit of the job is the court. I enjoy that. It's amateur dramatics really, anticipating the next question, thinking fast on your feet. I've got one friend, every time he tells a lie in the witness box, he pulls at his ear. Actually, I move my feet when I lie, but luckily you can't see. I'm always careful to put my hands on the box, so they're still in front of me and I don't give things away that way. Psychologists say your feet reveal everything, and so you should have glass witness boxes, but most juries are so bloody stupid they wouldn't notice anyway. I think you'd be better off settling cases by the throw of a dice.

DH: *Does all the lying ever worry you?*

Alan: No. Criminals lie all the time. To catch the clever ones, you have to lie better than they do.

DH: *Do you ever feel you get a case wrong?*

Alan: No. I mean, maybe one guy didn't do it, but so what? In the cases I'm talking about, he's bound to have a criminal record, which means he's probably done things he never got sent down for, so if occasionally they get sent down for one they didn't do, so what? I don't lose any sleep. Someone I know has just cost the commissioner £118,000 for wrongful arrest in a robbery case. One of them got off, sued him in civil court. But the other four went down. He got four out of five. And the fifth was the brother of one of the convicted, so I'm inclined not to believe he was innocent. My friend'll never hear any more about it.

Juries are ridiculous. You can usually tell what verdict they'll give. Back at once and it's guilty. Stay out and it's innocent. Don't look at the prisoner and it's guilty. But really, any gathering of twelve people is an indecision.

DH: *You sound pretty resentful all round.*

Alan: Police are angry, of course they are, because they're not supported by the law or the community. The question of police assaults is very serious because the attackers don't get the sentences they should, though mind you I have noticed it's the same officers who get assaulted all the time. If we are racist, sexist and thick, then probably it's a reflection on the society we come from. The racism is in the canteen, not directly to people's faces. We're the only group who actually have an offence of racial prejudice. You have to behave better than everyone else. I recently had a bloke in – he was lying to me, it's all on tape, of course – I started raising my voice and swearing, I was doing a fair impression of Bernard Manning, I tell you. But I was quite proud: he was black and yet I didn't refer to his race once.

DH: *You feel you get it from all sides?*

Alan: If you read what the police were set up for in 1821, it was, first of all, the protection of property. We're there to look after the middle class, who stole the stuff in the first place. Black guys, when they steal, call it taxing. And they're right. Everything was nicked somewhere along the line. Where did the Queen and the Duke of Westminster get their stuff if not by thieving?

DH: *Then why do it?*

Alan: Police work is attractive to young people for one obvious reason – you can, with very low qualifications, be earning £17,000 or £18,000 two years after you start. It hardly matters if it's satisfying or not. And where I am now, my attitude to promotion is that the Commissioner earns £70,000, he has 26,000 police in his charge and 30,000 civilians. I earn £30,000 and look after no one. There's no question which I'd rather be.

DH: *If PACE were repealed, would you be happier?*

Alan: What's unfair since PACE is that we have to take all the statements and send them to the CPS, so that the defence has to have everything we have. *We* have to show all our cards, but they don't have to show theirs. All the law demands is that we write down in full the questions leading to their confession, their confession itself, and then you're meant to be allowed to summarize everything else. But the CPS keeps writing back for more particulars, more statements, more red herrings. So the pool isn't clear, it starts getting all frothy.

DH: *But there are loopholes in PACE, aren't there?*

Alan: Sure. What happens at the point of arrest isn't recorded, so if the bloke then says, 'I did it,' *before* we bring him in, then that is admissible. If I then ask why, and he says, 'Because my wife is driving me crazy,' then I might just get away with introducing that in court. But if he confesses in the back of the van, you then transpose it, pretend he said it earlier when you arrested him. The only admissible evidence is at the point of arrest, so you move everything down to there.

The only place you can do the salesman bit is between the arrest and getting him back to the station. I'd never go in a van after an arrest, because then you've got some uniformed bloke in with you, and he might be anyone. You never say anything in front of a uniformed policeman. He may be full of high ideals, or thick, or just out of Hendon. No, take him in your own car. Then when you get back to the station, make sure there's a good sergeant on duty, because there are ways of presenting the arrested with their rights. The good ones sort of say, 'Look, just sign here, will you? You can have a solicitor, but I don't think you'll want one, will you?' Whereas the bad ones read it out very slowly to give everyone a chance to waste the tax-payer's money. You have a chance with the bloke who's never been arrested before. But any professional criminal knows that you have now lost your power to negotiate. So he will get a solicitor and sit there and say nothing. Nothing. At the tax-payer's expense. No comment, no comment.

DH: *Do you think other people agree with you?*

Alan: There are three kinds of policeman. Yobs, partial yobs, and the ones who go home to their wives. Everything I've said today about CID work, other people feel it, they just maybe don't say it. I say it, that's all. I've never thought that fabricating evidence against someone who's prosecuted is corrupt, taking money for it is corrupt.

DH: *You sound like you've given up.*

Alan: It's not *me* that's given up. Look, honestly, society is not indicating to me that it wants guilty people prosecuted. It has put so many checks and balances up against us that the message I am getting from government is: don't bother.

There's been a gradual wearing down. I don't think anyone's interested or got the energy to catch criminals any more, we're just a minor element of social control. I mean, are they interested in stopping crime in Clapham?

DH: *They say they are.*

Alan: No, no. They're just like everyone else. They just don't want it in their own street. They all drive in every day from Worcester Park or Surbiton, nice white middle-class suburbs, they don't *live* in Clapham, they don't give a damn what goes on there.

There was an African student I had in on suspicion of stealing a £2,000 ring, which there was no way he could have afforded. As he went into the interview room, the first thing I said on tape was that he'd confessed it was stolen when he was arrested. The student denied it. I said, 'Well, look at my notes,' and waved some paper in front of him. 'I now bloody well want to know where you're selling this and where you got it, and I'm giving you four weeks to tell me.' Of course, it's a bluff. Because basically, an uncorroborated confession on police evidence alone is unlikely to lead to a successful prosecution. But it's *me* that's taking a risk, because if he doesn't scare, then I've got to quietly drop the prosecution because I've got no evidence. I *ought* to send it to the CPS and *they* ought to make the decision. But it's risky. So if, as I think, the bluff hasn't worked, I've got to bury it. You see, there's no muscle now, just bluff. In the old days, I would have rung Catford, where he lives, and said go in at six o'clock and do his place over for drugs, please, as a favour, and be sure to tell him, 'Alan sent us,' which would really frighten him. But now nobody's in at six because they can't afford the overtime, and even if they did agree to do it – which they wouldn't – the first thing they'd say is, 'Sure, and we'll send you the bill.' It's got that bad. Supers are money managers, so they wouldn't thank me. So we do nothing. There you are.

Arthur

It was Alan who really introduced me to the idea of what the police themselves call 'noble cause corruption'. Another way of putting it: doing the wrong thing for the right reason. So I was keen, after spending time with Alan, to meet a friend of his, Arthur. They had started out together, and remained friends, yet their subsequent careers could hardly have been more different. Whereas Alan had opted resolutely to remain a constable, Arthur was on fast track, taking time out for three years to do a law degree at London University ('no problem'), and now in charge of huge and complex murder investigations in East London. Tall, moustached and very quick, he is part of an accelerated promotion programme which is intended to take him to the rank of commander.

Arthur: I'm sorry to hear what you say about Alan, because he is exactly the kind of policeman we ought to be able to keep motivated. He's just as good as I am. There's no difference between us. I love the police. It's done everything for me. It's given me the education I never had. And now they're putting their trust in me. I don't intend to let them down.

DH: *So what's gone wrong with Alan?*

Arthur: We've lost his enthusiasm. I know what's going on now where he is. There's no one to get him going. He just says, 'I'm late because I stopped to go shopping on my way in,' and they all think it's funny. That's Alan. But they don't notice he's a bloody good officer going to waste.

DH: *He says that society is not sending him the signals that it wants criminals caught.*

Arthur: Not society. The system. The system sends that message, I agree. Most people don't know anything about it and they aren't interested. Do you think anyone cares whether Hanratty was innocent or not? The only people who care are people who make a lot of money from writing books about it.

DH: *What Alan is saying is that since PACE . . .*

Arthur: Yeah, yeah . . .

DH: *The game is so rigged against policemen . . .*

Arthur: This is just stupid. There are always ways round any system. There are ways of getting things done. You just need some ingenuity, that's all. For instance, it is not a breach of PACE if you *lead* someone to believe something false. If you don't actually tell them a lie, but just allow them to draw the wrong conclusion, well, I'm sorry, but that's down to them.

DH: *Tell me some of the ways you can get round PACE legally.*

Arthur: The classic, of course, is in Northern Ireland. Or with the IRA here. You break into someone's flat, probably someone who isn't in the IRA. Then you say, in half an hour I am going round to pick up X, Y and Z, and you name three people. Well, of course, the guy you've bust into will know at once that X, Y and Z are going to think he's grassed. And for that they'll either break his kneecaps or kill him. So you say, OK, if you don't want me to go round there next, give me some other names. Or with a father, you threaten to put the children in care – though after the Cleveland case, that doesn't work as well as it used to.* Or if you see a piece of stolen property on the mantelpiece, and you've not really got evidence, you say to the bloke, 'Right, you're arrested, and I'm going to arrest your girlfriend for handling the property.' Well, that is a very powerful incentive for him to plead guilty, to get his girlfriend off the charge. Or – look – you use timing. For instance, if a bloke is looking after a gun for a friend, then you go into his house at six a.m., you take six armed policemen with you, you point your gun right into his face, with his wife lying in bed right beside him. No one can point a finger at us in those circumstances. It's all by the book. We're going in with armed officers, protecting ourselves. If a wife's got a gun in her face, the bloke's going to own up pretty quick. These aren't illegal methods. You need the gall to challenge the system, to make it work with you.

DH: *I understand it's getting harder to get officers to lie on behalf of other officers.*

---

* In August 1987 an inquiry began into alleged cases of child sexual abuse in Cleveland. The care procedures for the children during the period of the inquiry caused public uproar.

Arthur: Yeah, in the last fifteen years. Change in the nature of the intake – better educated. They know they can say no when an officer says, 'OK, I'll just say he took it out of his pocket.' More and more, it's officers blowing the whistle on other officers.

DH: *But there are still a lot of bad ones?*

Arthur: Of course. There are the taxi-drivers. Not even taxi-drivers, mini-cab drivers is what they are. They're just lazy, they don't even go looking for fares. The press ring up and they want a photo of an arrested man, and they'll pay £500. You see some guy's eyes light up, and he mutters, 'Anyone seen a photo anywhere?' Then you know. They're the ones I really hate. I don't mind what Alan does – lying in court, I mean. That's not nearly as bad. And Alan has great skills. He's brilliant with victims.

DH: *Are you?*

Arthur: I am. Very good. Mind you, like a lot of us, I enjoy meeting victims, because they're usually decent people. They're not swamp people, like most of the ones you meet in this job. Though in Clapham, of course, most of the victims are dross as well.

DH: *What police reforms would you like to see?*

Arthur: The most important is to have traffic police hived off. They're such ignoramuses, they should be a separate branch. It's them who approach the law-abiding citizen as if he's a criminal. It does us so much harm. The famous joke is when a copper's fallen off his bike and they say he's going to be brain-dead for life, and the other copper says, 'That's all right, he can join the traffic police.' I'd privatize it today.

DH: *And PACE? One side of PACE seems to work terribly well. The duty officer who actually tells you your rights.*

Arthur: When *you're* there, yes. You're not seeing anything at Clapham. It's all public relations. I know these people. Maybe for fifteen minutes out of three hours you see how it really is. But, basically, it's all a load of cod, what you're seeing. It's much, much rougher. They are putting on a certain tone because a middle-class person is present, and they're automatically adjusting.

DH: *Policemen do that instinctively?*

Arthur: Go to Holborn or Rochester Row or Ruislip. You'll see how they deal with fraudsters. It's all yes sir, no sir. And these are crooks who've taken millions and millions, far more than the little bloke who's just pinched ten quid. Because, of course, the police are socially aspiring themselves. They all live in Ruislip, so when a middle-class fraudster comes in, they all say, 'Oh yeah, he is a bit bent, but, you know, he's a member of the golf club, and it's not like street crime.' You ought to see that.

RECURRING THEMES

Nearly all the police I interviewed at some point complained that both their discretion and their effectiveness had been diminished by the reforms introduced to counter the element of corruption which had come to light in the seventies. Parts of the CID had plainly been out of control. Most policemen were willing to admit that Sir Robert Mark's subsequent measures to investigate abuses by the police had been necessary, and that public complaints procedures had had to be improved. But most of them also felt that the pendulum had swung too far. They regarded any prospect of civilians being allowed in on investigations into the police as being frankly farcical. But, more important, they felt the detecting skills of the CID had already been diluted in the fight against increasingly sophisticated criminals.

They objected to the new procedures of accountability on two grounds. First of all, an element of discretion had been removed from CID work. There had been areas of the law which were not entirely clear and which had enabled policemen to do things their own way. To put it at its most trivial, they had once been allowed to clip young offenders round the ear. Now, with the procedures which had been introduced to counter the abuses, they felt that they were spending more time making sure they obeyed guidelines than actually catching criminals. And, worse, they were victims of the quite inordinate amount of paperwork the new guidelines involved.

Policemen have always been managers. They have always had

to be planning officers and administrators as well. But over and over, I met policemen who felt that the balance of the job had shifted. The time they spent filling in forms was disproportionate to the time they spent on the street. There was a new figure in police legend called the 'seagull': this is the senior officer who flies in, shits over everything, demands a structural reorganization, and at once flies out again.

The police's demoralization had been furthered by the introduction of the CPS. Although everyone, indiscriminately, had a bad word for it, the most serious objections to it centred on its role as yet one more hurdle put in the way of criminals being delivered to justice. The police could see from the figures that the chances of any crime being dealt with in the courts were terribly low. There were so many filters between a crime and its eventual prosecution that they believed the public had become seriously disillusioned. People did not even bother to report crime any more, because they no longer believed it would be cleared up.

Like many interest groups, the police reserved their special contempt for the government. Nothing caused them more anger, in the Criminal Justice Act of 1989, than its provision that, for offences against property, no reference could be made to the accused's previous convictions. It was their belief that laws were now being deliberately framed with the express intention of keeping people out of prison. Whereas I, at least, saw this as a not wholly bad thing, they invited me to imagine its effect on their morale. It meant, in their own terms, that they no longer felt they were delivering a service. Crime rose all the time, and yet the obstacles to its detection and prosecution grew.

The extraordinary difficulty – as they saw it – of getting anyone sent down was little more than the cynical policy of a government which was trying to save money. A blind eye was being turned to small crime, not just because the expense of going to court was disproportionate, but because society was not willing to pay for the prisons they would then put criminals in. Penal policy was being determined not by considerations of justice, but by money.

It is true, as one officer told me, that policemen are like farmers. 'They moan and moan and moan, and then they go out and get on with the job.' But the most thoughtful policemen I met saw everything as a problem of balance. They wanted neither the rigours of a police state, nor, on the other hand, did they want the police so over-regulated that they were prevented from doing their job. It was, everyone agreed, a matter of where you drew the line. But nobody I met believed that the line was currently in the right place.

IN AND OUT OF THE POLICE

Ron Walker

Ron Walker is an ex-policeman who enjoyed considerable fame when he attempted to draw attention to the dishonesty of policemen and police practices in his area of Kent. He had found that the press's interest had battened specifically on the fiddling of the clear-up figures. Nick Davies of the *Observer* had then revealed that this practice was widespread throughout the country. In the publicity which followed on the revelation of police manipulation of their own achievements, Ron Walker nevertheless felt the lessons of his experience had not been drawn. Tall, thin and chain-smoking, he came up specially on the train to meet me at the National Theatre, and spent nearly three hours telling a story which had plainly obsessed him over many years.

Ron Walker: Look, you have to start from the proposition that the police are very aware of dishonesty and its uses. A good policeman uses a degree of dishonesty but he knows how to control it. You have to police yourself. Once you yield to temptation, there's a tendency for it to grow. If you steal a pound, you might as well steal a million. It's every day, the temptation. You have to be Jekyll and Hyde. Your work is with people who are rotten, but your home life is with people who are good. It's how you hold the two parts of your life apart that's difficult. That's why so many police are alcoholics, or have broken marriages.

You can be dishonest in the public interest. I can live with that. But it's evil if you're dishonest just in the Force's interest. We created this. We're not victims. You have to ask, why do we lie to the public? What's the reason? To benefit ourselves? Imbert said we don't want a police force, we want a police service.* I tell you what it really is: a police club.

I spent a year deciding what to do with the evidence after I first found the proof of the fiddling which was going on. All through that year I was thinking, shall I sacrifice myself or not? The first people I went to were three millionaires, because I needed to get my fight subsidized. I wanted to get a TV programme made, entrapping the people involved. The millionaires all said they couldn't help. I had to be very careful because I wanted to keep my wife and two kids. I was trying to make it secure for them so they wouldn't suffer financially or socially. But in the end, when the case did become public, it went on and on. We were lonely, there was no one.

I chose to make my case on the basis of the crime figures because there was paperwork which proved things. That gave me security. I mean, it was a personal success for me, because I came through it stronger. And it did make policemen think about themselves. But it wasn't a real success. I wanted to enforce the law among the law-makers. Let's face it, I wanted policemen arrested, convicted and put in prison. And to do this, I had to shop guys I'd been working with.

I was never interested in promotion. Everyone takes the sergeants' exam after two years. I failed, by two marks. In 1972, when I joined, no one joined for promotion or money. That's one of the things that's changed. There are policemen now with two cars, the BMW and the six-bedroom house in Putney. A lot of them go through the stages – the drinking stage, the mistress they can talk to – because of the tension. But the tension comes because the police force now represents itself, not the public.

I left for a while, in 1978, but in the outside world you don't

---

*Sir Peter Imbert was Commissioner of the Metropolitan Police from 1987 until he retired in 1993, shortly after suffering a heart attack.

feel you're taking part in anything. I went to work in a paper mill, but everyone thought about nothing, they believed in nothing. The police is interesting, you know. You come home, you don't watch TV, you think about the court case you're preparing, the people in the cells. Of course, some of it is boring – observation is the worst – but mostly it's very exciting.

So I went back six months later. Within two months they asked me to join CID. But we were all aware that the crime figures were suddenly shooting up like crazy, out of control. And we knew that other divisions were playing with the figures.

In some areas, they literally couldn't find enough crimes to clear up. The figures were so fake that crimes were being cleared up which hadn't even been committed. It was often because of the senior officers that they were all competing with each other. They wanted promotion – easiest way was to have the best clear-up rate. And, of course, they made it plain to the guys below them that if they play ball, then they'll move on up when they do. As he goes up, he takes people with him.

You must understand, you've really got to work to get a figure up to 60 per cent clear-up, because this was at a time when the real figure was under 10. They were inventing phantom crimes, even sending criminals to commit crimes so they could clear them up. They had to control the number of crimes they detected, because they were in danger of clearing up more than had been committed.

After all, you get someone of 17, he's been a teenage criminal, he's old enough to go to prison for the first time, and he'll confess to fifteen or sixteen burglaries, thirty or forty cars. He comes up at the Magistrates Court, the police don't oppose bail. They send him out knowing he'll commit more crimes. The people were creating their own crime waves. The protectors were enlisting criminals. It was evil. Then, when his trial does finally come up, they say he's a good character who's seen the error of his ways, and they put in a plea for his sentence to be reduced.

It was quite difficult for me. As it happened, at the time I had an inspector on my tail. It was just bad luck. That's something that happens all the time. Vendettas inside the police force.

Someone gets on your case and rides you. Some years before, I'd had trouble with this inspector, when we were all playing a game of police cricket, and he's in to bat, and although he's already won the game, he wants to go on batting to show off in front of his family. And I just drift off to the pub, dying of thirst. And everyone follows me. He was furious. I mean, this is real life, he's an intelligent man, but he wants to impress his wife.

Next day he's lecturing us on the media, and I say something like, isn't it better to tell the media the truth, because we need them, and they do sort of represent the public? Next thing I know he's screaming at me that I'm a fucking commie bastard and he's going to get me.

So there are a number of detectives who are fiddling figures and some of us who are straight. But of course the fiddlers want us to go over, because if you're running something, you don't just want zombies, you want the characters to join as well. Then I had a bit of luck. I got breathalysed, and I used it as a way of leaving CID without alerting people. I went back to uniform. And that's when my year of hell began, deciding what I should do.

We spent that year policing the miners' strike. I've never seen anything like it. They say a policeman should never leave the job, because as soon as you go away, you begin to realize what it is. The whole motorway was jammed with vehicles, closed just for us, hundreds and hundreds of trucks from all over Britain. Then 700 beds in an aerodrome. I'm really sorry for the young people who joined at that time.

When I got back, I got a job as a collator. I started photocopying material at night. I drew up a criminal complaint; it was twenty-eight pages. I typed it in the office. I was in turmoil. I rang Scotland Yard to put in an official complaint, but they told me it would have to be referred back to my senior officer. They also told me our conversation had been recorded. There was no going back. Then I decided to go to my own Police Headquarters to see a senior officer. He turned white when he read it.

The subsequent scandal lasted about three years. Eventually only one man was dismissed. There was a new Chief Constable and he went on TV and said people had been silly. By now everyone was bored.

It's now being seriously suggested that the Home Secretary is going to use clear-up figures as a means of determining the efficiency of police forces.* That's why I feel I didn't achieve a great deal. It seemed as if no one listened.

It's all manipulation of the public's concept of the police. Use the media to dupe the public. It's Saatchi and Saatchi, designer uniforms, social services, help the aged – everything except real policing. It's all down to individuals. A policeman takes an oath. He promises to keep the peace – we nearly do. To prevent crime – not very successful. To prosecute offenders – lost control of that.

Hayden

One of my most interesting mornings is spent watching young recruits at Hendon Police College. The police enjoy simulating real-life situations. At Heathrow they have built stage sets and called them Riot City to train policemen in techniques for controlling inner-city violence. And here at Hendon there is a heavy emphasis on amateur theatricals which take place in little Disneyland pubs and street corners. Pretend-drunks pretend-vomit over pretend-policemen.

There is a two-day selection procedure for prospective recruits based at Paddington Green. They then have to come to Hendon to run round a cinder track and prove they are physically up to the job. If selected, they officially become policemen immediately. But before they can go to work, they must spend some time at a police college.

For any student policeman, there is such an extraordinary amount of factual information to take in that mnemonic acronyms are used all the time to help them retain the different procedures.

*In July 1993 the Sheehy Report, which was intended to reform pay and conditions in the police service, recommended that a policeman's salary should be related to his arrest and conviction rate.

Which outer garments can be removed outside a police station? JOG: Jacket/Outer garments/Gloves. Power to search for certain items? SOAP: Stolen articles/Offensive weapons/Articles with blades or points/Prohibited articles.

My host for the day was Hayden, who was on a temporary attachment. He had been working as a community involvement officer and was now teaching the recruits. In pullover and brown corduroy jeans, he was in his mid-30s and plainly bright, keener to talk about the philosophy of policing to me than about training. If the college imagined they had chosen Hayden to give the recruits a hopeful vision of policing, they had certainly chosen the wrong man.

Hayden: There are two irreconcilable functions in being a policeman. You've got to be a help to people and you've got to arrest them. A shoulder to cry on, and a hand on their shoulder. A mixture of compassion and hold-on-I'm-arresting-you. You become immune to criticism. There's so much of it, you just start to assume it's all wrong. Most people, when they join, tell you what their reasons are – helping society, serving the community and so on. But it's not till they get out on the street they find their true motives out. Like maybe exercising power. They get to the station where they're going to work and suddenly they're out there, and they find all the things we've told them to believe in aren't believed in by the majority of officers on the street. So they discredit us retrospectively in their minds. That's why Hendon is contemptuously referred to as The Dream Palace.

DH: *You sound as if you hate being a policeman.*

Hayden: We will never be acceptable to society as a whole. Any authoritarian order is going to be unacceptable to most people. The complaints bandwagon is out of control. It's society's problem. Society says we want a certain quality of life, we want to be able to walk down the streets and so on, but we aren't willing to pay for it. So they direct all their complaints against the police. And we turn it back on the public, because there's so little reward. The result is a vicious circle of resentment.

DH: *Do most people here pass?*

Hayden: Oh, sure. Nearly everyone. Let's face it, it costs £20,000 to train a policeman. We're not going to throw them away.

DH: *Do you tell them the truth about the job?*

Hayden: (*Laughs*) How can you? What am I meant to say? They'll find out. Senior officers are all in the golf club most of the time. The men despise them, and rightly. Because they're politicians after a while, not policemen. Once you get to a certain level, above inspector, then the job's about keeping your desk clear. I mean, senior officers don't want to stir things up, they'll say to you, oh, don't look into that, it'll just lead to trouble. Avoiding trouble is what it's all about.

Most policing is just complete bollocks. It's to do with going into a situation, making a decision and then *winning*. The kind of policing we believe in is not making everyone bow to your authority, it's much more to do with saying, 'Right, let's look at this, who's right and who's wrong here?' You should be the catalyst, not the judge. It's an ideal, I'm not saying it happens all the time. I'm not bothered. I'm off to get a degree. It's a lot easier than trying to become a sergeant. The sergeants' exams are ridiculous. They take a certain quota and that's it, according to the year's needs. So you can get a very high mark one year and not get accepted. The next year someone gets a very low mark and passes. It's a lottery. I know one sergeant who failed his inspectors' exams with nearly 80 per cent. He was so angry, he quit. Now he's become a barrister instead. That'll show them. Or perhaps it won't.

PRIVATE ENTERPRISE

Hugh

Just as spending a few minutes in a police station quickly alerts you to the ways in which televised fiction can subtly get things wrong, so meeting your first real-life private detective can prove a surprising experience. I knew before I went that there was no chance of my portraying a gumshoe in my play, but the opportunity to meet one proved irresistible.

Hugh employs over a hundred people and runs his business from a room in Central London. His own office is completely undecorated. On the table, there is nothing but a few magazines on electronic surveillance. The operation is 24-hour, round the clock. Hugh is unmistakably an ex-public schoolboy, in his late 30s, John Le Carré-ish, and looking as if he plays a lot of squash. He is scruffily dressed. Thirty-five per cent of his cases come from lawyers, but 52 per cent from commerce. The rest come from government. His speciality is large-scale fraud.

Hugh: Ninety-five per cent of fraud cases never reach the courts, because the firm is aware it reflects badly on them. Needless to say, most fraud doesn't ever go to the police. A bank doesn't want adverse publicity. Most of them concern non-professional fraudsters who have seen an opportunity. We collect the facts, present them with them, get them to give the money back. If they won't, then perhaps we reverse the sting. Our job is to find out who did it, how much they got, and where it's gone. We have a unique ability to access that information.

DH: *Are you at the top end of the market?*

Hugh: There are three kinds of private detective. The lowest form are inquiry agents. They're used by solicitors to serve summonses, confirm addresses and so on. They're pretty cheap.

DH: *I hear you're £75 an hour.*

Hugh: Who said that? Who on earth said that? We're £35.

Anyway, the next level up is the private investigators. Adultery, motor accidents and so on. Then last come the so-called Rolls-Royce firms. If you're a visiting American you'll be told to go to one of these. They all claim to be nation-wide, but actually they work on a franchise basis.

DH: *How did you get into this?*

Hugh: I was in Intelligence. I left because I was offered a job at twice the money. But it involved foreign travel. So when I got married, I started this business. We're known to be uniquely good at acquiring sensitive material from Swiss bank accounts. I'm very strict about clients. If they don't come from lawyers, I prefer them to have access to legal advice, so I'm sure what we do ends up in the right hands.

Of the 128 people I employ, thirty are on the road in straight investigation, maybe going under-cover in jobs in the firms with fraud problems. The rest are in surveillance. Most of our work is at night, because individuals work by day. Night is when they do what we're interested in. Six people here work on photographic and technical, round the clock.

We had one chap who had defrauded in the US about $28 million. He had a raft of Panamanian companies. All we knew about him when he came here was that he'd applied for a Venezuelan passport in 1974 at the London embassy. But from that single fact, we traced every one of his bank accounts. People thought it was a fluke, but it wasn't.

DH: *If you wanted to find out what is in my Midland Bank current account, could you?*

Hugh: Yes.

DH: *How?*

Hugh: I won't tell you.

DH: *How many people could find out what's in my account?*

Hugh: (*Very long pause*) In the UK, about four or five other people know how to do it. I mean, of course, the local CID officer can always do it in a particular local bank through contacts – Freemasons, Rotary club and so on – but nationwide, it's four or five.

DH: *What interests me is that presumably you have to persuade fraudsters to give money back and not cause any embarrassment. How do you do that?*

Hugh: By employing techniques I learnt in Northern Ireland. You have to decide what will motivate the fraudster to co-operate. You have to work out what his weakest point is. Will he do anything to avoid prison? Does he fear his family being involved? Is he frightened to lose everything? You have to make him see that it's in his own best interest to do what you want. But you also have to make him feel he's finding a way out for himself, whereas, in fact, of course you're manipulating him.

DH: *This reminds me of my favourite political maxim, which is Enoch Powell's great statement: Do not enter the yellow box unless your exit is clear.*

Hugh: (*Laughs*) Yes, that's it. The whole art is to pretend not to be intelligent. You have to pretend to be dull. If you seem intelligent, they get competitive and start dreaming up alternatives. But if you're dull, it discourages counter-decisions.

DH: *I must say, I've spent a lot of time with the police and they don't seem to me to think in a strategic way.*

Hugh: (*Leaning forward, emphatic*) Technique is such a wonderful thing. And they have no technique. Right now there's a man sitting in a cell near here, not far away, and he's done a £2.3 million fraud. The CID have done well to get him, but now they've got him, they have no technique, they can't see the opportunity. He's ready to confess. It's down to the calibre of the individual officer. There is no direction, there is no control, the training is not scientific.

Take resources. Tonight in Vine Street Police Station, there are just twelve police officers from eleven p.m. to six a.m., to police the whole of Soho, Mayfair, half the West End. One inspector, two sergeants, an area car driver, a radio operator, a van driver, a gaoler. That leaves four blokes on the beat for the whole of an area crammed with stealable stuff and top bods. One CID bloke in the capital city tonight, in a major terrorist target. Do you know how many police are on duty in Sidcup tonight? Exactly the same. Twelve. It's just stupid.

DH: *You were in the police before you were in Intelligence?*

Hugh: I started as a policeman. Coming from the middle class it was an unbelievable eye-opener. A PC must have a knowledge of the law, he has to learn it by heart. He needs a comprehensive knowledge of first aid, got to virtually be a GP, deal with a heart attack, or a kid who's OD'd, or a major brain tumour. He's got to deal with the social services, the judiciary, old-age pensioners, domestics – and he has no qualifications. Tonight, there are sixty police officers standing outside Buckingham Palace. It's ridiculous – why not put guards out there? The Army knows how to challenge a terrorist, they know fieldcraft. Instead it's the police in bushes with bloody torches. It's not widely known, but the SAS did a mock raid on Buckingham Palace. They got straight in and planted the bombs and straight out, and set off just one perimeter alarm.

DH: *What do you think has made things so bad for the police?*

Hugh: The CPS has been a disaster. Before it the policeman was emotionally involved. He had to have a case he believed in. He presented it to the duty sergeant, who had to believe in it; the magistrate would indicate whether he believed in it, so the police-man had to have it sorted out in his own mind. Unless he was bent, ambitious or off his nut, he had to have a very good case and be master of it. Now he has no personal interest.

The things which really destroyed the police were, one: Robert Mark cleaning up the CID.* He destroyed infiltration techniques, knocked the informer on the head. Each officer had his own informer, just you and the inspector knew about him. Sure you paid him money, but such tiny sums. The most I ever paid was £60 for a tip-off on an armed robbery. In return you turned a blind eye to criminal activities. But now there's a central register on com-puter for informants. It's out of the individual's control. I wouldn't inform in these circumstances, would you? Two: pay review was a disaster, falsely raised expectations. Of course, the pensions are fantastic, but the vocational side has vanished. Three: media persecution.

Even more important, the police have lost their heart. They just feel they're the dustbin of society. The media are against them, the public are against them. They go through the motions, but they're now like American police: nervous, terrified of being sued for

*Sir Robert Mark was Commissioner of the Metropolitan Police from 1972 to 1977.

criminal or civil offences. I know what Gardiner said about it being more important that one innocent man go free than a thousand guilty be put behind bars. But he's wrong. The thousand are much more important than the one. Awful for the one, of course. But now we're reaping the highly moral whirlwind.

DH: *Are the police distrustful of juries?*

Hugh: Juries are fallible. The police have various terms for them. A *Fresh* jury is one which is facing its first case, so they want to be Solomon, they want to be fair and serious and responsible and merciful. They always acquit. The *Greyhound* jury want to be in and out as fast as possible. They say not guilty, so they can go home quick and have nothing on their consciences. The *Nobbled* jury – they're so obvious, it's laughable. I've even seen members of juries talking to the defendants in the corridors. I've seen defendants blow kisses to their wife in the well of the court when she's holding a six-month-old baby. Look, we're talking about a population that watches *Neighbours*. They like emotion, they think emotion's what it's all about. Of course it works.

DH: *To me the paperwork seems the worst thing about policing, the sheer bureaucracy . . .*

Hugh: God, yes. But also the police's biggest problem is that the people who support them are the people who never come in contact with them. I mean, in a way, everything we're talking about is reassuring. Perhaps it's good for democracy that the police and Intelligence services are pleasantly incompetent. If they were too efficient, they'd be quite dangerous.

DH: *Your job seems much more interesting, gathering information and then using it. Yet in what you say, and after all your life in Intelligence, I can tell you're very against freedom of information.*

Hugh: The real nonsense is imagining that people have a right to know. They don't. They have no bloody right to know. Information is valuable. To put it in everyone's hands is to debase its value. If you put it in everyone's hands, then all that happens is that they know everything, but they're powerless to make decisions which affect what they now know. So that just leads to frustration.

THE INNS OF COURT

Maurice

By an extraordinary coincidence, during the writing of *Murmuring Judges*, I opened my newspaper one morning and found that a film I had made was at the centre of a case in the High Court. A litigious politician had taken offence at a chance remark by an actress, in which she had glancingly compared the character she played to that of the politician. Since Clara Paige in *Paris by Night* goes on to kill one of her oldest friends, the politician was claiming that the comparison had caused her 'upset'. For this, she wanted money.

To lovers of the surreal, I can recommend no more interesting experience than entering G. E. Street's Gothic building in the Strand, hurrying along its hushed cloisters, and entering a court in which a fictional character you have created is being discussed by bewigged lawyers. As the jury went out, I heard one highly paid advocate lean across to the other. 'What do you think? Yours or mine?' The defence lawyer shrugged. 'Fifty-fifty, I'd say.'

I have never attended a performance of *Henry VI* in which Dick the Butcher's line to Jack Cade, 'The first thing we do, let's kill all the lawyers,' was not greeted with storms of applause. So it was fortunate that the first High Court judge I met was Maurice, whom I spoke to alone in a gloomy room at the top of the High Court. On the way up the lift broke, and my brief period of imprisonment in a darkened shaft added perhaps to my sense of a judge's isolation. White-haired, gentle and concerned, he explained to me the different functions of the Lord Chancellor, who is a political appointment and a Member of Cabinet, and the Lord Chief Justice.

Maurice: The Lord Chancellor is in charge of the administration of justice and once a year makes what is called 'the bid' in Cabinet for his department. He then reports to the Lord Chief on how much money will be available for buildings and so on. But it's important to understand the principle that each judge has absolute autonomy within his own court. It's his and no one else's.

DH: *How much worry do you have that a judgement you make is going to be overturned on appeal?*

Maurice: I'm not worried at all. On the contrary. It seems to me a great bonus to know that there will be a second chance to consider things, especially in a difficult case. For example, I gave a chap five years for aiding and abetting his girlfriend in suicide with drugs. This chap had tried to kill himself at the same time, but the prosecution claimed he'd deliberately given himself an under-dose and his girlfriend an over-dose. Well, when my sentence was reduced from five to three, I must say I was tremendously relieved, because it had been a most difficult case.

DH: *Do you realize what an unfortunate impression it creates when Old Bailey judges are wined and dined in full fig?*

Maurice: It's appalling. The Sheriff of London uses us as a means of entertaining his guests. You know, he says to foreigners, 'Come along and lunch with some judges.' Some of us won't go. My constitution would not enable me to go, and to do my job adequately, more than once a week. Mostly, I just have a sandwich.

DH: *Does a judge have to have an instinct for when people are telling the truth?*

Maurice: I think people who say they have an instinct for when people are telling the truth are very foolish. I tend to trust someone who says, 'Well, it all happened last year, so I can't be 100 per cent sure, but . . .' In a criminal trial the jury don't like people who make dogmatic statements. Cross-examination reveals them. Sometimes you feel the jury are on top of it; sometimes they're floundering. You know from the nature of the questions they ask. You can tell whether they've spotted the same issues you have.

DH: *Have you seen the attitude of juries towards police evidence change over the years?*

Maurice: Since the late sixties, police evidence has been distrus-ted. In London, juries tend to acquit in cases dependent solely on police evidence, or on things reportedly said to the police. Honest policemen have been tarred by the dishonesty. Mind you, they weren't straight in the past. But they were *believed*. That's the difference.

I started in 1955, and it now seems light years away. In those days, in Newcastle, say, quarter sessions used to sit four times a year, and the session only lasted four or five days. But by 1970, the assizes had become unworkable, and so the Crown Courts were introduced, sitting more or less permanently, trying criminal cases. I don't know what the answer is. All I know is, things are profoundly unsatisfactory. OK, you don't send someone to prison, you send them to do community service. Then they don't obey the order. What do you do? Of course, we send far too many people to prison, but tell this to the householder who's just been burgled and they get very angry. Custodial sentencing just is incredibly depressing. At least with dangerous criminals you feel there's some logic to it: you're putting them out of harm's way. But the real growth industry, I'm afraid, is in sexual offences. What possible advantage is there in putting fathers and stepfathers in gaol? But that's what society wants. It's down to hysterical treatment in the press, and encouragement from certain of our leaders – Mrs Thatcher in particular. Prison ought to be a deterrent, and for the middle classes it is. There really is some point in putting a company director in prison for thirteen months for drunken driving, because that really does deter.

DH: *How much are you influenced by public opinion?*

Maurice: Public opinion is always at the back of the judge's mind. You must pass a sentence that reassures the public. You've got to think about the victim. If the criminal lives locally, what will the victim feel if he's in and out in no time?

DH: *From seeing them in court, what impression do you have of the police these days?*

Maurice: Most of the police's problems recently are down to stupidity. It's because they're so stupid. They ginger up the evidence. These younger policemen get their attitude to life from the blackshirts. They're roughneck intake. God knows why, they've had blue-chip treatment in terms of pay. It's all so unnecessary. It's happened to all of us – we've all dealt with snotty, arrogant policemen on piddling matters. That's what I mean by stupid. Don't they know they depend on the good will of the public?

Oh God, I mustn't say any more.

Raymond

My second judge was a circuiteer, who splits his career between being an advocate and being a judge. Raymond was in his 50s, short and well-dressed, full of fun, telling me he wanted to write a play himself because he regarded most fiction about the law as misleading. It always has monsters in it, but in fact there are no monsters. When later Raymond referred to a particular judge as a bastard, I picked him up on it. 'I said there were no monsters. I didn't say there were no bastards. It's an entirely different thing.'

Raymond: Criminal work is muck, though of course criminal lawyers go hairless if you say as much. Not only is there more money in civil cases, but also you're putting your case to a judge. Persuading a jury is a very different proposition. I don't regard it as a great intellectual challenge, frankly. When someone says to me, 'Well done,' after I've made my case, 'that was a jolly good speech,' I say, 'Was it? We won't know, will we, till the jury pronounce?' That's what's annoying about jury trial. You may make all the best points, but you may miss the one which will sway a jury.

DH: *As a judge, are there certain areas of the country where the police are believed more than in others?*

Raymond: Oh, absolutely. Chances of conviction vary according to geographical area. Police evidence convicts in Surrey, but it doesn't in East London. And certain police forces are known to be bent. For instance, in Salford once, years ago, they asked a defendant to strip to look for grass seeds. 'I don't have any grass seeds,' said the defendant. The policeman replied, 'No, but you fucking well will by the time I've finished.'

DH: *Do you think a judge can sway a jury one way or another?*

Raymond: The judge can actually do very little to affect the outcome of a trial directly. He *can* admit evidence he shouldn't, but that can be appealed. He *can* interrupt too much. He *can* get his law wrong. He *can* be biased in his summary. But a clever judge does it in such a way that he doesn't get caught. He does it by looks and winks and nudges. That's what a QC is watching for all the time, and often you get irritated because your client and their solicitor never notice these little hints, which are the real indicators of how the trial is going. But a judge knows he is always subject to appeal.

DH: *Does this worry you?*

Raymond: It doesn't bother you in the slightest, it's a purely professional thing. No pride involved at all. The other day, a friend said to me at lunch, 'I hope you're talking to me, Raymond. I've just slashed a sentence of yours in half.' 'Good God,' I said, 'I didn't know I'd given one which *could* be cut in half.' I'd given someone six months for reckless driving. I had to give a lot because there'd been a big thing in the paper about it just before.

DH: *What you're saying is that appeals against sentence are not necessarily heard very objectively?*

Raymond: Not at all. This is something nobody understands. Say you're in the Appeal Court. Appeal comes in, and sure enough there's a mistake in the summing up, or the judge interrupted too much, or he only gave the defence half a page against fourteen pages for the prosecution. And say the crime is burglary. Well then, it's, 'Very sorry, chaps, but this was a mis-trial and we have to throw it out.' But if that same case was a really vicious rapist or paedophiliac, well, then suddenly the appeal judge will say, 'Oh, I don't think the summing up was so biased, do you?' And he will uphold the conviction. Because there is a double standard which no one admits. You only throw out the cases which you *dare* to throw out.

The press would call this double standard hypocrisy. But if the case is that of a rapist, who's to say it's wrong? You're on a hiding to nothing. The case of the couple who were in a tent on the Defence Secretary's estate, allegedly making plans, was thrown out because Tom King made a stupid, prejudicial remark during the trial about the right to silence.* But if King's wife had been killed, if there had been actual bloody bodies, do you really think that technicality would have prevented a successful prosecution? Of course not.

DH: *Are you very sensitive about the press?*

Raymond: I do get sick of judges being held up to ridicule by the press. There are a million judge-words a week, and of course judges say stupid things. The phrase 'Who is?' is a way of saying that you are refusing to take judicial notice of something, i.e. it *does* have to be proved. For example: Margaret Thatcher is Prime Minister. The judge takes judicial notice of that, meaning he will not need proof, everyone knows it. But 'Who is Paul Gascoigne?' is a way of saying that the judge will not *automatically* accept that Paul Gascoigne is a famous footballer. It doesn't mean he doesn't know who he is.

DH: *I've met a number of lawyers who say the first ability you develop is an instinct for when people are telling the truth.*

Raymond: What bollocks! What fucking arrogance! Do they really say that? What a fucking arrogant lot they must be! It's balls. Mind you, after a while you do have a pretty good idea.

DH: *I find extraordinary this lunch the Sheriff gives . . .*

Raymond: (*Groans*) Oh God . . .

DH: *At which judges are paraded like monkeys . . .*

Raymond: It's a free perk, so everyone takes it. It is truly objectionable. A typical gathering will be the Chief Whip, a couple of stockbrokers, perhaps an ambassador. Mind you, benchers' lunches are like that, too.

DH: *Is England run by small groups of men meeting in rooms?*

Raymond: Why just England? Everywhere is.

---

*In April 1990 the Court of Appeal freed three people convicted in 1988 of conspiring to murder Tom King, then Secretary of State for Northern Ireland. The Appeal Court judges ruled that comments made by Mr King at the time had prevented a fair trial.

Dinner at Middle Temple

It is Benet Hytner QC who is kind enough to invite me to one of the formal dinners at Middle Temple. Most readers, I think, will know that, in order to be called to the Bar in England, a student must attach him or herself to one of the four ancient Inns of Court. While pursuing a legal education in more modern surroundings, the student must also eat a certain number of dinners in their Inn. In each term at least one dinner is formal and distinguished guests are invited. There is often a smattering of ex-prime ministers.

Hytner himself, who was at the time representing one of the Guildford Four at the May inquiry, and who also represented families at the Hillsborough inquiry,* has a justified reputation as a humane and decent lawyer. He is strongly committed to a belief in the fundamentals of the British Bench and Bar, but he is also entertainingly aware of its shortcomings.

We meet first in his rooms, where he gives a thumbnail sketch of many of the distinguished lawyers I will be meeting in the course of the evening. At the cocktail party before the dinner, I find myself talking to Sir Peter Pain, who is discussing the annual meeting of the Society of Labour Lawyers. The association wants judging to be a part-time job, so that mothers can do it.

Sir Peter: It's a very hot issue. But if you've got a criminal case which lasts three days, how can you get through it in two, just so that the judge can go home and change nappies?

There is a call to silence as we assemble outside the Middle Temple Hall, then we process through the long benches to the High Table. A guest night for benchers, it's a regular dining night for students, and my impression is of a cosmopolitan mix of faces,

*At Hillsborough football stadium, Sheffield, in April 1989, ninety-five people died at the FA Cup semi-final between Liverpool and Nottingham Forest. The main cause identified at the inquiry led by Lord Justice Taylor was the failure of the police to contain the movement of supporters into the stadium.

gleaming with youth and intelligence. The Hall itself is Eliza-
bethan. According to Manningham's diaries, it is where *Twelfth
Night* was first performed in 1602. The dinner for those of us on
High Table is asparagus in pastry, lobster Newburg, roast veni-
son and crême brûlée. We drink champagne, Chablis, some stunning claret and a Sauterne. I ask Ben why all this ridiculous
dining business still goes on for the students.

Benet Hytner: I've looked into it in great detail, and what I've
discovered is that barristers come here for lunch, and that in itself
is not enough to keep the kitchens financially viable. To make
them economic, they have to work in the evening as well. So the
dining requirements for students are maintained in order that the
barristers can go on having a lunching facility. That said, they are
doing their best to make these occasions into something more
than just dinners. We have Moots, or debates, or just talks.
We've even had Ken Livingstone.

We are sitting opposite the Master Treasurer, who officially runs
the Inn, though he is in fact aided in his task by the Under
Treasurer, Rear Admiral Hill. I am not quite sure if it is the
surroundings or the Master Treasurer's own natural manner
which has us all discoursing in an orotund, High Victorian style
of speech. A Senior bencher down the table has caught the
affliction.

Senior bencher: I was once in my lifetime prevailed upon against
perhaps my better judgement to invest in a theatrical production
in what I believe is called an angel's capacity.
His guest: Not a fallen angel, I hope?
Senior bencher: (*Ignoring this*) I was wise enough to use one of
the smaller trust arrangements that I have at various times of my
life made on behalf of various members of my family. The play, I
believe, featured the actor who plays Alf Garnett in a popular
television series . . .
DH: *Warren Mitchell* . . .
Senior bencher: So that when the deplorable production did

indeed close, I was able to turn to my wife at breakfast and say, 'I am sorry to inform you that you have just lost a thousand pounds.' But it was a thousand pounds she had not even known she possessed.

As the lobster arrives, we fall inevitably to talking about the threat which had been posed to barristers by the government's proposals to merge their work with that of solicitors, and to deny them unique rights of access to the courts.* This proposal had, of course, been met with predictable outrage by the Bar, who had found powerful support among judges, most of whom are themselves ex-barristers. The Lord Chief Justice had famously over-reacted in the House of Lords, invoking images of the Nazis to describe the government's intentions. This had served to further undermine his already doubtful sense of proportion. But Ben and his friends had a much more sophisticated analysis.

Hytner: A Thatcherite wind was blowing through the professions. Thatcher was the voice of the lower-middle class, and she looked at the law and she saw it was an upper-middle-class profession. She wanted it to be 100 per cent competitive. But she was unable to understand that rules which promote integrity, I'm afraid, do necessarily inhibit competition.

Of course, I'm not saying there weren't restrictive practices. There were. The numbers of juniors you had to bring along with you, and so on. Mackay, the Lord Chancellor, was on to some of the rackets that were going on, and we've had to give way on all that.

But Thatcher never understood the fundamental point of the profession. She never understood what a profession is. I'm a lower-middle-class boy from the North. My generation at Cambridge was unbelievably serious, desperate to put the world to

*At the time of my writing *Murmuring Judges*, this issue, pressed by the Lord Chancellor, was dividing the whole legal profession. Although the Court and Legal Services Act 1990 theoretically broke the Bar's monopoly, solicitors are, at the time of writing this book, no nearer appearing in the Crown Court and High Court.

rights. And the way to do it was through the law. I'm sure I was impossibly pious and absurd, but the fact is I do still believe in professional values. And this place represents those values. I believe people here have different values and different standards than the standards of money. They are willing to turn round and make reasoned decisions, and they *are* interested in finding out the truth. And now politics is in the hands of people who don't give a damn about anything except their own wealth and advancement, professional standards are more important than ever.

Further down the table, an amiable QC in his early 50s has been listening to Ben and is now keen to join in.

QC: The whole Saatchi and Saatchi thing was farcical. We had a beauty parade and then appointed a public relations firm to put our case against amalgamation to the general public. We fell for it because it worked for the doctors. The newspaper ads were a complete waste of time because they involved issues way beyond the general public.

DH: *I heard they were full of spelling mistakes.*

QC: They were terrible. The PR people didn't understand what they were saying. And it showed in their work. Mind you, very few people did. The politicians were shocking. A Bar Council delegation went to put their case to one Cabinet Minister, and he spent two-thirds of the meeting discussing his chances in an impending reshuffle. I know for a fact that when the Lord Chancellor was asked to guess the turnover of a large firm of City solicitors, he was out by a factor of ten. This is what no one understands. The income of two firms of City solicitors already equals the income of the entire Bar.

DH: *Is this your basic argument? That the changes would make powerful, monopolistic solicitors even more powerful?*

QC: My basic argument against the proposals is that you need specialists. At present, any solicitor can call on any specialist. But if you have amalgamated law firms, they will make you take their man, who will know less on a particular subject. The public will be less well served. OK, a lot is wrong with the Bar, but if you say a lot is wrong with architects, you don't say, 'Right, then, let's get lawyers to do their job.' You say, 'Let's get architects better at their own job.' We are actually cheaper than solicitors.

As more food comes, I move the conversation round to the prisons.

QC: We all know the prisons are a disgrace. If we were the fifty-first State of the Union, they would be closed down because they constitute a 'cruel and unnatural punishment'. The judges need to take account of the fact that there are only 20,000 places in British prisons and work to that. But they refuse to. They go on convicting 46,000 people to go in them.

DH: *Why do they do this?*

QC: You do have to remember, judges are terribly lonely, you know. Have you been to their awful rooms? Some of them are in the basement. And they don't see anyone, they don't have secretaries, they don't talk to anyone. It's tragic.

DH: *Will you become a judge?*

QC: I was meant to become a judge, which, frankly, I don't want to, because unless they do something about prisons, then being a judge is an unacceptable profession as far as I'm concerned.

As we go on discussing the proposed amalgamation, everyone at the table is relieved that the threat appears to have gone away. But the friendly QC is still worried.

QC: Mind you, I do think we have to go on asking questions. We need to examine whether the Inns serve any function.

DH: *(Laughs.)*

QC: Why are you laughing?

DH: *Because the Inns will survive.*

QC: Why do you say that? There were once thirty Inns, now there are only four.

DH: *They'll survive.*

QC: Why?

DH: *Because in this country everything with silverware always does survive.*

The first part of the meal over, the students are dismissed and the rest of us move to a second, smaller dining room, where we continue the meal. There are fruit and nuts, with Kummel, brandy, port and coffee. For this part of the meal, I am next to a judge who has a court in the East End. He is huge, an ex-rugby player with a very loud voice. I shall call him Brendan.

Brendan: I believe in East End juries. They live with crime day in, day out. So they know about it. They're not sentimental about it. They're realistic.

Hytner: That's not what David's asking. He's asking if the police are believed.

Brendan: Well, obviously I have ways of guiding a jury to make sure the police are believed if I think they deserve to be.

DH: *You mean you can steer the case?*

Brendan: Of course.

Hytner: In that case I'm lost in admiration. I've never managed it.

Brendan: I once argued as strongly as I could for an acquittal in my summing up, and the jury convicted. If for a moment the jury *senses* that you're steering them, then you're lost. Forget it. They react against.

DH: *So you decide, do you?*

Brendan: No, I don't *decide*. A judge never decides. I would say there has never been a single case in my court where I thought a man innocent and he was convicted by the jury. There are plenty that have gone the other way. People I knew should be sent down. The fact is, 85 or 90 per cent of the people who come to the courts are guilty. They just are. My father once said to me, never lose any sleep over the ones you know are guilty but whom the jury acquits, because in the long run, it does nothing but good. It *proves* the judicial process is independent of the police, and the more often that is proved to the public, the better. Each time a guilty man goes free, it's a proof of the independence of the system.

At this point, our conversation is interrupted by Barbara Mills, who is later to become Director of Public Prosecutions, suddenly banging a gavel at the far end of the room. She, the Junior Bencher, then stands up to face the Master Treasurer at the other end of the room.

Master Treasurer: Master Junior, shall we drink to the Queen?
Junior bencher: Let us drink to the Queen.
All: The Queen.
Master Treasurer: Master Junior, let the toast be: Domus.
Junior bencher: Master Treasurer, the toast is: Domus.
All: Domus.
Master Treasurer: Master Junior, shall we now drink to absent members?
Junior bencher: Master Treasurer, we shall now drink to absent members.
All: Absent members.

The dinner moves yet again. We are now in our fourth room. In this last room, we stand or sit, drinking lemon barley water, beer or whisky. Brendan has become more voluble.

Brendan: No one realizes how jolly hard we work. They think we swan in at ten and knock off at four, and it looks like a very light day. It's outrageous. And what annoys me most is this bloody Home Office nonsense that we are trigger-happy about sending people to gaol. If you knew how hard we work to avoid custodial sentences when we possibly can. And I am sick of reading this damned, blackguardly, black lie that it's all the judges' fault. When it's the Home Office's fault for not having enough places.
DH: *But have you been in the gaols? They're just dustbins. You're consigning people to dustbins.*
Brendan: Don't blame us, blame the Home Office.

Duncan

During my visits to the Inns of Court, Duncan's name came up a number of times. Lawyers are sometimes too busy or too habituated to think much about the special character of their work. Like many of us, they get their thinking done young. But Duncan was known to be a QC who had managed to keep himself one step back from the Inns, and to have some perspective on his own role as one very small part of one very long process.

Duncan: Judges claim to be responsive to public opinion. But they are in fact extremely resistant to lighter sentencing. The magistrates are notoriously worst of all. Given a chink of discretion they will always use it to lock people away. This is only one aspect of the whole legal culture. Most lawyers try consciously not to think about the issues raised by their work. The vulgar idea is to think of judges as Tories in ermine, but in fact, although the law has a conservative dynamic, it is quite different from political conservatism.

DH: *Presumably judges have influence but not power?*

Duncan: Judicial power in the law-making process is essentially negative. Some have the power, through their place in the Lords, to give the thumbs-down to legislation, but they are never guilty of putting anything positive in its place, because they do not want to be accused of running the country.

DH: *Where do you think the government's proposals to reform the Bar originated?*

Duncan: Nobody has ever been able to get at the truth of this. The rumour always was that the Lord Chancellor recruited all the mandarins from the Department of Trade and Industry who had broken trade union power, smashed up the state monopolies and saved money in the process. That is the general belief, but the Lord Chancellor does deny it.

DH: *You know, when the Bar Council decided to hire public relations people to fight the proposals, the million pounds they needed to do it was raised in four days.*

Duncan: (*Laughs*) Not only is that a measure of the panic, but also we're talking about men who are not noted for their willingness to part with money at the best of times.

DH: *Why do you think the proposals were successfully resisted?*

Duncan: The Bar's arguments against the Lord Chancellor's proposals to reform it would not have prevailed if barristers alone had put them forward. The crucial thing was, *the judges supported them*, because the judges themselves were all ex-barristers. The judges pointed out that the rights of audience in a court were not granted by Parliament but by them. The Inns of Court act on behalf of the High Court judges. To insist by Act of Parliament that the licence to appear in court be changed would be to provoke a constitutional crisis, for it would take away historic power from the judges.

DH: *Ben Hytner has a very brilliant defence of the Bar, which he identifies with the idea of professionalism itself. Truth before money.*

Duncan: The difference between Ben and me is that he thinks the system is full of honest people doing their best. I don't. I think it's a fount of intellectual dishonesty, and that interpretation of the law is swayed by personal bias at many instances. For a long time there was one judge who was known still to be angry about the war. If you had a German name, you simply could not get a judgement in your favour.

DH: *By and large, you avoid criminal work. Why is that?*

Duncan: I always say, because I'm not good enough. It needs extraordinary practice and sensitivity. Which, unfortunately, it never gets. Sentencing should be the most difficult thing in the world, and instead it's treated as if it's routine – once you know the tariff, you've got it. This is terribly wrong. I used to worry all night, that the bloke would be convicted and he'd have a record because I hadn't done a good enough job. It's not professional, taking your cases to bed with you. You're wound up and tired, you don't do a good job.

DH: *But if people like you won't touch crime, isn't there a problem with who will?*

Duncan: The sad thing is that, in criminal law, the experience in this profession goes exactly the wrong way, because it's the most *in*experienced who are handed the briefs at shortest notice. It's in the Magistrates Courts that you're suddenly bunged something ulcer-making which you have to do on the hoof. But to be able to fight a case at thirty minutes' notice is precisely when you need years of experience. The law on something like threatening behaviour in a public place is terribly complicated. Then the solicitor gives you an inadequate statement from a witness (because of legal aid cutbacks, preparatory work is pared to the bone), you maybe haven't seen the police evidence, so the policeman gets up and describes a case which bears no relation to what your client's told you. Well, your only hope of an acquittal is to have the experience to know how to find inconsistencies in police evidence. Your only other hope is that your client is middle-class and well-spoken, so you can ring seven bells of sympathy with the magistrate, who thinks, 'Oh, this must be a terrible mistake.'

DH: *I've begun to realize that the law is tripartite. The judiciary, the police and the prisons. And it depends for its essential character on the fact that each part of it is mutually ignorant. Nothing – nothing – causes such horror to any one part of it as the suggestion that they should find something out about the other. My favourite remark so far has been from the judge who told me that he didn't want to know what prison was like because then he would be able to imagine where he was sending people when he sentenced them. This, he said, would affect his judgement.*

Duncan: Well, there you are. The whole system of crime and punishment stays off the ground by some strange levitation. It's all pulls and pushes. At least people are beginning to realize after Strangeways that a pressure-cooker penal system is expensive. If the doves are in the ascendancy at the Home Office, it's because they can point to Strangeways and say, 'There, I told you so.'

Bernard Simons

Early on in my researches I enlisted the London solicitor Bernard Simons to help me with any detail of the law I didn't understand. He was excellent company. I never tired of his scurrilous stories of self-important people coming a cropper in the courts. He belonged to that rich English tradition which sees the law as a first-rate source of human entertainment. His account of Dennis Potter's successful libel action against Mary Whitehouse was a special gem. In his early 50s, owl-faced with thick glasses, he met me first in an expensive restaurant of his choice, where he began by encouraging in me a healthy distrust of everything lawyers would tell me.

Bernard Simons: It's a bad thing, I suppose, but with the years I find more and more I don't believe that what people tell me is true. It's inevitable in my job. I mean, very occasionally, it even happens that when you've got someone off, they say, 'That was a wonderful job you did,' and then it's pretty clear what they mean. They were guilty. But I can't say it happens very often.

DH: *What's the most important gift for a solicitor?*

Simons: The solicitor's job is to choose the right QC. Courtroom technique is far more important than knowing the law. The law you can always bone up on. But persuading the jury is a real art. If the evidence is fifty-fifty, then the jury will decide according to which barrister they prefer. They don't listen to the evidence, they listen to the way the evidence is put.

Defence lawyers *want* a case to last a long time, because then the jury gets to know the defendant. The longer they spend in his company, the less likely they are to find him guilty. After all, after a while he becomes familiar, a friend even, and nobody wants to send their friend to gaol. If they see him briefly, then they have no feelings about him.

DH: *Can you read a jury?*

Simons: No. People claim to understand juries, but they don't. The only ones I fear are when it's clear they want to get home and cook the lamb chops. They are dangerous because they simply aren't listening.

DH: *Do you get very involved in your cases?*

Simons: I no longer feel passionate about criminal law. I just do cases for friends. After a while you get to know the magistrates and you know what they want and you give it to them – usually a speech about how your client has made one mistake and has now learnt their lesson. At one time, I made the same speech about drugs all over the country, and grew so used to making it that once, in Leicester, I found myself as if dictating it, complete with instructions: 'Has learnt his lesson comma and will not do it again full stop, new para.' The magistrate said, 'Well, that was very interesting, Mr Simons.'

DH: *Am I right in thinking all serious attempts at penal reform have been abandoned?*

Simons: Everyone's just given up. There's no evidence penal reform worked. And besides, it's expensive. I don't think there's any doubt that judges are too fond of sending people to prison. Most people need a very short sentence indeed. All they need is to hear the clang of the prison gates. The prisons are now so ridiculously overcrowded that if you do criminal work you spend all your time travelling – to faraway prisons to find your client. If it's bad for us, imagine what it's like for the relatives.

DH: *Do judges still try to guide juries?*

Simons: There's much less of that. It's counter-productive now that jury is open to all. When it was just property-owners, then juries were much more deferential. But now they're diverse and sceptical, they resent being guided.

DH: *You're going to be a Recorder yourself. Do you have mixed feelings about that?*

Simons: Some. I have come to realize that judges do see the right to send people to prison as the real source of their power, and they will fight to retain that power. They don't want to give it up for anyone. A lot of the problems come from this current Lord Chief Justice, who in order to standardize sentences – in response to press criticism that judges are inconsistent – tends to lay down guidelines in appeal cases. And all the junior judges want to follow him. But what Lane rarely points out or mentions is that you don't *have* to use prison at all.

DH: *What seems so disastrous is the judiciary's distrust of probation officers.*

Simons: The worst thing a probation officer can do is indicate a recommended sentence for their client. As soon as they do that, the *judge balks and sees it as a threat to his power. He becomes nakedly territorial and discounts the report.*

DH: *Judges all tell me that having their sentences overturned is no disgrace.*

Simons: Oh, they always say that. They always tell you that only a weak judge is never overturned. But when you think about it, what that actually means is that if you sentence high, there is a chance you will be appealed against. If you sentence low, no one will question you. Motto: only weak judges sentence low. It's depressing.

DH: *It wasn't till I started work on this play that I realized how unusual it was for a defendant to get the barrister they were expecting.*

Simons: It's almost unknown. Barristers are always unexpectedly tied up on cases going on longer than they anticipated. Or a case is called very suddenly. The result is that 75 per cent of criminal briefs are returned the night before the trial. I must say, it does make things very difficult.

HER MAJESTY'S PLEASURE

Chris Whitehead

A year or two before I had thought of writing about the law, I had been invited by a group of prisoners to see a production they were putting on in the lifers' wing at Wormwood Scrubs. If, like me, you have never seen a play by Steven Berkoff, then I cannot imagine a better introduction to his work than first to see it presented by an all-murderer cast. The performance was startlingly assured. But the most chilling moment came afterwards. When I told the leading actor just how good he was, he begged me not to praise him. 'Because I have to go back to my cell,' he said, 'and I have another eleven years to go. And if you tell me tonight I could actually make it as a professional actor, I think I will go mad with the longing.'

It was Dostoevsky who said you may judge the state of a country by the state of its prisons. Over the years, each section of our Criminal Justice System has developed highly sophisticated reasons why it is right to blame the other sections for the deterioration of the prisons. The judiciary, of course, say the prisons are no concern of theirs. The government blames public opinion and the unions for their resistance to more humane working practices. The unions blame understaffing and underfunding.

To obtain permission to go into prisons, I had to visit the Home Office and meet the press officer, Chris Whitehead, whose office is high up in the hideous modern building at the back of Victoria Street.

Chris Whitehead: We're building a new prison in Woolwich – it's got an astro-turf playing field, full-size. That's better than most schools. The architecture of Victorian prisons was ideal from a security point of view: you had a central point from which you could observe everything, whereas the dormitory prisons of the fifties and sixties were much harder to police. But the Victorians had a different idea of prison. You were to repent the error of your ways, so you were banged up without integral sanitation. The Home Secretary has promised that by 1994 three-quarters of prisons will allow access to sanitation. That's a tremendous advance. It's a question of resources. You can't just build more prisons, or rebuild old ones, because where do you put people while you're building. Money itself isn't the sole answer.

DH: *Is the expectation of an ever-rising prison population?*

Whitehead: Yes. Well, the projection is, but the peculiar difficulty of prison planning is that projections are always wrong. Actually, at the moment it's falling. We expect the new Criminal Justice Bill to recommend more non-custodial sentences for small offences. We did try electronic tagging with fifty volunteers. Every prison reform group was down on us. It is astonishing to me, it's a cultural thing, but people would rather go to prison than be tagged.

DH: *People think tagging is humiliating.*

Whitehead: Well, that then gets you on to the question of what prison is for in the first place.

DH: *Well, plainly it does not reform.*

Whitehead: Quite.

DH: *Nor does it rehabilitate.*

Whitehead: No. We accept that.

DH: *So surely if it's about punishment, the loss of liberty is the punishment. You don't need to humiliate people as well.*

Whitehead: Yes, absolutely. In a way, the longer your sentence, the better you're treated. The worse you behave, the likelier you are to be Category A, which means you have your own régime. What we can and must do is help remand prisoners.

DH: *Well, you're hardly helping them by the recent rule which forbids food being brought into the prison.**

Whitehead: That was so that everyone should be equal. So the rich weren't better off. It was an attempt to level down.

DH: *Yes, but when you're on remand, you're meant to be innocent, until you're proved guilty.*

Whitehead: (*Laughs*) You'd have to talk to the judges about that. Why do they put them on remand? Again, it's partly financial. They're on remand because they can't afford bail.

DH: *How do you see conditions in prisons being improved?*

Whitehead: The crucial humane issue is how long you're allowed out of your cell. There are 123 or 124 prisons – it depends if you count Strangeways – and each is run by its governor. In Lincoln, the governor has done a deal with his staff and the result is the men are let out of their cells for a really good proportion of the day; there are classes and activities and so on. Now, if they did it in Lincoln, why don't they do it elsewhere?

DH: *Well, why not?*

Whitehead: Everyone knows. There is a problem with the union. In spite of the Fresh Start programme,† they go on asking for more men. It's a perpetual battle. For new practices, they want more staff.

DH: *You can't blame the unions. It's a terrible job.*

---

*In the late 1980s the right of remand prisoners to have food brought in by family and friends was withdrawn by the then Home Secretary.

†Fresh Start was a new attempt, in 1987, to rationalize pay, overtime and allowances and to introduce a new style of group working in British prisons.

Whitehead: Is it? We don't have any trouble attracting recruits. Half are people who like uniform and power, the other half are socially conscious. There are some wonderful people in the service.

DH: *Doesn't a prison depend for its tone on the flavour of its regime? Strangeways went up because it had the toughest screws in the country.*

Whitehead: Yes. Well, Wandsworth did get badly out of control as well. The warders introduced a slash across their peak caps – like a para-military organization. That was stopped. It's natural, in a way. It's pride in your prison. 'We do things differently from Brixton,' that sort of thing. It's group loyalty.

DH: *So will you take more staff on now?*

Whitehead: We are recruiting more staff because of Strangeways.

DH: *So the riot was a great success, really. It achieved its aims.*

Whitehead: (*Correcting himself*) No. We're speeding up the advancement of a process of recruitment. To progress, we need the right level of staff, the right buildings and a change in trade union practices. At the moment they're refusing to let us farm out minor jobs like video monitoring or court escorts to non-union members.* They want to protect their jobs and their status.

Justice Stephen Tumim

Inside the Home Office, giving advice directly to the Home Secretary, but licensed by a Queen's Warrant, is Her Majesty's Inspector of Prisons. The first, and so far only, holder of this post is Justice Stephen Tumim, whose job it is to report on those particular prisons which he feels fall below an acceptable standard. The authority and diligence with which he does this, and the consistency with which he manages to keep the respect of all sides in the arguments about crime and punishment, are all the more remarkable for the fact that he is himself a product of the very judiciary of which he is so critical.

*In 1993 some prison escort work was transferred to a private security firm, Group 4, with farcical results.

In person, he is physically like a classic public school master, complete with the shock of white hair and the trouser flies seemingly worn on the outside. Maggie Hambling's portrait of him, which was for a time exhibited at the National Portrait Gallery, captures a good deal of his vitality and warmth.

Stephen Tumim: The Woolf Report, following the Strangeways riot, is going to have the same theme as the play you're proposing to write. How do we get the different parts of the judicial system to talk to one another? At the moment, you couldn't even call it a system. The judges are difficult. Woolf will propose interdisciplinary commissions or boards, and the judges will want to chair them, or not join them.

DH: *You visit prisons and report on conditions inside?*

Tumim: My job is to be independent of everyone. My job is to advise ministers on prison conditions. When I go round to listen to prisoners, I tell them I'm reporting, and I say, 'Imagine you're writing the report and tell me what should be in it.' I sometimes take a guest inspector with me, but I see prisoners in the absence of staff.

DH: *You know better than I that judges resent any interference with the running of their courts.*

Tumim: Judges sometimes confuse independence with ignorance. They think it means they needn't read anything. NACRO [National Association for the Care and Resettlement of Offenders] produces wonderful reports, but often they do not read them. Oh no. They do it all internally, through Judicial Studies Boards, where senior judges advise younger ones on sentencing. For instance, few of them knew about the experiment in Germany, where they have taken an average of 10 per cent off custodial sentences in the last decade, and it has had no effect on the crime rate whatsoever. I look at all these distinguished grey heads when I address the recorders and circuit judges, and I start by saying, 'There are seven different types of prison.' And I see them all bowed, writing, taking notes. And I think, 'You don't know the difference between a local and a training prison, for a start.' These are the sentencers.

DH: *What is the judges' defence?*

Tumim: Their defence is to say that the Court of Appeal does not allow them to say what kind of prison an accused should go to. So their answer is, 'Once the prisoner goes out of the court door, it's no business of mine.' The mutual ignorance of the judiciary and the prison service is shocking. At least in the old days, an assize judge would knock off for an hour and say, 'Right, I'm going round the local gaol now.' It was all very patronizing, there was a lot of, 'And what are you in for, my man?' sort of stuff. But it was something. Now judges often claim they're too busy.

DH: *What are the practical measures you're interested in?*

Tumim: I advised the Home Secretary that for about £40 million we could end slopping out by 1996. There was a lot of reaction, people saying target dates were undesirable because they were a hostage to fortune, and pointing out there's no point in putting lavatories into buildings which are due, only a few years later, to be ripped down. So when Kenneth Baker came in and asked when slopping out was going to be ended, I said the present estimate is 2007. He said such a late date would be politically unacceptable. He decided on 1994.*

DH: *This internal sanitation thing mystifies me, because right now at Wormwood Scrubs they are rebuilding A-wing with no internal sanitation.*

Tumim: This new Scrubs building has, I believe, inadequate architectural advice. The new prison at Woolwich I went to see appears to have serious design faults, perhaps due to the good architect being inadequately briefed. He's built too many cells for two. In each cell, at great expense, there is a bronze latch on the window. A perfect ligature on which to hang yourself.

DH: *Is sanitation the worst problem?*

Tumim: Not really. I do get a little tired of what I call the Eeyore mentality. You know, *Winnie the Pooh* – Eeyore stands saying how dirty the pool is, but he's swishing his tail in it himself. My preferred aim is to attack three general areas in prisons: Lack of Sanitation, Overcrowding, and Lack of Occupation. Of these

---

*At the time of writing, this target date for ending slopping out still holds.

three, the most important is the third. I mean, lavatories are valuable and so on, but unless you get people working where are you? People are proud of this thing called association, it's considered to be marvellous if you have a lot of it, but what is it? What I want is remedial education. Not sewing mailbags, which still goes on, but proper City and Guild certificates in welding and so on. I want family conditions improved. Outside any London prison, you see all these poor women with their babies, the rain slanting down on them as they wait. We need proper visiting areas with carpets and crèches and tea and buns and biscuits. *Dramatically* better visiting. Because it's crucial. If a prisoner could earn £10 a week then we could *make* him give some to his wife outside. The censorship of mail is unnecessary. The mail should just be opened and shaken out in front of the prisoner, to make sure there's no drugs, and that's it. Except spies and terrorists, obviously.

DH: *Why are so many people in British prisons in solitary confinement?*

Tumim: I don't know. Sexual offenders need protection, of course, but so do the maladjusted. Graham Greene got this right. One of his characters says, 'The world divides into the torturable and the non-torturable.' What can you do about it? Prison culture is so deep. A prisoner often says proudly to me, 'I survived Wandsworth.' This is a prison with a reputation for a fierce staff.

I want the end of slopping out, not only for hygienic reasons, but to raise morale. The best thirty pages ever written about prison are by Evelyn Waugh in *Decline and Fall*. He got it right – it's a nasty public school. Go to the washhouse in Brixton. It's like Kipling or the Indian army. In Wandsworth the men line up naked, then the whistle blows and all the showers come on at once. They shower. Then the showers go off.

I can help deal with the smelly side and the washing up. All that's easy. The hard thing is the sentencing, and that will only ever be sorted out by contact between governors and judges. They don't lunch together very much. But what is a governor like? There's no typical prison governor. Mr Justice Streatfield said in the fifties, 'You can either think of prison as looking back to the offence, or forward to re-entry into normal life.' And he said, 'We've got to look forward.' Now everyone looks back. This new bill sees prison as punishment. But the converse of punishment is reward. People talk about stick and carrot. I see the stick, but where's the carrot? Punishment is now the aim of prison, and it costs £20,000 a year per prisoner. Fifty per cent recommit. Among young men, 80 per cent recommit. You simply can't say punishment is an end in itself. It's got to be a means to reform. That means proper training, not courses in bricklaying that last four weeks and you never lay a brick again. At one prison you can do bookbinding as a course, but at the end the prison has no books to bind. I want men occupied and interested. I want more briskness.

DH: *God, you do sound public school.*

Tumim: I must find a better word than briskness. But it is what I mean. The worst thing I ever saw was B-wing at Hull. Fifteen- and 16-year-olds thrown into cells to spend the whole day lying on their beds, with 20-year-old criminals in the same cells to teach them all about crime.

DH: *Has your job given you much respect for politicians?*

Tumim: The problem is, some of them are so busy they have no time to master the arguments. They simply can't make informed decisions. But others think out the position more carefully.

Wormwood Scrubs

Many people who read this book will have visited one of the larger London prisons. They will be familiar with the depressing surroundings; with the knots of families waiting patiently outside for their turn to be allowed in; with the cheerless reception rooms; with the shouting and screaming which goes on as night comes down; and with the stench of cheap food which permeates everywhere. In one prison I visited, the entire kitchen had been reclad in stainless steel at a reputed cost of £1 million. But in the two years since the refurbishment, the rats had already eaten their way through the metal, and the job was being started again.

Anyone fond of prison literature will know, of course, that people adapt. Everyone involved – prisoners and screws – finds resources of humour and character to deal with the atmosphere created by the surroundings. The card at the entrance to Wormwood Scrubs, reading 'WE ARE IMMUNE TO GLOOM', spells out the first law of survival. The graffiti in Strangeways – 'DON'T COMPLAIN YOU BASTARDS, YOU'VE ALL VOLUNTEERED' – fills in the other side of the picture. A sign I saw in the Wandsworth Prison Laundry – 'WE ARE THE UNWILLING DOING THE UNPLEASANT FOR THE UNGRATEFUL' – belongs somewhere in the middle.

On my first guided tour of Wormwood Scrubs, I am accompanied by Tim Beeston, Governor 5. There are five levels of governor and his is the most junior. We meet in what he calls the sterile area, which is that part of the gaol to which prisoners have no access. He is in his late 20s, in a grey suit, one of a new breed who have entered the service as a graduate. The Scrubs has four main wings with approximately 250 in each. A-Wing: short term; B and C: remand; D: lifers. The lifers do their first three years at the Scrubs in order to be assessed, given help to come to terms with their sentences, before being dispersed to other prisons. I am later told this process need take only twelve months, which is how long a lifer needs to adjust, but the term is often spun out artificially. A startling number of lifers are first offenders.

Most gaols are on a radial system, all wings emanating from a central circle, but the disadvantage is that the sun never reaches certain parts and you get problems with rotting. Sir Edmund du Cane designed the Scrubs so that the sun reaches all the cells at some point in the day. But, because of this, it is scattered over a large area.

Tim Beeston: The prison is supervised by a board of visitors, who are appointed by the Home Secretary. They have two roles: watchdogs on the prisoners' behalf, and adjudicators in the discipline procedures. These roles are, of course, in some sense contradictory. They have automatic access to prison – a right they share only with JPs and the bishop of the diocese. They are composed of people 'involved in the community'. Anyone can apply and have their name vetted before being put forward to the Home Secretary. A new grievance procedure has just been introduced. A wing governor has to answer a prisoner in writing within seven days. All movements from prison to prison are controlled by the Tactical Management Unit, which is based in Birmingham and which decides who goes where. A governor has to accept whoever he's sent. The board of visitors has twenty members, of whom sixteen will be at any one meeting. They deal with two or three cases a month. One member comes in to check the prison, on rota, every week. They have a statutory obligation to taste the food.

We then start our tour of the prison. The visiting areas first. Because of the huge numbers on remand, there are desks about seventy feet long with chairs either side. Remand prisoners have a right to one meeting a day of fifteen minutes. Convicted prisoners have two a month of at least thirty minutes – usually all afternoon. The remand prisoners' right to have food brought in was stopped for two reasons: the immense resources needed to check everything for drugs and weapons; and the problem that the poor were spending more on the father's prison diet than on their own children outside. The sensitive issues to a prisoner are canteen, mail and visits. The censorship of mail at the Scrubs, I am told, is less than in many prisons. All mail is opened, but only 5 per cent is read.

As you move from wing to wing, you cannot avoid the small packages of shit which litter the ground, and which the prisoners throw from their windows in order not to have to spend time in their cells with their own excrement. The shit accumulates alongside soft-drink cans and all the other garbage that rains down from the cells.

Beeston: If you talk to the men, sanitation's not all that important to them. They're much more concerned to get television in the cells. I think this would be a bad thing. There's a lot of talk about how we would control the cable, so that they would only be able to watch so many hours a day, but if you let people sit in their cells watching TV all day, you really are renouncing all claim to be preparing them for life when they leave.

DH: *But how much rehabilitation is going on in the Scrubs anyway?*

Beeston: Oh, lots. They're seeing professional experts who are assessing them. There's work, there's sport.

We go on to the remand wing. Here you may wear your own clothes. An indigestible tea of cold-looking spaghetti and meatballs is being served. Everyone will tell me that the atmosphere on remand wings is much worse than elsewhere, because there is so much uncertainty. On other wings, people are more or less resigned to their fate. But on remand, fights break out and people grow jumpy because they do not yet know what their fate is.

Behind us, a white prisoner is abusing an Asian.

Prisoner: I've decided you're a fucking cunt.

Asian: Why am I a cunt?

Prisoner: You're a cunt and I don't want ever to fucking see you.

We all ignore this and move on, as if it's not happening. We also ignore the man who blows persistent raspberries at me because I'm a visitor. (Later, visiting another prison, Richard Eyre, Bob Crowley and I are startled to be greeted with a cry of, 'Oh, look, three cunts in coats.' But we decide later it's a fair description.) In the fifties, I grew up on films about 'old lags'. But now they are in the minority. I suppose the thing that most shocks me is how young everyone is.

When we get back to the sterile area, I run in to Paul Schurer, who is chairman of the board of visitors here. He is preparing for a visit from the Prison Inspectorate, who will soon spend a week here. Schurer is in his 40s, and has been involved with the Scrubs for fourteen years. He used to help run Help the Aged in his local area, then decided he wanted to be even more involved in the community.

Paul Schurer: I'm not sure why certain things don't happen, things you argue for year after year. Is there any point going on arguing for them? We make these recommendations and nothing happens. Like integral sanitation. It's an absolute scandal. It's disgusting. Everyone says they're in favour, but it doesn't happen. They say it's the Treasury. It looks more like incompetence to me. I mean, to spend a million on A-Wing here and *still* have no lavatories, it's crazy. You're given the plans. You can't imagine how slowly the department moves. You think, if I object to these plans, then any changes we force on them will mean the whole scheme is postponed for another two years. Or will never happen. So you let them browbeat you into accepting them, although you know they're wrong.

There are 1,000 men here in a prison which was built for 750. The only reason there aren't 1,200 is that the Prison Officers' Association would strike and refuse to admit them. So when I hear people going on about how backward the unions are in prisons, I think, yes, but they do actually stop the Home Office just cramming in as many as they want.

DH: *Do you know any prisoners individually?*
Schurer: Honestly, no. Remand prisoners come and go so fast. A lifer I might meet once or twice. Finally, I do sometimes help individuals – when someone went up on the roof, I went and talked him down. But bringing about change, that's impossible.

Schurer, Beeston and I walk back through the darkening grounds; the Alsatians are out now, the cream wire lit by floodlights.

Schurer: Actually, we're not even standing still, we're going backwards. Like they said, the workshops were underused, so they decided to close them down. They said remand prisoners were too busy worrying about their trials to do anything. They said they had to see their lawyers and their minds were on their cases. Well, that's just balls. You see the lawyer for an hour a week. What are you meant to do with the rest of your time?

Lynn

Opponents of prison reform regularly accuse liberals of ignoring just how unpleasant and vindictive many criminals are. To give myself a powerful reminder of the day-to-day problems of dealing with prisoners, and especially those with life sentences, I spoke with a senior probation officer at an unnamed gaol. In her early 40s, Lynn was quiet and soft-spoken, but as she talked her strength of character became clear. Although we were in the sterile area, the telephones had been taken out and locked away for the night, for fear prisoners should riot and break in to contact the outside world.

Lynn: The first twelve months, most people are appealing, so they're claiming they're innocent. Then, after the appeal, most of them admit they did it. The more serious the offence, the longer it takes to appeal. They deal with the less serious ones at once. We've got one at the moment who has gone on protesting his innocence and we all believe him. We just know he is. I asked one of my team, why are you so sure he's innocent? They said it's something to do with his dignity.

DH: *How many people in the gaol at the moment are innocent?*

Lynn: I can't say for sure, but I know three or four about whom I have no doubts at all. Everyone knows who they are. It's unmistakable.

DH: *Do you have a programme here which you administer for lifers? How does it start?*

Lynn: Any lifer who has killed someone in a brawl, say, first and foremost has to analyse what circumstances made him do it, because unless he is willing to do this, how can we, as probationers, recommend his release without the worry he will do it again? So, even after nine years' resistance, the prisoner will finally realize that his chances of getting remission depend on our reports and they'd damn well better do something about it. Reports on individual prisoners go to the Home Office.

When a prisoner arrives, he has an induction week. They happen four times a year, and in that week you meet representatives from the chaplain, psychologists, education, probation, the uniformed staff and medical. The week is to tell you what to expect in prison and how to deal with it. Then in the induction unit there are three long-term boards, after six months, eighteen months and three years, where the prisoner comes in person and talks to representatives of all these disciplines about his crime and his attitude to it. He'll then be debriefed by his probation officer on how he's done. We then have some extremely hard arguments among the board about whether someone convinces us of their attitude to the deed or not.

DH: *You want them to come to terms with what they've done?*

Lynn: The murderer must learn about himself. The central thing is to examine the act. What was it within me? If they don't reach that, then they will flip again. Of course, the easy thing is to be angry all the time in prison – at the system, at the other prisoners, at the officers. It's easy to be angry with other people.

DH: *Some people resist?*

Lynn: They resist like blazes. If you're the kind of person for whom prison is an occupational hazard, the easiest way to get through is to stay angry. Angry at the conditions. Angry at the staff.

DH: *Are you saying your work is to make them angry with themselves?*

Lynn: Yes, it is. It bloody well is. And when you do actually realize you've killed someone, and the effect that will have on their family, then there will be a tide of guilt and grief and anger.

DH: *But take people's anger away and aren't you taking away something which makes them want to live?*

Lynn: What's sad is people become institutionalized whether they want to or not. The institution always wins, the individual never wins.

DH: *But in a way it's healthier to keep your anger.*

Lynn: For the tearaway in a children's home, yes, I agree, it's probably better for you to stay a tearaway and refuse to conform. But in a prison, you'll lose remission and be put on segregation, which makes your problems worse. You're branded as a troublemaker, which is a name that sticks. No, prison never loses, always the people. What's the first thing they do when they take you into a religious order, or a mental institution, or a prison? They take your clothes away. First thing. And your name. They take your individuality. It's all part of sliding you through.

DH: *And you think that's wrong?*

Lynn: Well . . .

DH: *I can tell you do. I can tell you think it's a stupid way to treat people. Do you ever let a prisoner know you think that?*

Lynn: No.

DH: *Why?*

Lynn: Because if I made him indignant, what could he do with his indignation? It would be cruel. The fact is, we take away their individuality and expect them to conform. The clever ones play the system. If you're shrewd you get a job in the library. It's warm, good books, pleasant and so on. You use the education, you get on with it. That's one type. Another type becomes passive, loses their will, droops, becomes a victim. Then the ones who frighten you are the ones who internalize their anger and are permanently depressed. They're the potential suicides, though there's most suicide on remand.

DH: *How bad is victimization in the prison?*

Lynn: I don't think it's worse than in the outside world. Some people are born victims, and that's what they become in prison.

DH: *What hampers you most in your own work?*

Lynn: What you have to understand is the whole system is monstrously inefficient. Monstrously, totally. It's Dad's Army. The other day there was to be a fire drill. We'd all been warned. Six fire engines will sweep on to the main concourse. Only no one had told the man on the gate. So he wouldn't let them in. Always, always there's someone who hasn't been told. Perhaps there's a vacuum in all large organizations. Things never happen on the day they're meant to. Never. It's well-meaning and chaotic. And the Home Office is just as bad. The worst problem is clothes and towels. I mean, there are weeks when we simply can't clothe the men. Or find them towels. The laundry never sends back what it's been sent. It's an absolute nightmare.

DH: *What are the rewards of your job?*

Lynn: They're few and far between. Occasionally you do really good things for someone, they go out into the world, they write and say thank you. Most of the time it's exasperation with the system and with the men themselves who have all this ability they don't use. I mean, one man was actually complaining to me because he'd perfected a way of opening parking meters. He said, 'Do you know, I had to get up at five o'clock to do it, often in the wet, and do you have any idea how bloody hard it is carting pails of coins around all day?' It's hard work, he kept saying, and nobody appreciates it. He had all the ingenuity to work out how to do it, and to tell the bank he worked in an arcade, and he wanted *me* to feel sorry for him because he worked so hard.

DH: *But crime is hard work, that's why so many people give it up at 30.*

Lynn: It's true. Lots of criminals are stupid, but some are very clever. The ones who frighten me are the clever ones. They're very scary. Because they plan their murders. It isn't a bottle picked up in a pub. It's *planned*. Unbalanced and very clever, that's a lethal combination. We're always arguing with the doctors because they don't agree on where the line is between unbalanced and mentally ill.

Probation officers are the grit in the machine, because we're empowered to ask questions. That's why you shouldn't stay in the job too long, because you lose the power to ask them. Far too many people are on remand in prison, and far too many people are here for silly offences. I'd throw the lot of them out tomorrow and concentrate on the people society really does need protecting from.

DH: *Well, everyone agrees with you except the judges.*

Lynn: Oh, the judges! You can chip away at every aspect of the system. You can improve it all. But the judiciary is totally immune. You can't chip in there.

PART THREE

The Absence
of War

The Labour Party is like a vehicle. If you drive at great speed, all the people in it are either so exhilarated or so sick that you have no problems. But when you stop, they all get out and argue about which way to go.

Harold Wilson

Student politics are the most vicious kind of politics that exist, because the stakes are so low.

Henry Kissinger

I have no quarrel with fox-hunting, Ascot, the Monarchy or Bernard Manning; I prefer the *Daily Telegraph* to the *Independent* and I go a bit funny when I think of Churchill, Nelson, Shakespeare, the Authorised Version, Celia Johnson, Jack Hobbs and Richard Hannay. I do however draw the line at the Conservative Party.

Stephen Fry

One is punished for being weak, not for being cruel.

Baudelaire

Prime Minister, of the three candidates you have suggested, I much prefer the two who are dead.

Halifax to Churchill

Never underestimate the British economy's capacity to disappoint.

Sarah Hogg

The vision thing can come *after* we have frightened the voters.

A John Major scriptwriter, 1992

David Owen: History will judge whether my attitude to the Peacock Throne was right or wrong.
Peter Tapsell: I think history will have better things to do with its time.

Debate in the House of Commons

There are two kinds of problem in my life. The political ones are insoluble, and the economic ones are incomprehensible.

Sir Alec Douglas-Home

Nixon's no fool. If the country wanted moral leadership, he'd give them moral leadership.

New Yorker cartoon

THE STATE

I was some time deciding the subject of my third play. By now my
methods had been established and there was no shortage of volunteers stepping forward to offer their own institutions as possible
subject matter. Nothing surprised me more in the whole five years
of my work than to find myself at a cricket match sitting next to a
man who worked for the Queen. After telling me how much he had
enjoyed the first two plays in my trilogy, he then turned benignly to
me and said, 'Who are you going to do next? Us?' He then offered
me all the co-operation I might want.

I cannot say a play about the House of Windsor especially
interested me. I was much keener to write about the Army, which
seemed to me to be the last trade union, and therefore, like all trade
unions, under threat from the government. But then I realized that
soldiers were singing me all the tunes I had already heard from
policemen. The Army had ceased to be a vocation. It was no longer
valued. There was no *esprit de corps*. The individual regiment was
of less and less importance. No longer did everyone follow the great
Football League supporters' motto of Club Before Country.
Instead, the professional soldier had been replaced by a phenomenon known as the 'yuppy in a beret', who left his wife at eight in
the morning and expected to be home by six.

It was, therefore, with some sense of inevitability that I looked
around for a way of writing about the State. The subject seemed so
impossibly all-embracing that I was not at first sure how to
approach it. An admirer of *Yes, Minister*, I saw no way of
improving on its distinctive view of the struggle between the civil
service and government. But, as usual, it was a chance encounter,
this time with a couple of Labour apparatchiks, which made me
realize that I should abandon any absurd ambition I had to describe
the workings of the State. Instead, I set out to capture that strange
moment at which a small part of the State is compelled, for a few
weeks at least, to offer itself up to the public's inspection.

THE GENERAL ELECTION

The General Election of 1992 was unusual in that it had been so long anticipated. Although a British government is technically allowed to run its full five-year period, it is commonly expected that an incumbent prime minister will use the advantage of surprise to go to the polls well before the end of his term. But because in late 1990 he had suddenly inherited the leadership from the markedly unpopular Margaret Thatcher, John Major had judged that he needed time to establish the authority of his own régime before risking it with an appeal to the electorate. The result had been a long and slightly unreal period of waiting.

It was during this phoney war that I had written to Neil Kinnock, the Leader of the Labour Party, and to Chris Patten, the Chairman of the Conservative Party, asking if I might be allowed to sit in on their deliberations. I wanted to find out how you plan and fight a general election. I did also consider approaching the Liberal Democrats, and yet I admit, perhaps shamefully, that I was stopped by the intuition that I would be meeting characters with whom I was already familiar from my time in the Church of England.

As soon as I attended my first Labour Party strategy meeting, I realized how stupid I had been to imagine I could watch both parties from the inside. With characteristic generosity, Neil Kinnock had offered me access even beyond that I had asked for. Knowing as much as I did of Labour's campaigning plans, it would have been impossible for me to attend equally confidential meetings at Tory Party Headquarters, even if the Conservatives had shown anything but the most veiled signs of wanting it. For this reason, I followed the Tories with a more distant eye.

The commonest complaint about the 1992 election was that it was boring. Journalists claimed that the preparations for it were too long, and that by the time it began officially, there was nothing new for either party to say. When the whole thing was over, it was widely believed that Labour had lost the initiative way back in

January when they failed to meet the challenge of Maurice Saatchi's 'TAX BOMBSHELL' posters which convinced voters they would each be £1,000 worse off under Labour. It became the common wisdom that Labour had lost before they began.

I am not sure about this. When people say something is boring, it sometimes means that they themselves cannot find a fresh way of looking at it. Because it was new to me, I found everything about this election interesting. Not for the first time, I found myself envying journalists their extraordinary privileges, while wondering at how little some journalists value them. For these four weeks at least, their profession seemed to offer the most wonderful life.

Monday, 9 March 1992

Election planning meeting

For some months now a group has been meeting once a week to make strategy for the inevitable election which John Major must call before July. The group is made up of senior members of the Shadow Cabinet, together with representatives of the Labour Party from Transport House, and members of Neil Kinnock's own private office. Although I have been invited to attend, I am kept waiting outside in the Leader's warren of rooms, because I am told parts of the meeting are too sensitive for me to witness. When I am let in, everyone is sitting round a large table in what turns out to be the Shadow Cabinet room at the House of Commons. Like most people, I have read something of the old-fashioned surroundings in which British politicians are forced to work. But nothing has quite prepared me for just how depressing the brown-panelled walls would be. Opposition to the government of the day is plotted from a room which looks as if it might be the dining room of a particularly down-at-heel Tudor hotel in a fifties British film. You expect Alec Guinness or George Cole to appear any moment as the head waiter, with soup on his napkin. An attempt has been made to cheer the atmosphere by hanging a banner from the South Wales

Miners' Union. Later, I will often be told by cynics that this election is about nothing more than who will have the right to be chauffeur-driven in Rovers for the next four years. It seems to me at once that it is also about who will have room in which to work.

When I am let in, the Chairman of the Campaign, Jack Cunningham, is asking Roy Hattersley – one of the few members of the Shadow Cabinet old enough to have been in government – when and how a prime minister is allowed to call an election. Cunningham, a Geordie in his 50s with a science degree and a reputation for stoutly defending British Nuclear Fuels, then leads a discussion about how Labour can get some news coverage in a week in which the Conservative Chancellor will present his Budget.

Jack Cunningham: With the Budget coming up, they're going to have Wednesday. So we have to get Thursday. I don't want them running away with the whole week.

At first I recognize only the faces I have seen on TV. But within twenty minutes I have worked out that there are three main groups represented at this meeting. First, the professional politicians, like Hattersley and Kaufman, who seem to be slyly enjoying the relaxed atmosphere of the meeting. Secondly, the members of Neil Kinnock's own private office, which is partly financed by the tax-payer specifically to deal with the workload created by a Leader of the Opposition, and who seem to have the strongest and most developed views on all the tactical issues which arise. And thirdly, the representatives of the Labour Party itself, who take charge of all the practical arrangements, and who seem by nature the most cautious and nervous of the people here.

It is a condition of my presence at these meetings that I will later disclose only the broadest outline of their content. No political party, however fair-minded and benign, will agree to an outsider sitting among them and slapping down all the stupidest things they say. Later, the pace and ferocity of events will put people under considerable pressure. Nobody, in such circumstances, wants to go on the record. But I give nothing away if I say that my first experience of *realpolitik* is listening to a rather meandering discussion about the question of endorsements.

Young man: We have the endorsement leaflet on Tuesday with some eminent people coming out for Labour. Steve Cram. Erm. I can't think of any others. David Puttnam.
Roy Hattersley: Oh God, we can't have the same old faces, that really won't work.
Gerald Kaufman: It can't be 'round up the usual suspects'.
Woman: It sounds more like a rally than a press conference.
Man: It seems to me that Neil has to be statesmanlike. Being statesmanlike doesn't go with celebrities.
Woman: Neil can be statesmanlike on Wednesday. Thursday's the day for celebrities.

There follows a discussion of who is speaking where and on what during the week. It is essential to any political party that everyone else knows not just when and where people are going to speak, but what they are going to say.

Hattersley: I'm speaking in Bolton on Sunday.
Cunningham: Good. I'm in favour of that. I'm in favour of you speaking where there are lots of Tory marginals.
Hattersley: I'm going to speak about the threat from the new Premier League to 3rd and 4th division clubs.
Cunningham: You mean 3rd and 4th division clubs in marginal seats?
Hattersley: Yes, but I'm not going to put it like that.
Man: Is Terry Venables coming out for us? Is Gary Lineker?
Another man: The Lineker endorsement. Perfect.

Already bleepers are going in pockets. Politicians' assistants are coming in and out of the room. One person has even started up a conversation in the corner on their portable phone. Cunningham is keeping going, talking about the list of speakers for a meeting on Saturday.

Man: As it's London, to avoid any aggro, what about a woman?

But Cunningham is fighting a rising tide of activity which seems to be lapping into the room. This is something I will become familiar with in the coming weeks, and which seems to me, more than anything, to characterize modern politics. At every meeting, another meeting is beating against the door.

Tuesday, 10 March 1992

Budget day

In addition to the weekly strategy discussions, Cunningham also chairs a much smaller, more informal meeting every morning at nine a.m. in his own office at the House of Commons. I am now beginning to recognize some of the members of the group. The most dominant is Philip Gould, who is in his 30s, quick, in an ad-man's baggy suit, with long curly hair. He is given to rambling, energetic sentences which die suddenly in mid-air. Gould runs the Shadow Agency, which not only controls the Labour Party's advertising, but also takes a strong directive role, commissioning and interpreting Labour's own private opinion polls. Although neither party publicly admits to it, secret polling has a huge influence on their respective strategies. Alongside Gould, I recognize Julie Hall, who is Neil Kinnock's own press officer. She is blonde, an ex-ITN reporter in her early 30s. Also present are Dave Hill, moustached, trenchant, who is head of communications for the Labour Party itself, and Gez Sagar, his younger, thinner assistant, still, I think, in his 20s. Sagar is in charge of contact with the press.

It is generally expected that the election will be announced on Thursday. This will allow two days after what the Tories hope will be the positive reception of today's Budget. But because nobody yet knows for sure when the election is coming, Gould has had to resort to ringing round to see if there is any sign of the Tories buying space in newspapers for potential election advertisements. But, strangely, nothing is yet happening.

The group then runs through the list of speakers who will have to be ready to go on radio and television to react to the Budget later today. Cunningham, with half an eye to me, explains that for any leader of the Opposition, replying to the Budget speech is the hardest parliamentary occasion of the year. The Chancellor has had months to prepare what he has to say, but Kinnock, with some help from his colleagues, will have to think on his feet.

Cunningham: Neil will get the bull points fed into him.

The atmosphere among this smaller group is extremely relaxed – a group of professionals well on top of their job. Cunningham even takes time out from the endless detail of the day's business to reminisce about the bad times in the early eighties when the running of the Labour Party was considerably more chaotic.

Cunningham: If David wants to write a play, then he should have done it in the old days when there were Clause Five meetings and everyone on Labour's NEC and everyone in the Shadow Cabinet was allowed a say about what should be in the manifesto. You would see whole swathes of Labour Party policy removed in nano-seconds. Fifty people writing on little bits of paper and trying to paste them into the manifesto. It was hilarious. Julie, isn't that where we first met?
Hall: No, we met at Meet the Challenge, Make the Change.

The discussion becomes more serious when everyone realizes that they have been given a disastrous venue for a big Labour Party meeting on Saturday. The Tories are planning an event in Torquay. It is vital to the rhythm of election strategy that whenever you know your opponents are planning something which will get a lot of coverage, you counter with something equally telegenic. But Labour is currently booked into a warehouse at the side of the Business Design Centre. It is too late to build a set to put inside it by Saturday.

The same problem obtains should the Tories decide to

announce an election on Thursday. Labour has no suitable venue for its own first press conference. Some people are in favour of the ICA or the Festival Hall, but the press officers are concerned that there will be no trees or grass around – just a concrete wasteland. Cunningham likes the idea of the Festival Hall because it is associated with a period of post-war change. But Gez Sagar points out that the Festival Hall went up before he was born. Its image is out of date. He prefers the idea of Leith's – the glass building which looks out on to Hyde Park.

Cunningham: I don't think the Labour Party election effort should be launched from a restaurant.

Budget afternoon

In the afternoon a friendly newspaper smuggles me into the Press Gallery as a reporter and I watch John Major doing Prime Minister's Question Time. He reads from a huge ring-bound folder answers which other people have prepared for him. The Budget which follows is equally uninspired, not seeming to me to offer any of the dramatic measures the Tories need to relaunch themselves for an election. Kinnock's answering speech is adequate, but inevitably bears the marks of having been prepared for any possible contingency and only adapted at the very last moment to what the Chancellor actually said.

Immediately after Kinnock's speech, Julie Hall comes to collect me from the gallery, saying Neil would like to see me. I am rather surprised, saying surely he must be very busy immediately after the Budget. As we go down, I ask Julie why Kinnock saddles himself with the impossible task of writing all his own speeches.

Julie Hall: I think it's very like the Robert Redford film *The Candidate*. You know, the one in which the candidate is manufactured and says other people's words. When he first got the job, Neil said he was determined this should never happen to him.

When I go into his room, Kinnock is extremely cheerful, opening a bottle of champagne, with five or six people, and calling out comments at the commentators on the TV. He rehearses his arguments in reply to the television.

Kinnock: No, no, no. You see, we've got the extra billions, because ours will be a borrowing for investment, not for tax-cuts . . .

There is a good poll due tomorrow morning in the *Guardian*, putting Labour three points ahead. When I ask Kinnock if this will be enough to give Labour an overall majority, he asks me if I know what the Kellner curve is. When I say no, he grabs a scrap of paper and starts, rather obsessively, drawing a curve on it to demonstrate what he calls Kellner's theory.

Kinnock: You see, Gallup's always out of line. So Kellner says with Gallup you always have to add three for us and two away from the Liberal Democrats. Now, let's see if that's right.

I am becoming a little self-conscious, feeling the leader must have better things to do with his time than explain the Kellner curve to me.

DH: *What will you do tonight?*
Kinnock: We'll go home to bloody Ealing.
Hall: There'll be a lot of photographers tomorrow, if the election is announced. You'll wake up with them.
Kinnock: They were there on Sunday. I couldn't put my spring bulbs out. I thought, I'm not going to do my spring boxes and give a picture to the bloody Torygraph.

Jack Cunningham comes into the room, which is now emptying, and asks what reply he should give to the question of whether Labour will repeal that afternoon's Tory tax cut.

Hattersley: That's what I'm waiting for. I need to watch the BBC at six to get the exact words John Smith uses so I can use the same ones at seven on Channel 4.

Cunningham: I'm doing News at Ten and that's what I need.

Hattersley: Well, wait for John.

DH: *Do you really have to be as careful as that? All mimicking the Shadow Chancellor, word for word?*

Kinnock: This is it, you see. We've only got to use three words different and the press will say there's a split.

Everyone smiles at me, then watches John Smith's reply to this question on the Six o'Clock News.

Kinnock: It's how the press work. In every profile of Brian Gould you read they now say he's back with Kinnock again. He was never out. But it's become a fact. All along he was my best bloody friend.

I look round and see that, by chance, everyone else has left. I am alone in the office, just shooting the breeze with the Leader. It is something else I notice, the inevitable converse of how busy everyone in politics is all the time. You suddenly get these strange, little, unplanned bubbles of time in which they are lost, doing nothing, directionless. Kinnock and I are silent for a full two minutes, just watching the telly. Then someone comes to the door.

Thursday, 12 March 1992

Labour launch

Under the rules of our unwritten constitution, the government has no obligation to notify the Opposition of when it plans to call an election. So the Labour Party has learnt the news in the same way as the rest of us, in fact by a telephone call from a friendly journalist reporting John Major's intention to make his way down the Mall towards the Palace. In some haste, the Labour Party has prepared one of its slightly ambiguous events, which is part-launch, part-photo opportunity, and part-parade of all its most distinguished showbiz supporters. Needless to say, these seem to me to be exactly the 'usual suspects' I heard them say they wanted to avoid.

The event is at the International Press Centre in Shoe Lane. Backstage everyone is issued with red roses. Then Neil Kinnock does his piercing imitation of a referee's whistle to call the politicians and celebrities to order. They march on to the stage, where the press and television people are already assembled. Hilariously, the celebrities are put on a strange little dais at the side where nobody can see them. A large sign which will eventually read 'IT'S TIME FOR A CHANGE' is currently reading 'IT'T FO A CHA'. Workmen are still putting the letters up.

At the back I find Philip Gould and talk to him about an ad Labour have placed, blaming Tory health cuts for the death of a young girl. The *Mail* has devoted the whole of its front page to the ad, calling it the first smear of the campaign. But Gould is delighted. Although the *Mail*'s story predictably excoriates the Labour advertisement, nevertheless, somewhere deep in their ravings, the journalists have had to admit that a girl was indeed twice turned away from Great Ormond Street Hospital and that, subsequently, she did indeed die. So from Gould's point of view the ad is a success, not just for what it says, but also for altering the agenda. It has swept the Tory budget off the front page.

The meeting starts. Although the photographers are now ringing the stage in such a way that the celebrities' presence is superfluous, nevertheless the stars all sit with hopeful and attentive expressions on their faces as if everything Kinnock and Hattersley are saying were magical. As soon as Kinnock is through with a short speech, the photographers head in, shouting, 'Over here! Over here! Neil! Neil!' In fact I notice none of their pictures appears in the papers next day, but at least I learn a new expression. When photographers ('monkeys') cram in six deep, each one behind the other, it's known as a goat-fuck.

Friday, 13 March 1992

Poll tax press conference

Today, in the Vickers building by the Thames, there is to be a press conference about the poll tax. In fact the official campaign will not begin until the following week, but people seem to feel that any activity is better than none. I am beginning to understand the routines. Immediately before each meeting, there is what is called a 'pre-meeting', where people decide what they will say. At this one, typically, everyone is drinking Nescafé and eating Hob-Nobs. David Blunkett, the blind Labour frontbencher, has his speech ready in Braille. They are all delighted that the Tories are at sixes and sevens about whether John Major and Norman Lamont should debate on TV with their opposite numbers ('we've got them arguing among themselves'), but the truth is, everyone knows this is all small beer, and far too early to mean anything at all.

The press conference itself is poorly attended and very badly presented. Bryan Gould and Blunkett do their best but there is a confused feeling that the poll tax, as an election issue, cannot be ignited again, least of all by the sheaves of worthy statistics which are distributed to the few journalists who have turned up. Everyone knows that there is no chance of the damning figures appearing in any newspaper next day because they are . . . well, let's face it . . . *dull*. The result is a general listlessness, and the growth of that most dangerous of all journalistic feelings: the general conviction they should be somewhere else.

Afterwards I talked to Gez Sagar to discover the next week's agenda and to ask him whether he could put his hand on his heart and say there is anything he would have done differently.

Sagar: Absolutely nothing this week, we've won every single day. Each day has been ours.
DH: *Do you believe that if I asked the same question of your opposite number at the Tory Party they would be able to put their hand on their heart and say the same thing?*

Sagar: I don't. I think they're badly shaken. It's really going badly for them. I think they're demoralized and it shows.

Gez, like others on the campaign, sees himself as involved in a day-to-day battle. Each day there is a result. The exact analogy is with boxing. If you win every round, you have a fair chance of winning the whole fight. But underneath these tactics runs the memory of an ominous failure. Although everyone in the strategy group believes that Labour ran a wonderful campaign in 1987, it is also an article of faith among them that this campaign ran out of steam in the last seven days. When I ask Roy Hattersley why that was, he replies: 'Two reasons. One, they got us on tax, and I'm determined that should never happen again. Two, they spent a million pounds in that last week.'

In all the tactical meetings I attend about this election, the underlying question for Labour is: 'How do we prevent that happening again?'

Monday, 16 March 1992

The Shadow Budget

On Monday afternoon John Smith, the Shadow Chancellor, is presenting his Shadow Budget at the Institute of Civil Engineers. This is part of what is seen by Labour as a pre-emptive move to try and present itself as a sober and reliable party with whom you can trust your money. The Institute of Civil Engineers has been chosen as a suitable background, suggesting probity, reliability and utter seriousness. Labour's economic plans are presented as much like the real Budget as possible, in order to make the personnel seem like a government-in-waiting. Somehow everyone seems to understand this except me, and I am the only person in the hugely crammed room not wearing a tie.

Kinnock sits beside Smith, letting him rip. The press want to trip Kinnock up and address questions to him, hoping he will demonstrate what they think is his ignorance of economics. But

Kinnock refuses to speak, deferring all the time to Smith, whose classlessness is much helped by his being a Scot. All the politicians in this election are pretending to be bank managers. John Smith is very definitely trying to be area manager, and what's more, with Barclays, not the Midland.

Tuesday, 17 March 1992

Tory press conference

The Tories are having one press conference at Smith Square before their manifesto launch the next day. Outside the building at seven-thirty a.m. there is a furious crew from Thames Television. Thames have lost their licence to broadcast in the London area in the recent ITV carve-up. It is widely believed they have been punished as a company for their journalists' brave investigation of the SAS killings in Gibraltar. Now this news crew have been knocking furiously on a blue door for half an hour. They have been told this is where they are to collect their security passes for the press conference inside. Thanks to Tory policies, this group of angry technicians are all out of a job. But I am rapidly able to discount any idea of conspiracy for them when I launch my attempt to get my own pass. I have telephoned the day before to make sure I have been cleared, but now I am here I am sent upstairs, then downstairs, told to wait, and then sent somewhere else. The Party of Free Enterprise is notorious among journalists as a distinctive mixture of incompetence and red tape. They have lost my pass. After three-quarters of an hour, I give up and leave.

Wednesday, 18 March 1992

The Labour manifesto

Labour is to launch its manifesto at its new Campaign headquarters on Millbank. My research assistant has made six calls to the Tory

174

HQ the previous day, so now I go to Smith Square to make a second attempt to collect my Conservative pass. There is the usual security nightmare before I find a twin-setted woman behind a desk.

DH: *I don't understand. You can just walk straight into the Labour Party.*
Woman: Nobody wants to blow them up. We're much nicer than they are.

Bewildered by this non-sequitur, I head on to the new Labour HQ, which has been specially installed in order to fight this election. It looks as if it could be the premises of the American Democratic Party – muted carpets, faxes, mobile phones, young women in designer outfits. The Shadow Cabinet have been put in the conference room in which all strategy meetings will now take place. It is dominated by a huge grey table and full of modern tubular furniture. Everyone is being briefed by a man who is saying, 'I'd like to take you through this morning's choreography, if I may.' Hugh Hudson, the director of *Chariots of Fire* and of various Labour Party political broadcasts, is trying to penetrate the room with his camera crew.

Press officer: There should not be a fucking camera in there. It puts a pressure on them they don't need.

The press officer wanders away. In the next five minutes, Hugh Hudson's crew gets in and then is thrown out three times in a row. I talk to Gerald Kaufman, Labour's Shadow Foreign Secretary, who once worked closely with Harold Wilson in Number Ten.

Gerald Kaufman: You know you're winning an election when you're not going towards people, but people are coming up to you. Everything at the moment is going our way. I've never seen an election where Labour candidates managed to get their literature out so quickly. I worked nine years on the *Daily Mirror* when it was a real newspaper, under Hugh Cudlipp who was the greatest popular journalist of the century, and he taught me one thing – you can't make people think what they don't want to think, but if they're already thinking it, you can nudge them along.

I walk into the main press conference room, which is filled with a hundred journalists and thirty television cameras. I run into various of the younger Labour apparatchiks who are in a state of high excitement, reassuring me that Labour is five points ahead and that the Tories are 'a dead ticket'. The newly composed Labour anthem starts to play deafeningly loud, and through the crowd comes a solid phalanx of dark suits and red ties: the Shadow Cabinet triumphant. As the announcer's amplified voice booms out 'And now the Leader of the Labour Party, Neil Kinnock', a yuppy reporter on her mobile phone comes chiming in: 'Hello, Dick, it's Katherine here . . .' She is quickly silenced.

As Kinnock speaks, I start reading my copy of the manifesto, which is prefaced by a bad Adrian Henri poem. Blue winter is going to be ended by red roses on a bomb-site – or some such. It is depressing the way culture is being commandeered for pseudo-presidential politics. Ever since Kennedy produced Pablo Casals and Marilyn Monroe, politicians have been seeking equivalents. Kinnock is nervous, not at his best, picking his words with the air of a man who is anxious of being called verbose. You never quite feel secure. There is always the danger the wheels will come off. Today he is more tightrope-walker than orator.

The Tory manifesto launch

I go straight across to the Queen Elizabeth Hall where a sticker saying 'Press Pen' is stuck on my identity tag. The first person I run into is the *Independent* journalist Mark Lawson, who tells me the Labour anthem was written by Michael Kamen. When he asked Dave Hill what the music was, Hill had rashly replied, 'Well, it's a bit of everything.'

Lawson says that everything is going Labour's way and that the Tories are badly rattled. The *Sun* is planning to fight back in the final week and they have a piece already prepared which has a diagram of John Smith's heart to prove that he will have a heart attack if he gets into government, and the accompanying article by a doctor is already in proof.

Lawson tells me that John Prescott, the Labour transport spokesman, was kept off the platform of the party launch because polls show that he frightens voters. Lawson has also been to see Michael Heseltine, once the Tories' star speaker, perform in Torquay.

DH: *How was that?*
Mark Lawson: You know the sort of thing. It's like late Olivier. He knows he's not a great actor any more. He gives you an echo of what he used to be, then winks at the audience as if to say, 'I'm not much good any more, am I?'
DH: *How are the Tories feeling?*
Lawson: The worst news for them is Andy and Fergie breaking up. It happened to work in their favour today because the Labour five-point lead was wiped off the front pages, but if this story runs for the next couple of weeks, it's going to wipe Major's initiatives off the front pages and that's very bad news for him.

I go into the hall. It is very lavish and has two enormous, extremely badly printed photographs of Major behind the stage. Norma Major arrives to sit in the audience. At once attendants look for people to sit next to her, so that on TV she will not look isolated. They find her what they call 'noddies' and they slip in beside her. Then, after some music, by Andrew Lloyd Webber this time, the Cabinet arrive and file on to a platform which is set out so that they look like the game-show guests for *The Krypton Factor*. There are four rows of them and they look as if they should have buzzers and lights. The effect is somewhat comical because the seats are rather low and their little heads only just pop up over the desks. There is only one woman on the platform – Gillian Shephard – and she has been pushed to the front.

John Major steps forward to make his keynote speech. It is quite extraordinary that a man who has so much charm in private appears to have no public antennae at all. He is a hopeless judge of a public occasion. There are some odd things about his speech patterns. I have read already that he is very sensitive about the way he pronounces 'want' as 'wunt'. He regards it as snobbery when people draw attention to this, and yet he seems to use the phrase 'we wunt' all the time. It is particularly noticeable that Major never talks about thirteen years, presumably (a) because thirteen is an unlucky number and (b) because it brings back memories among the older electorate of 1964. For that reason he talks about the Tories ruling 'for twelve or so years'.

Anthony Bevins from the *Independent* is extremely animated and determined to challenge him because he says that the total burden of tax has grown under the Tories and not diminished. Major starts to tell him that his figures are wrong and Bevins wants to get into an argument with him. Chris Patten, the Tory Chairman, intervenes to say, 'This is not socratic dialogue, it's question and answer.' When talking about something called 'the red book' and 'stepping up reserves', there is no doubt that Major understands what he's talking about in a way that I don't and I think that most people in the room don't. But even then he is prone to energy-sapping sentences like 'I needn't tediously bore you all with my reasons.' When John Sweeney from the *Observer* raises the question of Mark Thatcher's role in the super-gun affair, Major becomes extremely resentful. Whereas five minutes earlier he promised to take away what he calls 'the cobwebs of secrecy' from government, he has no intention of doing it on the spot.

At one point, Major matches Kinnock by trying to drag culture into everything. He manages to refer to London as 'the music centre of Europe', somehow for me summoning up images of men walking down the street with transistor radios on their shoulders. He also makes the first of what I will come to recognize as his many references to the state of British Rail stations, and in particular, to the wasted land around them, which for some reason attracts his special displeasure.

However, the atmosphere is much more relaxed and easy-going than at Labour's press conference. These people are dressed in power and it makes them witty and confident. When Andrew Neil, the editor of the *Sunday Times*, asks what appears to be an irreverent question about the absurd length of the Conservative manifesto, he nevertheless nods and grins through the reply, saying, 'Yes, Prime Minister,' more than once. It is interesting how authority, at least for a little while, is still working its magic.

There are two crass errors – of which only one is remarked. When Major is asked about Gillian Shephard, he replies in language so out of date and out of touch ('Don't you think she makes an attractive acquisition?') that even this audience hisses. But the more outrageous answer is from Heseltine, who, when asked why he doesn't want a Greater London Council, replies, 'I don't want a local government that's only interested in opposing us.' The contempt for democracy implicit in that answer takes my breath away. But it goes unchallenged.

Tuesday, 24 March 1992

Labour press conference

I now have a routine. I get up at five forty-five a.m. and drive down to Labour headquarters, where by six-thirty a.m. there are already some campaigners sitting round the big grey table, reading the papers and drinking coffee. At six forty-five the Labour strategy meeting starts. At seven-fifteen the meeting about that day's press conference follows. At seven forty-five I attend the Labour press conference, then at eight-thirty I walk over to watch the Tories.

Over the weekend the press has been strategically anti-Tory, claiming that they are in real danger of losing unless they improve their campaign. This does not fool anyone for a moment. Everyone knows that in two weeks' time they will be running around licking Tory bottoms in the usual way. It is a game they play, to pretend that they are seriously concerned about Tory prospects. This way they hope to demonstrate their power, and to goad Tories into being nastier about Labour.

The press conferences are heavily circumscribed by the fact that journalists are only allowed to ask one question each. Ostensibly this is to allow as many people to speak as possible but in fact, of course, it is a way of making sure that nobody comes back at the politicians' answers. The atmosphere at the Labour press conference today is markedly bad-tempered as John Smith tries to prove that tax has actually increased during the thirteen years of Tory rule. The journalists don't much like Jack Cunningham, and there is none of the obsequiousness they show to the party in power. Anthony Bevins, the loose cannon from the *Independent*, who last week was waving papers above his head and hectoring the Prime Minister, has now discovered a discrepancy between two Labour documents. When the Labour spokesman, Tony Blair, stands by what is in the manifesto, Bevins shouts at him, 'So this one is a lie, is it? It's a lie. It's a lie.'

The same journalists are called all the time. The major networks can always get a question in, because television is understood to be at the top of the pecking order. But then Charles Reiss is always called next by the Tories because they can rely on a pro-Tory headline in the *Evening Standard* at lunchtime. After that, it's always George Fuchs of the *Telegraph* and Andrew Marr of *The Economist*. Peter Jenkins and Robin Day appear to have *droit de seigneur:* they may intervene at any point.

As John Smith bangs away at his narrow point, I begin to understand what campaigning is and how it has nothing to do with running the country. It is simply a form of verbal point-making. A piece of ground is chosen (say, the Tories have/have not overall increased taxes in the last thirteen years), and on that ground a verbal construct is made by one side, then by the other. Two teams of verbal gymnasts then go in, trying to knock each other's constructs down. No attempt is made by either side to get above the ground, or to give any strategic sense beyond that ground. You are reminded of the First World War, where intense, costly battles were fought over barren, symbolic tracts. As in the Somme, breakthroughs are well-nigh unknown.

The press reports this battle by giving Major what used to be called, in pre-feminist language, the masculine role. In other words, he is always given the active verb. *The Times* will always give Major a male verb – 'Major attacks', 'Major commands', 'Major fights'. The passive role is always given to Labour – 'Labour surrenders', 'Labour yields', 'Labour holds on'. Needless to say, Labour never commands.

Tory press conference

Major arrives at the Tory conference looking physically exhausted and attempts to establish foreign affairs as an area of Tory expertise. No sooner have I noted the use of male verbs in newspapers than Major starts firing them off from the platform: 'We need to command the new nuclear generation.' He introduces Douglas Hurd, the Foreign Secretary, whose speech is a mixture of diplomatic gibberish – 'We operate directly and we operate through organizations' – and an attempt to talk up Britain's influence in the world. British influence is like the classic definition of style: if you need to refer to it, that just proves you don't have it.

As Hurd tries to emphasize Major's growing stature as a statesman – 'I have looked through the Prime Minister's diary and I have seen seven meetings in the coming months which we need to attend' – Major fiddles with his tie and teases his chin. This is a gesture he shares with Chris Patten. But whereas Patten does it in the characteristic way of the middle-aged man who fears he has too many chins – the Chinese will later nickname him Fat Peng – Major is camper, resting his chin on a single finger. He is embarrassed by Douglas Hurd's encomium: 'I have seen John Major build his influence. I have been in a room and seen it happen.'

As he answers questions, Major seems better, the real man coming through now he's tired. But there is a contradiction in what he is saying. His central claim – an absurd one – is that Thatcherism has ended the Cold War, and the world is therefore going through a unique period of safety. But his subsidiary claim is that the world is uniquely *un*-safe, and that only a Tory administration can guide you through it. Again, this contradiction goes unchallenged.

Wednesday, 25 March 1992

Labour strategy meeting

The Labour Party has put out a party political broadcast, directed by Mike Newell, dramatizing the plight of young girls who have to wait for an operation for glue-ear, a condition of which I at least have hitherto heard very little, but which it now appears afflicts large parts of the junior population.

As people straggle in for the six forty-five a.m. strategy meeting, there are lots of glue-ear jokes. Dave Hill, the director of communications, is slightly taken aback at the ferocity with which the newspapers have attacked the broadcast, but he has taken the precaution of calling the father of the girl on whom the film was based.

Dave Hill: All I can tell you is that he said to me, 'You and I are singing from the same tree.'

Cunningham has to throw out some cameras from *Panorama* – 'We can't talk while you're here' – but they remain outside the glass door, filming as the meeting starts with Philip Gould presenting what are called the overnights. The news he brings is that 'our negatives are leading theirs. Ours are nine to three, theirs are nine to one.'

Once you understand these figures they are extremely interesting because they are in answer to the question, 'Are you now more or less likely to vote for Labour/Conservative than you were at the beginning of the campaign?' The negative figure (in this case the nine) is always higher than the positive. It is understood and accepted by everyone in politics that they will turn more off by what they do and say than they will turn on. You will also have more success stopping people voting for your opponents than you will making people vote for you.

It is Gould's job to report every day on how these figures are moving, to note where men's views differ from women's and where young people differ from old. He speaks in a kind of gabbled shorthand which everyone in the room understands ('On managing the economy, we are excellent to good on thirty-one. The Tories are down at twenty-six. Our main negatives are taxes, mortgages, and where's the money coming from?'). The underlying message he brings today is that, although John Smith's shadow budget has done something to convince the electorate that Labour will not put taxes up immoderately, nevertheless the Tories start with such a huge in-built advantage on the question of tax that Labour does well to get off it as fast as possible.

To an outsider, this perhaps is the most surprising and controversial part of Labour's thinking. It would seem logical that if 60 per cent of the electorate believes that 'Labour will raise taxes on people like you' then your time will be well spent either explaining to people why tax rises will be necessary – a strategy long since ruled out – or, alternatively, in seeking to reassure them they have misunderstood Labour's intentions. But no. Labour strategists regard tax and the economy as issues on which Labour simply *cannot win*. They start from too far behind. Their advice, therefore, has been to raise these 'losing' issues early, in the hope of getting them out of the way, and to move on to the more fruitful subjects of health and education – the 'caring' issues – on which Labour has a corresponding in-built advantage. The plan, then, is not to change people's minds – too late for that, they say – but to control the agenda.

A regular participant in these meetings is Patricia Hewitt, a clever and articulate Australian who used to be Neil Kinnock's press secretary. She is now in charge of the Last Week Unit, a team of people who are meant to come in fresh, seven days from the end. This way they hope to avoid the dip of energy the campaigners suffered in 1987. Although Hewitt is theoretically meant to be holding herself in reserve, she is already working compulsively, drafting and redrafting the Leader's statements. At meetings which are already fairly hectic and highly pressured, she has a noticeable habit of conducting mini-meetings of her own, which go on at the side of the room in none-too-hushed tones. Today, as always, her particular concern is with Kinnock, and with making sure that everything in the campaign is directed through him and his personality. She is worried that each evening Major is planning a big speech. She speaks of the need to 'counter with a Kinnock challenge every evening'.

Meanwhile there is a plan that when the Tories launch a poster this afternoon, the Labour Party is going to drive into Smith Square with a rival poster – a spoiler – which is going to say 'After 13 years, you'd think they'd have something more to boast about than this.' Somebody raises the point that ITN is a bit confused and wants to know generally how what's going on at Labour HQ meshes with what happens on the road with Kinnock. There is mass laughter at this.

Dave Hill: Yes, we'd all like to know that.

The laughter illuminates a simple geographical problem which both sides have. All day, their leaders are out storming round the country, and in the mornings they attend their own parties' strategy meetings only fleetingly. In spite of the British Telecom bleepers, which all leading Labour politicians carry, with crystal displays of what the others are saying, problems of communication inevitably arise.

This morning it is particularly important that Labour is confident to deal with all questions raised by its controversial broadcast. It is agreed Cunningham is the best person to deal with this, and now, carefully, he rehearses his lines: the ad was prompted by a letter, the research has been vindicated, the father is resolute, there is a Tory candidate whose daughter would have had to wait seven months for the same operation but who put her on to private health.

The strategy meeting breaks up, or rather dissolves into the press conference pre-meeting and I find myself talking to Harriet Harman, one of Labour's Health team, about what it's like to be accompanied everywhere by a minder with a portable phone.

Harriet Harman: The Conservatives are used to having lots of civil servants to tell them what to do all the time, so when the election arrives they're lost, because suddenly they're more or less alone and without the usual vast back-up. But for us, well, we're used to being in ones and twos, and at last it's an advantage. We've always had to struggle, and campaigning's no different.

Neil Kinnock has arrived, and now the room is full of people watching William Waldegrave, the Health Minister, trying to attack the Labour broadcast on TV. There is so much laughter at his floundering performance that a man has to come running in to tell everyone to quieten down because they can be heard by the journalists outside. As the hapless minister finishes, one politician points at his fading image on the screen.

Politician: You're stuffed, Waldegrave.

Cunningham calls the new meeting to order and starts running through the press conference's main points, but before he gets very far Labour's chief Health spokesman, Robin Cook, arrives, fresh from defending the Labour Party's broadcast. Everyone congratulates him, but he sits down, furious.

Robin Cook: Yeah, but it would have been easier if I hadn't been dropped in it in the first place.

There is a sudden silence. The broadcast had gone out without first being shown to Cook, and now he is in the position of having to defend something about which he is plainly uneasy. Cook wants to know if there are going to be any more, similar broadcasts based on real cases, and to make sure that, if so, he sees them first.

Taxi home

In the taxi on my way back home, the driver asks me if I'm following the election.

DH: *Yes. How do you think it's going?*
Taxi driver: Well, I'm not going to vote Labour because they're going to put up VAT.

185

Now since this is in fact the exact opposite of Labour policy, and the only party who might possibly put up VAT are the Conservatives,* this remark puts some of the last couple of weeks in perspective.

Taxi driver: It's incredible listening to these phone-ins, isn't it? I heard a politician the other day and he didn't answer one of the questions.
DH: *Who was the politician?*
Taxi driver: Alan Freeman.
DH: *Ah.*

Thursday, 26 March 1992

Labour strategy meeting

As I arrive at six thirty-five a.m., a large number of people are already sitting round the big table, their heads bowed over the screaming headlines. There is a profound silence as they contemplate the impact of an event which is in danger of spinning out of control. The mother of the girl on whom the broadcast was based has objected to her case being used. The father, on the other hand, is happy. A related argument, about how and when the hospital turned her away, is leaving everyone nervous.

There is a general sense now, backed up, as ever, by overnight polling, that Labour is so exposed in its claims about these operations that it has no choice but to go on seeing the resultant issues through. They have to cross their fingers and hope they're right. Although they are considerably cheered by a *Guardian* front page which carries a letter from a consultant who confirms the basic factual claims of the broadcast, they also know that in some sense it is as important that something is convincing as that it is true.

*In March 1993, the Conservatives announced their intention of imposing VAT on heating fuel.

As they try to predict the day's developments, they reassure themselves with the memory of the Monmouth by-election two years earlier, in which they made the dangerously bold claim that the Tories were planning to privatize the National Health Service. Although they then lacked concrete evidence, their strategists went ahead and based their whole campaign on this charge – with spectacular success. As they now remember, it did not matter that they could not prove their case. It was enough that people felt that it corresponded with their own personal experiences. As someone puts it now, 'It was what they *knew* was going on.'

In the general nervousness, someone has come up with the idea of opening a hotline on which members of the public will be able to ring in with details of their own problems with getting their children's ears looked into. There is a slightly farcical discussion of whether Labour can get a line organized in the next couple of hours and how they will man it. And the increasing tension is reflected in the fact that this telephone idea, which appears to have arisen spontaneously and without much preparation, is being run next to another idea, whose exact source is also hard to trace: later this morning Labour will go public with ten dossiers of substantiated cases which confirm the general claims of the original broadcast.

There are enough people in the room who are not yet exhausted to point out that it will be counter-productive to produce dossiers which later fail to stand up. But somehow everyone is now working at such speed, and so much discussion is curtailed so quickly, that these objections get lost. As the meeting starts to break up, someone's reassuring announcement that 'not all the cases have to be grommet, they can be widget as well' is already lost in an equally urgent discussion of why the Labour Front Bench look so small at press conferences against such a big set.

Neil Stewart

For some days now I have noticed the contributions to these discussions of a Scotsman called Neil Stewart. He has the classic manner of ex-student politician, burly, authoritative. It is almost impossible to guess his age. He turns out to work in Kinnock's office as an apparatchik, representing Kinnock's views to the Parliamentary Party and to the party itself at Walworth Road.

Now, during a lull in the meeting, Stewart asks me how I find the election, and I reply by saying that I am very confused as to why everyone thinks it worth while to work these ridiculous hours.

Neil Stewart: It's true. In the old days, prime ministers started work at nine and packed in at five.

DH: *Macmillan read novels in the evenings.*

Stewart: I'm not sure all this frantic activity gets you anywhere. I was looking at the legislation for the 1945 Parliament – the most important reforming government of the century – and yet in a single year there were only about five major acts, with perhaps a couple of single-page bills in addition. But basically the business was done in just a few words. Now the legislation – partly thanks to Europe – takes volumes and volumes and volumes.

DH: *To me, it's a substitute for war.*

Stewart: What do you mean?

DH: *People overwork like crazy and hope it will give them some sense of personal worth.*

Stewart: Well, certainly, I was close to the NHS, and those people, who know what they're doing is valuable, are the people who dare to knock off at eight-thirty in the evening and read a novel – because they don't question their worth, they get it in their work. Some people got it in the Gulf War. In two months, they got a sense of personal value and knowing they'd done something that mattered, and that will have set them at peace in a way my generation never can be. Look at Denis Healey – the fact is, if you've been a beach-master at Anzio, no one can question your worth.

DH: *Do you think this applies to Neil?*

Stewart: No, Neil's not like my generation. He's more like Healey. He's been tempered. He's been through personal barriers. Nobody's been through what he has these eight years. You reach a certain barrier and Neil has gone past it. A friend of mine, who had been a journalist for years, was helping bring John McCarthy back to England, and even he was shocked. Nothing prepared him for the full blast of the media. He himself had been part of it, but when he was on the receiving end, he saw how different it looks. You need extraordinary composure and nerve.

DH: *It's the people from the Labour Party who seem wobbliest.*

Stewart: Yes, but that comes from Walworth Road.

DH: *You mean it's a timid organization?*

Stewart: Have you asked yourself why the Leader's Office needs to exist? Why does Kinnock have to have his own staff group? Why doesn't the Labour Party run the campaign itself? Why is there this strategy group? Because things wouldn't get done. Because Neil's determination would get diluted.

DH: *Everywhere I go I hear this. Last week I was talking to senior Tories. They all say their party organization is hopeless.*

Stewart: Do they?

DH: *What I find over and over in politics is that two lots of people are doing the same job. It all seems to be belt and braces. When it comes to government policy, it's the same. The Prime Minister has to have something called the Policy Unit, headed by Sarah Hogg. But I thought the whole job of a minister was to make their own policy. Isn't that what a Minister is?*

As we talk, we hear the Michael Kamen fanfare in the background and, over the loudspeakers, the sound of Cunningham's voice.

Cunningham: A. B. Mortimer had adenoid trouble and glue-ear, and maybe she needs her tonsils looked into, too.

Conservative press conference

I go across to the Tories, where John Major is doing his rather pious best to present the whole thing as a moral issue. 'I do not believe this kind of broadcast would have been sanctioned by Attlee, Gaitskell or Lord Callaghan.' One of the favoured tactics of the Tories is to pretend that the Labour Party was once an honourable part of our democracy, but no longer. The Labour Party equivalent is to pretend that the Tory Party was once run by gentlemen who had a sense of decency, but is now in the hands of unprincipled estate agents. Major does have a very effective phrase, when he calls Labour's broadcast 'shroud-waving'. This, however, is not as good as Jon Snow of ITN, who refers to Labour's hotline as 'a sort of telephonic Lourdes'.

The official subject of this press conference is the unions, but you can tell nobody's heart is in it. In response to one question, the Education Secretary, Kenneth Clarke – who for sheer lack of humility about his own ignorance is increasingly becoming my favourite politician – cannot remember the name of the man he has put in charge of deciding the future of teaching hospitals.

Kenneth Clarke: This committee is chaired by . . . an extremely distinguished chap from the North.

After the press conference I talk to the personable Adam Boulton from Sky News.

Boulton: The whole thing is too close to call. From where they started, the Tories should have won, but they've done everything they can to balls it up. Remember, we were at this for four months before this campaign even started, so I suspect you'd find that 90 per cent of journalists aren't going to vote because they're so turned off. The only Tory hope is to go for Kinnock. The rat pack is out to get him. Basically, they want him to hit someone.
DH: *You mean literally?*
Boulton: Yes. He's violent and he's longing to clock someone on the chin – and that's now the Tories' best chance of winning.

Emergency strategy meeting: 9.45 a.m.

Immediately after the Tory conference I go back to the Labour Media Centre and find an emergency strategy meeting going on about how to move the week's agenda off the disputed broadcast, which is now rapidly taking over everyone's time. They are all looking at a chart in which the planned subject of each day has been mapped out. Sunday: Condition of Britain. Monday: The Family. Tuesday: Education. But now something dramatic is needed to divert attention from an increasingly futile argument. It had been planned that the following week Robin Cook would announce that he would cancel the proposed prescription charge rise when Labour gets into power. So now they intend to try and bring this announcement forward. As people plan an alternative week's strategy, they keep using the phrase, 'I'm very relaxed about this.' It always makes me smile, because invariably it means, 'I'm nervous about this.'

The meeting stops to watch Robin Cook giving a speech in Nottingham on television. For some reason, the hotline is now called 'a dedicated number'. When Cook finishes with a challenge to Waldegrave to apologize to the nation, there are cheers from everyone in the room, because his rhetoric is so polished. Obvious expertise cheers everyone up.

Second emergency strategy meeting: 2.30 p.m.

The story has developed disastrously. Kinnock has given a press conference in Nottingham in which he denied that anyone from the Labour Party had named the girl on whom the broadcast was based. A journalist alleged in reply that Julie Hall, Kinnock's own press secretary, had given him the girl's name. At this, Julie Hall had done something rather unusual for a press officer. She had got up in public to deny she had used the child's second name. She had, she said, only referred to her by her Christian name, Jennifer. Julie Hall had then made a highly emotional speech in defence of the NHS, describing her own personal experiences, when she needed eye operations as a child. When she moved back among the press, a heavily built journalist from a hostile paper had tried to detain her, and Kinnock was seen on television to say to her, 'Don't talk to him, he's not big enough.'

Back at HQ, voices are being raised at a hastily assembled strategy meeting. Not only are people worried by this apparently dangerous breach of political etiquette – a press officer intervening personally at a press conference – but there is also a fear that the dossiers themselves, which were passed on the nod yesterday, are today unravelling. A woman in Hexham is saying she asked for no publicity, and yet her name has been broadcast.

As if this were not enough, there now seems to be a plan to produce some of these victims of NHS waiting lists at yet another press conference which is, for some reason, due in a quarter of an hour's time. One member of the Shadow Cabinet is arguing vociferously for letting these members of the public on to the platform. Another is arguing, equally vociferously, that Labour has had quite enough of the unexpected in the last forty-eight hours, and that to produce real human beings on a political stage with fifteen minutes' preparation is to invite disaster.

The ensuing press conference is predictably disorderly, but Cook makes a good show, trying to turn the whole story against the Tories. Adam Boulton leans forward to whisper in my ear that the Tories have just opened a hotline for people to ring in and tell them how delighted they are with the NHS. Meanwhile I read in the list of Shadow ministers' engagements for the day that Gerald Kaufman is sampling Nino's home-made ice-cream in Rhos-on-Sea.

Friday, 27 March 1992

Labour strategy meeting

It is in a somewhat sobered and chastened mood that the strategy group meets next morning at six forty-five a.m. There is mixed news from the overnights. Labour negatives have gone from nineteen to four. The Conservative negatives are only eight to two. Yet in spite of this, Labour's overall poll lead has gone up from 1 per cent to 4 per cent in the course of the week.

There is a good deal of lively debate about whether the row – now called 'Jennifer's Ear' – is working for Labour or against it. One member of the Leader's office is keen to point out that if you read the regional press, the broadcast has done Labour nothing but good. It is only in London that it is raising doubts about Labour's trustworthiness. The irony, says another, is that the previous week they ran a smooth campaign on tax and got nowhere. This week they are running a disorderly campaign on health, and their poll lead is climbing.

Much of this is hard to hear, because of a particularly noisy printer in the next room. When Julie Hall arrives, she is greeted by a discussion of what is now known as the 'Nottingham contradiction' – the fact that she said one thing, and her Leader said another. But whatever the frisson caused by her appearance, it is nothing next to the arrival of Robin Cook, who makes no secret of his anger at what has happened in the last few days. As far as he is concerned, all the Labour Party has done has been to let some innocent people in for some unwelcome publicity. 'We have landed them in it', he says, 'from a great height.' He is therefore proposing that Labour apologize and withdraw the dossier.

This particular suggestion is greeted with stunned silence. Plainly no one wants to cross such an angry man, but on the other hand the tactical wisdom of admitting error in the middle of an election campaign appeals to nobody. It is Bryan Gould, the New Zealander who chaired the 1987 campaign, who finally replies to Cook.

Bryan Gould: Robin, I have absolutely no doubt that you are right on the morality of this. What happened was not defensible from a moral point of view, but I have to ask if you're right on tactics.

At this point the door bursts open and Neil Kinnock stands there in a towering rage. His entire appearance in the room lasts eight seconds. He has just learned that someone on the campaign had spoken to the consultant in the Jennifer case without telling him.

Kinnock: I want to know who that was. Someone on Tuesday night spoke to the consultant. And they did not tell me. I want to know who that person was.

Someone nervously volunteers they took a call on Tuesday night from the consultant.

Kinnock: Right, come with me.

The two men go out. The door is slammed shut. There is an electrifying silence round the table.

Cook: I understand Neil's fury and in good part I share it. We have let four people down. A public apology is what we need.
Bryan Gould: If we apologize, that becomes the issue. We hand the Tories their issue. And all our good work is wiped out.

As they contemplate Gould's unanswerable point, an election strategist at the far end of the table tries to remind everyone that, underneath it all, Labour has had a good week.

Conservative press conference

Over at Smith Square, there are usually posters on the platform behind the politicians. But the Conservatives have taken so much stick for running a negative campaign that they have decided to cover over their negative posters. Unfortunately they have no positive ones. So instead they are using black lining paper. For the same reasons they have changed the subject of today's conference. Originally billed as being about tax, it is now about something called 'vision'.

It is interesting how the attitude of the press has changed in the past week. They are now much more aggressive, as if the Conservatives are no longer the government. Respect is no longer automatically accorded.

The John Major Battlebus

With some difficulty, I have arranged to spend a day on the John Major Battlebus, which leaves every day from outside Central Office to go to a destination which, for security reasons, cannot be disclosed. The price of a day ticket is £350, regardless. As the bus leaves and makes its way west out through Victoria, the assembled journalists, most of whom have now been careering round the country for two weeks, shout at Vanessa Ford, the Conservative representative whose job it is to usher them through the day. She is a PR woman in a power suit, whose good nature shows no sign of being worn down by their relentless sexual jokes.

The journalists are joined in a kind of desperate camaraderie, which comes from everything John Major does being so dull. They shout at Vanessa, 'Just tell us where we're going', 'Just tell us what the story is . . .'

Journalist: It's our livelihood, you know.
Another journalist: I'm dying of by-line starvation.

Vanessa reads out a list of the day's activities. We are going to visit a GEC aeroplane plant at an undisclosed location. We will watch John Major unveil a plaque somewhere else. We will see him inspect a microchip factory on an industrial estate. Then we will attend a John Major talk-in at an unnamed leisure centre. These informal occasions, where Major sits on a stool and addresses three hundred loyalists in the round, are known as Val Doonican sessions.

As we move down towards the A40, the journalists are in a state of reckless mutiny at the tedium of the prospect. 'Another totally fucking boring day'. Someone shouts at Vanessa: 'Can't we have a Kinnock-style row on this bus?' Quite a number fall to discussing Russell's Twix Bar – whether he's eaten it yet. Another journalist is telling others about how his cat's off his Brekkies. Meanwhile I hear someone describe a fellow journalist as 'the Julie Hall of the *Independent* – she'll burst into tears at the slightest excuse'.

We reach RAF Brize Norton and are kept in our bus as Major and Norma get out of their limousine to walk across to the aeroplane. 'Oh, there she is!' all the journalists and photographers scream in falsetto. 'There's Norma! There's Norma!' We board the plane, and as we settle down in our seats, a voice comes over the loudspeaker.

Voice: The Conservative Party welcomes you aboard this aeroplane.

After a short flight, we are put on another bus, journalists still desperately trying to work out where they are.

Journalist: Are we going to visit the factory that makes our lunchboxes?

Behind me a slightly desperate journalist is trying to dictate his story into a mobile phone: 'The PM sought to breathe life today into his flagging campaign . . .' We alight at an aircraft factory where I run into Neil Libbert, the *Observer* photographer. He informs me that I am in Wales.

DH: *What are we doing in Wales? He isn't going to get any votes in Wales.*
Neil Libbert: He's not going to get any votes anywhere, so we might as well be here.

We are kept at such a distance from Major, as he tours the factory, that our presence is almost completely pointless. Across the factory I see John Simpson, who has recently distinguished himself as the BBC's most brilliant reporter during the Gulf War.

DH: *Is it always as boring as this?*
John Simpson: This is a good day. We've got red wine at lunch and I've heard there's shortbread for tea.

In the afternoon we are being traipsed round the microchip factory on a featureless industrial estate in mid-Glamorgan. Once more the only people who can hear the Prime Minister are the sound recordists with their socks on the end of long poles. The rest of us are penned off by the young men in striped shirts who are running this campaign. They even have, working under them, teams of students in tracksuits who jog from spot to spot with ropes to keep us – and the public – at bay. When I ask one of the yuppy minders from the Tory press office what is actually made in this factory, he has no idea.

Journalist: The head is cut off but the chicken is running around.
Minder: That isn't fair. This is a place where modern technology is being developed.
Journalist: What for?
Minder: Helping the economy.
Journalist: In what way?
Minder: I don't know, but I'm sure it's helping the economy.

In fact the only thing I recognize is a kitchen machine. You put a potato in one end and a crisp comes out the other. Suddenly behind me there are raised and angry voices as another journalist finally cracks at the superciliousness of the Central Office minders.

Journalist: (*Shouting*) That's what we're bloody told everywhere we go. Nobody knows what we're doing and nobody knows why we're here.

Later in the afternoon we are bussed to a leisure centre and led into some squashcourts where the doors are closed and we are made to wait. They give us some biscuits and we wait some more. I look round. What is so funny is that earlier in the day the journalists were full of mutinous humour. Now they have been worn down, and have reached the stage where they will do anything they're told. After just eight hours of this nonsense, we all have the concentration camp mentality. Funniest of all is to see John Simpson – the hero of Baghdad – sitting at the side of the room with a look of utter desolation on his face. The spirit which Saddam Hussein could not extinguish has been snuffed out by the Tories in the space of hours.

When we go into the sports centre itself, I countermand orders and go and sit in the audience. The Prime Minister's talk is prefaced by two warm-up men. First, vice-chairman of the Conservative Party, Sir Geoffrey Pattie. Then Jeffrey Archer, who makes self-deprecating jokes.

Jeffrey Archer: As you may perhaps have heard, I've once or twice been in a spot of trouble myself.

There is ingratiating laughter, at this presumed reference to his gift of money to a prostitute. When John Major comes on, everyone grins inanely, embarrassed to find the Prime Minister so close. Contrary to what I have been told, the session is extremely professional and effective. But there is something about Major which all the time has you noticing his verbal mannerisms. Today he repeatedly uses the word 'raft', as in 'a whole raft of reasons'. Like most Conservative politicians, he is terrified of the word 'class', and has to go round the houses for a suitable euphemism. People instead come from 'varying backgrounds and interests'. He once again reveals his fascination for the railways, in a passage about the need to clean up the 'dirty areas around our railway stations'. As if anticipating my pleasure in this recurring theme of his, Major stops to elaborate.

John Major: People say I've got a bit of a thing about railways. But Margaret Thatcher had a thing about council houses and look what happened to them.

Back in the bus, the journalists are not as impressed by his overall performance as I am. One is dictating a story which begins, 'At four o'clock this afternoon, John Major visited a sports centre . . .' Then he turns to a colleague.

Journalist: You know the story is a stinker when the time of day is in it . . .

Later we are put back on the plane and made to sit watching John Major eat some fish and chips on the tarmac outside. A photographer remarks that never once in eighteen months have they caught the Prime Minister taking his glasses off. When we take off, Major comes into the back of the plane and the photographers, who have been so rude about him all day, suddenly start fawning.

Photographers: Oh sir, please sir, please sir, help us with our pictures. Please give us a chance sir.

Major: It's just that every time you snap, I think – my God, what caption are they going to put under this?

Photographers: Oh sir, honestly sir, honestly, we're not trying to stitch you up. Except him from the *Mirror*, sir. The rest of us, we're all for you sir. We promise. We just want to do a good job.

John Major moves behind me to talk to John Simpson, and I suddenly realize he is asking him for professional advice. Scraps of their conversation drift across to me.

Simpson: . . . not sure about your campaign . . . not sure you're showing yourself to best advantage . . .

Major: No, I agree. I agree.

Simpson: . . . all seems a bit pointless . . . ways in which you could be better presented . . .

Major: I know. I know. What do you think I should do?

After we have landed, on the bus back into London, one reporter is heard filing a story about fish and chips. At once there are groans throughout the bus.

Journalist: I thought we'd all agreed not to do that one.

So they all start filing the story – each one embellishing more.

One journalist: At Llancunnoch – oh God, I can't spell that, call it Cardiff – this evening, John Major got his fingers sticky . . .

Sun journalist: John Major may have victory on a plate, but last night he tucked into an appetizing plate of fish and chips.

Monday, 30 March 1992

Labour strategy meeting

I have had the weekend to recover from my trip to Wales. There has been some comment in the press over the weekend about John Major's decision to wrench his campaign away from yuppy control and to take charge of it himself. To this end, he has taken to speaking from a soapbox. But when I arrive at six-thirty on Monday morning, I find the Labour strategy group laughing, apparently cheerful. They are playing up the sense that perhaps the worst is over. People are firing again on all the usual subjects – how to stage a special event which will capture the electorate's imagination, whether to move now or later on to Education, whether Tessa Blackstone would or wouldn't be a good person on a platform with Neil Kinnock and John Smith. ('I think we need someone who isn't a Baroness.') A good deal of time is spent making sure that everyone's answers on public sector pay will tally with what Bryan Gould is going to say in five minutes' time on the *Today* programme.

Although the energy is febrile and business-as-normal has superficially been restored, I find, for the first time, that there is something depressing in the atmosphere: as if they all know in their hearts that Labour should have broken through in the polls by now. Underneath, everyone is disturbed that it hasn't. We are going through the motions, as if we know that the daily round of press conferences and Kinnock charging through miscellaneous schools and hospitals will give us an *impression* of activity, but will not actually deliver. I have learnt that the most dangerous thing about an election campaign is that there is always something to do.

Tuesday, 31 March 1992

Labour strategy meeting

This morning the atmosphere seems a little better. Everyone enjoys a joke about a report in the *Daily Express* which says that Labour has had a 'wobbly Monday' and that Larry Whitty, the low-key Secretary of the Labour Party, has been brought in to replace those currently running the campaign.

Larry Whitty: Quite right.

As Philip Gould does his normal report on the overnights, he goes on to remind everybody that it has always been planned that Labour's big slogan for the last week will be 'IT'S TIME FOR A CHANGE'. He is instructing everyone that they must use the phrase relentlessly. Every sentence everybody says has to begin 'It's time . . .' He is sure that only by saying 'it's time, it's time, it's time, it's time . . .' over and over will they get the momentum which will get them above forty.

They buzz through the usual meeting headings, reporting on press and television, what the Tories have been saying. It is part of Labour's overall strategy that this week should be about education, yet they are having trouble hitting the right tone. Jack Straw, the education spokesman, is so keen to stress that Labour will not be financially irresponsible that he tends to hedge in all his promises for schoolroom improvements with the proviso that they will happen only 'as and when resources allow . . .'

This is obviously making for a less than inspirational speaking style – one person notes that Straw sounds more like a Treasury spokesman than an Education minister. But it also points up a larger dilemma for Labour. An off-the-record briefing from a Tory strategist had confirmed for me what I already suspected. When they replaced Margaret Thatcher, the Tories had been faced with a public relations choice. They could either emphasize the difference between Margaret Thatcher and John Major – a new, more 'caring' kind of Conservatism – or stress continuity. After a good deal of debate, the Tories had opted for continuity. Although they saw the apparent allure of dressing up Conservatism with a kinder face, they had bowed to the expert opinion which told them that Compassion and Economic Competence were not, in the public's view, compatible. You could *either* be Caring, or you could be Capable. But there was, in electoral terms, no logical way of being both. What's more, it was Capable which had won the Tories the last three elections. And it was Capable they were determined to be again.

It was this brutally simple choice which Labour were, by contrast, unwilling to make. Instead they were trying to maintain a much more unwieldy balance, forced to convince people that justice and efficiency were somehow aspects of the same thing. Not surprisingly, they were forever finding themselves veering too much in one direction or the other.

Meanwhile, as the strategists try to correct Straw's tone ('We gave him a very good script, and he uses it more often than not'), Jack Cunningham is becoming more impatient to get the meeting over. He has to speak at the press conference in half an hour on both public sector pay and Labour's education plans. He needs briefing on both. Even before this meeting is over, experts are brought into the busy room. As everyone else gets washed away in overlapping activity, the advisers start to run Cunningham through the facts. He stops them all the time to check he understands everything they are saying. The room is full of a hundred people doing a hundred different things, but Cunningham goes on and on through both briefs, taking notes, checking and finally asking: 'Can we deliver on this?' Security men are at his feet, running metal detectors under the table, as Cunningham finally looks up, satisfied. I think for the first time I have some sense of what a politician has to be able to do. Cunningham has just absorbed a complex brief in impossible circumstances. At the press conference, his command of the facts is faultless. Like a film actor, he has put himself into the heart of a script at a few minutes' notice. But my guess is that, like an actor, he will have forgotten it by nightfall.

Wednesday, 1 April 1992

Labour strategy meeting

There is sudden, unanticipated excitement. From nowhere, poll leads have appeared putting Labour seven points ahead. Jack Cunningham comes in, laughing and waving the *Daily Express*. The whole atmosphere of the meeting is totally transformed, with everyone particularly pleased that the figures show Kinnock so far ahead of Major as an effective compaigner. The talk now is of avoiding triumphalism, of trying to position Labour somehow above the fight, as if it is now up to the Liberal Democrats and the Conservatives to continue with the squalid business of scrapping for votes, while Labour watches serenely from above.

Everyone knows that this is the moment at which most damage can be done by what they call free enterprise – individual candidates coming up with lines of their own. Now, more than ever, it is essential that nobody goes AWOL. Everyone must stick to the line. One strategist notes that there is 'only one line for key campaigners. The line is – positive, cool, calm, women, doubters.'

This last rather opaque reference is to the fact that it is women who are responsible for the movement in the polls, and when the meeting breaks up I manage to ask one of Neil Kinnock's most senior female advisers why this is.

DH: *I must admit I'm intrigued by the way it's the women who are moving.*
Adviser: Yes, I'm afraid they're more easily swayed. I don't know why. I regret it, but it's true. I've had terrible trouble making politicians realize that half the electorate are women. Jack Cunningham got into a dreadful row on Radio 4 with Michael Howard, and that's exactly the kind of behaviour which puts women off. I sit them down and say, 'You're not talking to some macho journalist, you're talking to women. Imagine the public are women.' I told Jack to do it the other day and he did the most beautiful interview.

When Neil Kinnock arrives, he is a mixture of irrepressible cheerfulness and physical exhaustion. He is both so ill and so happy that it is almost impossible to get him to concentrate, his conversation a fast-moving stream of impersonations and jokes. One senior Labour politician arrives and tries to get someone to tell her what the current line is on defence. She is met with nothing but impatience. I have noticed before that the men in the Labour Party all leap down the women's throats if they are even one beat behind. But this is the most ill-tempered yet, as if in this rare moment of sweet confidence, nobody wants to be bothered by details, least of all from a woman. Only Kinnock is patient as ever, even adjusting the collar of an NHS doctor who is to go on the platform with him.

The Michael Kamen music starts to play as the team waits in the wings. Once more, the music swells and the team heads into the press conference.

The Sheffield rally

I drive up to Sheffield for the biggest rally of the campaign. The Sheffield Arena is an astonishing 12,000-seat building which has been put up with the help of a grant from the EEC. As I arrive, there is a projection of a rose endlessly furling and unfurling. Sniffer dogs are going down the rows of seats. With nobody present, they start to rehearse the moment at which Kinnock's helicopter will touch down.

Commentator: And now, here they are inside the Sheffield Arena, please welcome Neil and Glenys Kinnock.

Two follow-spots travel the entire length of the hall, with no one inside them.

Commentator: Soon to be the man to restore confidence in the British economy – John Smith!

With time to kill, I take a break and walk out into the streets which lead off from the Arena. This was once the manufacturing heartland of Britain, where the steel industry grew and prospered. Now there are only small red-brick parades of shops and desolate, crumbling factories. As I walk past the little, doomed windows, I look at the lard cakes, the fish and chips, the chip sandwiches. Eventually even the crumbling buildings give way to a huge piece of wasteland, pockmarked with a pitch-black sump of polluted water, in which polystyrene pieces are floating. On abandoned land, small groups of vagrants are huddling round fires. For a second, Sheffield looks like Benares.

I walk across this bleak landscape to a massive new shopping centre half a mile away. The Meadowhall Centre stands, isolated, like a massive monument to the days before the recession, stuffed full of Dixons and Rumbelows and Boots and W. H. Smiths and Tandy and Debenhams. It is almost entirely deserted. Here you may buy food from all over the world. There are fresh oysters, and restaurants full of Kentucky this and Mississippi that. But there are almost no buyers at all. I feel, as always, the immense engulfing sadness of capitalism; the sadness of consumption, but the even more powerful sadness when consumption comes to a halt.

Back at the hall, people are pouring out of buses and cars to flood into the Arena. I realize of course how distant I have been from the people that this election is about. And now that I see so many gathered together in the hall, and hear them cheering as the video screen image projects Kinnock's helicopter landing about three hundred yards away, I feel my eyes watering and my throat thicken.

The first speaker in the enormous hall is Roy Hattersley, who at once adopts a tone which everyone at that morning's strategy meeting had sworn to avoid.

Roy Hattersley: We stand on the brink of a great and historic victory.

I am surprised that he appears to be saying Labour has already won. Later in his speech, I notice the thing which gets the largest response from this audience is any reference to crumbling classrooms, or the lack of schoolbooks. He is followed by John Smith, who is not a sparkling public speaker. As he rambles on, I see that Philip Gould's signs, which everywhere say 'It's time for a change', have been amended by some bright spirit to read, 'It's time for a drink'.

The former Secretary of State for Employment and Productivity and old-time Labour campaigner, Barbara Castle, follows. She receives an overwhelming ovation, to which she responds.

Barbara Castle: Thank you. You have proved this is the party of conservation.

She makes a speech in a completely different class to anything I have heard in this election, making the claim that she has detected the same groundswell of excitement and passion for change that she found in the electorate in 1945. The audience rise to her. There is a strong sense that most of what is decent about this country is represented in this hall tonight. For thirteen years people have been waiting patiently, effectively dispossessed, their values laughed at and their interests unrepresented. Now at last they are ready, on the brink of having a voice again. However, there is at the same time a sense of duty in the audience, a rather sophisticated understanding that it will be their job to provide pictures for the television, and to provide the noise which will rock the television audience back.

And sure enough, as Neil Kinnock arrives with his wife and walks the immense length of the hall, people stand up and scream and cheer, partly because they do genuinely like him, and partly to make sure the right image goes out on the Nine o'Clock News.

As always with Labour, it is a little unclear what the occasion is. There are musicians, there are filmed endorsements, there is the sense of a tub-thumping rally, but there is also serious politics.

And so, after greeting the crowd with cries of 'A'right, a'right', Kinnock launches into what is one of his less inspired speeches, whose subject is hard to discern. For some reason his slightly manic energy, as he joins Courtney Pine with a modern version of

Jerusalem, reminds me of Lenin: 'It doesn't matter what is said at a political meeting. All that matters is who is there at the end of the meeting.'

Thursday, 2 April 1992

The BBC

The next morning, I read the post-mortems on Sheffield. Matthew Parris, an ex-Tory MP, has a nasty little column in *The Times*, saying that Sheffield represented a sinister new development in British politics, the introduction of American packaging, the triumph of the image over real issues. Is it laziness which has prevented him from noticing, or bias which has prevented him from mentioning, what was most conspicuous about Sheffield? Not the razzmatazz, not the bands, not the speeches, but the rare expressions of hope on the faces of the audience.

Sheffield is also being discussed as I arrive at the BBC to watch how the election news is put together. The meeting I attend of top News executives is extraordinarily academic. After the fever of the campaign it is rather reassuring to sit among such calm people, who discuss like dons the shortcomings of their own coverage. The care with which they do this is immediately attractive. They debate at length whether they have or haven't given the Greens a fair crack of the whip. It's restful in the senior common room.

News editor: You're saying you've never eaten a bagel?
Director of Current Affairs: I didn't say that. Not at all. I said I'd never *knowingly* eaten a bagel.

There is general laughter.

News editor: You're astonishingly inexperienced if you haven't eaten a bagel.
Director of Current Affairs: I'm obviously not expressing myself clearly. I didn't know this thing was called a bagel when I ate it.

The general expectation at the meeting is of a hung parliament. The Cabinet Office has made it known that, during any period of negotiation, briefings will be done through the lobby.

News editor: Martin will do the packaging. The hardware will be plugged through to the London hub if there's a hung Parliament.
Bearded man: If Kinnock wins, we'll stay live in Islwyn.
Another man: Can I have Islwyn live for the Six?
News editor: Fine, and I'll beef Belfast up. Lance Price is preparing a film on Kinnock's history should he become Prime Minister.
Bearded man: Is Lance Price the right man to do this?
News editor: Lance Price is the right man to do this because he's the only one who can be given an Espace, and he can tweak it from Downing Street.

Tim Gardam

After standing in the gallery watching a couple of news bulletins go out ('Don't bale out until I hit the key . . . The weather's been crashed out . . . Run B, animate! Run Y, animate! Run Z, animate! . . . Page 35, France rewrite next . . . Drop Bishop, page 78 . . . there's a re-write of 59, Lurgan to come . . .') I find myself back upstairs with Tim Gardam, the editor of *Newsnight*. He is tall, thin, and still only in his 30s. In his brilliant command of argument, he comes across as his own chief presenter's intellectual twin, though with less of Jeremy Paxman's public aggression.

Tim Gardam: I think our brief is very different to that of the newsgathering team downstairs. News bulletins have to make sure they don't miss events, it's not their first responsibility to ask awkward questions about them. It's true that BBC News programmes have a further job – to provide analysis. On *Newsnight*, it is my view that it is too arid to see analysis as an end in itself; it is a tool. Our job is to provide insight – that's maybe a more volatile and less comprehensive brief, but it means our style of reporting is more interrogative. I do think we hold ourselves a little bit away –

partly for programming reasons; that is, if people have already watched the News, as two-thirds of our audience has, they want us to come in from a different angle. A Tory minister said to me privately, 'We don't care what is said on *Newsnight*, because the people who watch *Newsnight* are capable of making their own minds up.'

DH: *All politicians seem to be obsessed with television, but I'm not sure it really has the impact they think it does.*

Gardam: I'm afraid my feeling is that, as TV becomes more and more prevalent, it becomes less and less important. As the audience is segmented, the politicians can mould and homogenize what they say. David Mellor once boasted to me that he had done thirteen interviews in a day. This plethora makes for a pointless stalemate. Interviews aren't real conversations, questions are framed by the journalist just to get the right clip to fit into a package. We all do it. Sometimes, it is rehearsed beforehand. This is the danger of news as analysis, it can get stuck on the first four letters of the word.

We have allowed a complicity between interviewer and politician. How often does a three-minute interview get anywhere? But if you break the ritual, try to make an interview a real engagement, make time for it, you sometimes don't get it. Some senior politicians, Labour every bit as much as Conservative, refuse to come on *Newsnight* because they say they only want to answer a couple of questions for News.

DH: *Television seems to have been neutered in the last ten years.*

Gardam: I don't think that any of us has quite come to terms with the change that happened through Thatcher in the period from the late seventies. The language of politics changed. It wasn't possible to cover politics properly if you weren't economically literate. A lot of us weren't. From that moment, a generation of television journalists lost their edge. Oxford Union repartee couldn't deal with supply-side economics and the PSBR. It cut through the clubbiness, the chumminess, the sense that politics is just about personalities. But it brought a real problem for the broadcasters. The power struggles that counted were being fought out in a language that the audience didn't understand.

Most people who watch TV don't understand economics, so a lot of what is said is thought boring or incomprehensible.

DH: *I'm not sure many politicians understand economics.*

Gardam: It's in economic theory that most of the political battles have been fought in the last ten years. In this last Parliament, it wasn't really a contest between Labour and Conservative. The division that mattered most in my view was between Number Ten Downing Street and Number Eleven. Thatcher was ousted by a Treasury plot. If you look how she fell, it came about because of her reluctance to join the ERM. Before Madrid, Geoffrey Howe and Nigel Lawson went to her and gave her an ultimatum that she had to agree to join the ERM. So she agreed against her will, and from that moment on she was obsessed with a burning resentment that she'd been made to do something she didn't want to do. The following summer she dumped Howe, and then later she dumped Lawson. But it was from the seeds of that argument, between the Treasury who wanted us to go in, and Thatcher who didn't, for economic as well as political reasons, that her destruction came. However, the difficult thing for us to accept is that probably Thatcher was right and it would have been better for the British economy to stay out of the ERM.

DH: *To me this current election is about fear.*

Gardam: In what way?

DH: *Fear of losing power on one side. Fear of making a mistake on the other.*

Gardam: Oh, sure.

DH: *You say you're bored by the poverty of the discourse, yet to me this is your fault. Or rather, it's Fleet Street's fault. Because both parties are deeply divided. The Tories over Europe, obviously, and Labour over many other things. But nobody dares discuss these differences in public.*

Gardam: That's true.

DH: *You all say politicians are being shallow. Yet what choice do they have when to talk of real issues is to risk being called split? Whose fault is that? Yours. The media's. The politicians and the media are locked together in a dance of death. And that won't change until the media stop worshipping power.*

Gardam: In one sense, the press will always worship power, and they will whichever government gets in. The instinct of some political journalists is to hunt with the pack but to keep in personally with people in authority. Otherwise they might miss the story. To be honest, we are all captivated by the spectacle of power; we can't take our eyes off it. In this election, what *Newsnight* has been trying to do is to get outside London and to report the election from the regions. A lot of people in the country are angry at the self-enclosed world of the press and the politicians they see at the daily press conferences.

It's the basis of my belief that if you talk to people intelligently they will respond intelligently. Indeed, that's what the BBC is there for. BBC journalism has the authority and the specialist knowledge; what it can lack is eloquence. The kind of journalism I'm looking for, which has disappeared, and which if you like is represented by *Granta* magazine, is informed, passionate reporting. Now the fact is, you get a certain amount of that about foreign countries on the BBC, but why do you no longer get any of that reporting about England? Where do we look for that kind of thing?

DH: *Do you see either side as freer with ideas than the other?*

Gardam: The danger is that, in preparing themselves for power, the Labour Party have made themselves uninterested in ideas, and when they get there they won't know what to do because they've done no intellectual groundwork. The Wilson government, so much despised, nevertheless did contain people like Crosland, like Jenkins, who had done a great deal of hard political thinking – they had some overview, they had some sense of history. But who has any sense of history now?

DH: *Do you ever feel ashamed of your own contribution to events?*

Gardam: I must admit, I felt we wasted our time last week. We had an excellent film on law and order that went beyond normal party point-scoring. It showed that the crime rate in Scotland was not as bad as in England. When the film was over, Hattersley and Baker were asked for their reaction in the studio. They simply ignored it; perhaps because they hadn't been briefed. Nor was it in either of their interests to say that the crime rate is better in Scotland. So they just didn't deal with it. I thought, at the end, why did we bother to have politicians at all? Why not just run the film?

Friday, 3 April 1992

Labour strategy meeting

It's the last weekend. When Philip Gould reports on his overnight polls, the most significant changes are in people's expectation of which side is going to win. Those expecting a Labour victory have gone up from twenty to twenty-eight. Those expecting the Conservatives to win have gone down from twenty-seven to fifteen. The overall shift of twenty points is unprecedented in one day's polling.

It has always been part of Labour's overall strategy that in the last week of the campaign they will introduce a promise to look sympathetically on Proportional Representation when they get into power. A large part of this morning's meeting is therefore spent with the group reassuring themselves that Neil Kinnock was right to put the issue of PR on this morning's front pages. Labour believes that it is still haunted by people's memories of past Labour governments, and of the extremism which overtook the party in the early eighties. For that reason, they have always believed that, as the prospect of a Labour government drew near, it would be necessary to reassure the electorate of its consensual intentions. Although it is statistically demonstrable that Labour governments since the war have been at least as economically successful as Tory ones, if not more so, the Labour Party is agonizingly convinced that its own prospective success strikes fear into people's hearts.

Everyone now wants to convince themselves of the rightness of their thinking, and there is a long, general discussion in which nobody dissents from the view that raising PR has been a tactical masterstroke. It is an indicator not just of what Labour's policies will be, but of the manner in which it is going to govern. It has made Labour look like a potential 'listening' government, and it has made John Major look hard and unyielding. One strategist is particularly pleased with a phrase Kinnock has used about 'a more modern constitution'.

Strategist: I like that line. It's a nice, friendly line.

Underlying the need to make Labour appear softer is the fear that there will be a backlash once people realize Labour is going to win. One person points out that 'electoral history is littered with campaigns which were ahead on Friday and lost the following Thursday. Once it is understood that Labour may win, there will undoubtedly be a shift back to the Conservatives. And what's more, they will start to hit the tax thing very hard.'

Perhaps I alone find it strange to be sitting in a room with a group of people who are so convinced that the electorate does not want them, or rather will not want them in anything like their true colours. But then, I have not known the horrors of thirteen years' powerless opposition.

When Neil Kinnock arrives, it is clear the tension has reached him as well. The exhilaration of Sheffield has gone. He goes into a corner with an adviser.

Kinnock: Well . . . Are we on course?
Adviser: Just. Just. Personally you're way ahead of Major.

Kinnock nods grimly, as if he expected no less.

Adviser: It does make people uneasy that we're ahead.

Sunday, 5 April 1992

Conservative rally

Security is so tight for the last big event of the campaign that I am twenty minutes wandering round the car park in Wembley stadium before I find a small notice reading 'Political Event'.

Inside, a woman in a pastel suit is leaning down to her 5-year-old daughter, who is in patent-leather shoes.

Woman: Darling, you'll see the Prime Minister and the Home Secretary. Here's a copy of John Major's speech.
Child: Thank you, Mummy.

The Conservatives have built a 360-degree tent in which to stage their final event. You are encompassed by a slide show. For some reason as you come in there are pictures of rugby players on the screens. The first speaker is Tim Rice.

Tim Rice: I'm the Conservatives' Jeremy Irons.* I pledge that if I win an Oscar I will not say anything political. As Conservatives you feel you mustn't politicize events, but when you see socialists claim the high moral ground, I think it's important people come forward for John Major.

He makes an analogy with cricket.

Rice: It's like Botham at Headingley in 1981. Hammer them all over the shop in the last three days.

He is followed by Geoffrey Pattie, who has introduced John Major all over the country. Pattie praises the Lloyd Webber setting of Purcell, which has been the Tories' theme tune.

Geoffrey Pattie: There's something about this music which is very conservative, because it takes something traditional and it makes something modern and dynamic from it.

The final warm-up man is Tim Farmer, Chairman of Kwik-Fit. He seems to have been chosen to make John Major look like a great orator. He uses the line, 'These are exciting times for

---

*At a BAFTA awards ceremony earlier in the year, Irons had criticized the government's parsimony towards the British film industry.

Kwik-Fit . . .' A film is then shown with John Major in the Gulf. To the troops he says, 'It's been an absolutely fabulous job you've done . . .' I notice this is one of his favourite words. (He used it about the fish and chips the week before.) When Major finally appears and walks along a line shaking hands with Donald Sinden and Elaine Paige, the reaction is muted – in a deliberate attempt to avoid what Tories see as Sheffield's excesses. When he reaches the stage, Major refers to the soapbox he has been carrying with him round Britain.

John Major: I hope you like the set – we couldn't build a soapbox.

This joke fails. What is odd is that I have heard this joke fail before and am puzzled why he is using it again. Afterwards, one of his advisers tells me, 'John is comfortable with it so we don't mind that it doesn't work.'

Major: We've had some fabulous [*that word again*] rallies, rallies which I would compare with what happened in Sheffield. Did you see that gathering? To me, there was something un-British about it.

This is one of the oddest moments of the campaign. Sheffield was the most profoundly British occasion I have been at in years. But I realize of course that there are two Britains. The Britain I like is in a scruffy anorak and its hair is messy. It isn't frightened of emotion. But here I am now in the other Britain.

Major: Neil Kinnock thinks he can get into Downing Street. Well, either he's been drinking Carling Black Label or he's been reading *Fame is the Spur*.

This incomprehensible joke is received with open bewilderment, even by this audience. John Major is off script. We have all been issued with his speech, and are looking one to another nervously as he free associates through all the remarks he has acquired on the road. His problem is acute. As he makes inept jokes about Gerald Kaufman, I find myself for the first time disliking John Major. You suddenly realize that he depends for our esteem on being what he seems: a genuinely decent man who has become Prime Minister. But this necessarily means he is hopeless at personal abuse. The more he attempts it, the more distasteful he becomes. He looks like a weak man whose advisers have talked him into being unpleasant. Because he has no wit, the personal attacks seem lame and ugly.

Major: I believe this is a *great* country and I am tired of listening to the opposition running it down.

As he goes on in this vein, I stare at him with renewed fascination. In private, a number of Tory ministers are admitting to journalists that they are expecting to lose. Off the record, they have said as much. The atmosphere in the Conservative camp is dire. Yet Major himself seems untroubled. Watching him now, it is impossible to tell if his apparent indifference to his possible defeat stems from a kind of courage, or from sheer lack of imagination. Does he simply lack the nous to understand how deep his problems are? Or is he calm, but in a dream? Is he, in that wonderful Scottish expression, 'in a dwam'?

The speech itself does have some substance. Labour's decision to talk about PR and to raise the possibilities of constitutional reform has given Major the opportunity to counter with a speech on the horrors of devolution. Unsurprisingly, he is against the break-up of the United Kingdom. For once there is evidence of some personal passion as he defends the Union. All Conservatives look good when wrapped in the flag. But the ideas are trapped under ice, because the rhetoric is so full of 'it-is-my-opinion's and 'let-me-tell-you-this's. His Chairman, Chris Patten, sits behind him, too tired even to remember to clap.

THE STATE

Monday, 6 April 1992

Labour strategy meeting

The Tory newspapers have loyally declared Wembley a brilliant success. On the other hand, they have deliberately ignored Labour's rival event, a gathering of musical and theatrical celebrities which the *Express* contemptuously tucks away as 'Labour Luvvies Gather'. This particularly outrages Neil Kinnock, who is in early this morning, complaining that the *Daily Telegraph* has managed 'to take the two greatest Shakespearean actors of the day and write them out of the script altogether'. There is something extraordinarily touching about the personal depths of his outrage that the *Telegraph* has not mentioned Ian McKellen or Antony Sher.

As Kinnock leaves the room to write his speech, Dave Hill reports on the polls. Although there is a rolling lead of 4 per cent, there are a couple of alarming signs. People's second choice is moving from Liberal Democrat to Conservative, which implies that the Tories are picking up waverers. But, worse, the number of people believing that a Labour government will mean higher taxes is actually growing every day.

These slightly ominous figures lead the strategists into another of their unwieldy balancing acts. Labour is not attracting the uncommitted, so, on the one hand, it must sound as if it will offer a consensus government with which the Liberal Democrats can live. But on the other hand, it must not sound so wishy-washy that it puts people off. Although the group are pleased with the mixture they struck over the weekend ('I don't know if you noticed, but yesterday we toned Neil down, and he didn't sound as if he was taking the voters for granted'), they are still searching for that elusive formula called 'strong consensus government'.

The other danger for Labour is now from hypothetical questions. Everyone in the country is said to be expecting a hung Parliament, so that all journalists are now trying to lure Labour politicians into 'what if?' scenarios. Robin Cook had nearly been snared into a damaging discussion of what he would do if he became Health Secretary. Would he sack the chief civil servant, who was generally felt to have shown a mite too much personal conviction in implementing Tory NHS reforms? Cook had managed to avoid answering, but in one person's words, 'We were half a second away from disaster.'

The pressure from hypotheticals is mostly, as ever, on Kinnock himself. The press wants to ask him who he will and will not be willing to work with. The whole subject is a potential minefield and also smacks of all the backroom plotting which the electorate is said to dislike about minority government. So everyone is pleased with Bryan Gould's verbal solution: 'I used a line – I don't know if anyone heard me – Neil will do his constitutional duty.'

There is much amusement at Tory denials that a hung Parliament is possible. Everyone has heard the story about Kenneth Baker, who, immediately after John Major had given a press conference saying the Tories refused to contemplate such an outcome, went up to the constitutional expert David Butler and asked him if he could help with their planning for exactly that eventuality.

As the Shadow Cabinet arrive to begin another meeting, which will merge with this one, I find myself discussing Sheffield with Neil Stewart.

Neil Stewart: Well, you know what the Tories want, and what Tory journalists want – they want the television companies to replay that bit where Neil calls out 'All right?' and the crowd calls 'All right' back.
DH: *Was that bad?*
Stewart: It wasn't bad if you were there, but it plays very badly on television. It looks awful, so the more they play it, the happier the Tories are.

Tuesday, 7 April 1992

Labour strategy meeting

Two days to go. As I come in, now drawn by a sort of compulsive routine which has taken over my life, I run into a senior Labour peer. He asks me what I will do at six in the mornings when all this is over.

DH: *Sleep, I suppose. What will you do?*
Peer: Govern.

The atmosphere is, however, extremely jumpy. Rather to everyone's surprise, John Major has launched some sort of personal initiative and appeared the previous day on every London TV and radio station. The suddenness of his decision also allowed him to exploit his right to be balanced only by leaders of other parties. All junior Labour spokesmen had therefore been bumped, and Kinnock himself had not been available at such short notice to counter Major's offensive. Nor will he be available today. He is too locked in to a predetermined programme.

Philip Gould reads out the overnight figures and reports that John Major's personal popularity is suddenly up. Although he emphasizes that this figure is for Major, and not for his Party, his voice suddenly trails out as he remarks that he doesn't like Labour being at 38.7 per cent after all the ... He shakes his head, not wanting to finish the sentence, because he means all the effort that everybody in the room has put in. A Labour press officer tries briefly to restore morale with news of the largest poll yet, on the previous night's News at Ten, which has kept Labour in a three-point lead. But he also admits that the more detailed figures were presented in a way that was overly favourable to Labour, and that if he had been working for the Conservatives, he would have been on the phone like a shot to complain.

As the meeting breaks up, I find myself alone in a corner of the room with Dave Hill and one of the people advising on polling and press.

DH: *This is so peculiar.*

Adviser: What is?

DH: *This lull, this most extraordinary lull in the election. I can't explain it, but it almost seems to have come to a stop. I don't like it. The calm unnerves me.*

Adviser: We're all so haunted by the memory of the last election, where we were so exhausted we ran out of steam. But this time it seems to be them. They seem to have accepted they're going to lose.

Hill: They should have been throwing stuff at us. Every night I watch the TV and I expect it. And it never comes.

DH: *I've got an idea about this. They took so much criticism in the press for negative campaigning, they decided 'we've got to be positive'. So in trying to be positive, they can't go for Kinnock as much as they'd like.*

Hill: You're right.

Adviser: They listen to the press, they listen to journalists . . .

Hill: Which is always a bloody stupid thing to do. You should never listen to journalists in an election.

Adviser: Negative campaigning works. It works. And they abandoned it.

DH: *Yes. That's the one thing I've understood in this election. Negative campaigning works.*

Kinnock comes in, singing 'Embraceable You'. I am of course watching him as much as I can now. I am by now desperate to see whether he thinks he is going to win or lose. But his cheerfulness is so natural, and so touching, that I actually can't tell. All I know is that he *has* decided, one way or another. For now, he is doing his Churchill imitation, which is pretty good.

Kinnock: (*à la Churchill*) The lights are going out all over Europe. Oh no, it wasn't him who said that, was it? It was someone in the First World War. Asquith. As-quith me another.

I have started reading an article in the paper by a doctor who claims that the supposed tedium of this election is down to everyone involved suffering from sleep deprivation, when I hear Kinnock talking to a friend.

Kinnock: Did I tell you about my cousin Colin? He rang me on Sunday. He said, I just wanted you to know Alyson and I are thinking of you. We send our love and we promise you we'll still speak to you when you're Prime Minister.

Everyone laughs at this, then starts discussing a late Kenneth Baker speech in which he has (*a*) suggested that Labour will encourage mass immigration and (*b*) said that Proportional Representation leads to the undue influence of extremist parties.

Hill: For sheer preposterousness, to wait until two days before the election to run this one is truly pathetic.

Hill goes through the questions Kinnock is likely to be asked at the press conference.

Hill: You may get the 'migrant flood' question from Baker.
Kinnock: I will say that it doesn't . . . how shall I put this? . . . it doesn't grace his office. I could say something much ruder, but I shan't.
Hill: Next question. Does PR lead to fascism?

There is much laughter.

Kinnock: I'm going to say what Roy said yesterday. The British people are insulted by the suggestion that they want to vote for strong right-wing parties, or strong left-wing parties. There's never been any evidence of it. I've got a joke I want to use. To me the letters PR stand for Permanent Recession.
Jack Cunningham: No jokes, Neil.
Kinnock: All right, all right.
Cunningham: Cool, cool. Play it safe.
Kinnock: You're telling *me* to play it safe? You're telling *me* to play it safe? I'm the only man wearing a bloody corset over his mouth.

When the press conference starts, the back-room team sits down and watches it on television. Robin Cook draws attention to the fact that, since his awful performance during Jennifer's Ear, William Waldegrave has vanished from the campaign.

Robin Cook: I promise that when I become Secretary of State for Health on Friday, my first action will be to send out a search party to save and rescue William Waldegrave. (*Then, with lethal timing*) Resources permitting.

As everyone cracks up, Neil Stewart thumps the table.

Stewart: That's right. Laugh at them, laugh at them . . .

Wednesday, 8 April 1992

Labour strategy meeting

With twenty-four hours to go, there is nothing anyone can do except go through the motions of the last press conference. Because it is too late to affect the outcome, there is a last-day-of-term spirit at the final strategy meeting which precedes it. 'We're all de-mob happy,' someone cries. Philip Gould is in especially good spirits, reporting to the room at large that Major is down, Kinnock is up and all the overnight news is good.

However, people are rather taken aback by the newspapers. Although Labour is well used to the venom of the right-wing press, even they are standing stunned at the sheer volume of this morning's onslaught. 'The *Sun* has nine pages on what a nightmare it would be if Neil got in, similarly the *Express* and the *Mail*. The *Mirror* front page is excellent, and in our unbiased view the best of the lot. And the *Guardian* has finally decided, in the last paragraph of an endless editorial, that we should get a majority government if it's not too big.'

Cunningham: So the message today is – no triumphalism.

Larry Whitty: On a practical matter, these offices come down at twelve o'clock and this place will cease to exist.

The business of the meeting, which normally takes thirty minutes, is today sped through in five, and most of that is jokes. There is some cursory discussion of who has given the Tories their endorsements ('I shall never watch that bitch Cilla Black again') and whether Harriet Harman will be saying the right thing on an imminent appearance ('There is no worry. She is a disciplined sister').

All the Labour Front Bench appear in order to have their photographs taken, and when the cameras leave, one of the most senior politicians starts to brief his colleagues on how to behave in the coming forty-eight hours.

Politician: It's essential the line is circulated from Walworth Road. Whatever we're going to say must be adhered to. There must be no variation. There must be no confusion. There must be no private enterprise. John Smith will be the person who speaks about the economy, and all other people should preface their remarks with the words, 'As John Smith has said . . .' It's essential we all hold the line tomorrow on the economy. There will be two big exit polls tomorrow night and we must have a line on those. What I do not want is colleagues speculating. We must maintain the coherence we have had in the last few months. In reaction to these polls, two different possible lines will be prepared in advance, and then, at a moment's notice, we will be able to decide which line we're going to use.

The talk is then all of avoiding triumphalism. If there is a minority government, there must be no gloating.

Kinnock: We need to be sombre. Remember, Palm Sunday was followed by Easter.

The politicians go to their last press conference, and Kinnock is at his wittiest and most relaxed, a man for some reason profoundly at peace with himself.

Journalist: Only 1 per cent of industrialists are saying the Conservative campaign has been well run.
Kinnock: I think that 1 per cent may be a sampling error.

Almost as a footnote to the whole campaign, Cunningham calls a Nigerian journalist who asks a question about aid to the Third World.

John Smith: That is a very important question which has not come up much in the campaign.

As the politicians pour off the set, Cunningham sees Philip Gould standing at the side.

Cunningham: Philip!

Gould spreads his arms and raises them above his head, echoing Cunningham, calling out 'Jack!'
    Behind me, Harriet Harman is still explaining the likely outcome to someone.

Harman: . . . the anti-Tory vote will hold solid, and there's the question of whether the Liberal Democrats will move . . .

As the room finally empties, Harman notices that I am left alone.

Harman: We're all going on a boat, David, from Westminster. It's our last photo-opportunity. Are you coming?
DH: *No. No thank you, Harriet. I'm not coming down the Thames.*

Thursday, 9 April 1992

Election day

All day I remember going about my usual business – writing, taking a script to be duplicated, visiting the theatre – with the awful sick certainty Labour was going to lose. The newspapers had run headlines that morning saying the parties were now neck and neck. When I visited the polling booth to deliver my own vote, there was something in the atmosphere that made me certain of the result. If you make a film and you want to know if it's going to be a success, all you need to do is to watch from across the street as the audience arrive for the first matinée. If they hurry towards the cinema, you will do well. If they straggle, you are finished. I watched proud Tory ladies moving determinedly towards the polling booths in my own constituency and knew that Labour was doomed.

When night came, I moved across to Walworth Road. I had arranged to spend the night with party workers, watching the results come in. I walked up the steps of the Labour HQ at exactly ten o'clock. A receptionist smiled at me and said, 'Oh, I hate this bit, I wish it was all over and we knew.' On a television in front of her, ITN gave the first exit poll. Hearing it, I realized that I could not bear to spend the night in this building. I am not a journalist and I had reached the voluntary limits of my research. The prospect of a night's shared despair held no delights for me.

I went home and sat up in bed watching through the night. At five o'clock in the morning, conceding defeat, Neil Kinnock gave the best speech of the campaign. I flew off for an Easter holiday with my children. The following Wednesday, I finally found a German newspaper in Essaouira, the beautiful Moroccan seaside town in which Orson Welles filmed *Othello*. What I read did not surprise me. Neil Kinnock had resigned.

FAMILY GRIEF

Julie Hall

In the coming weeks it was noticeable that many of the people most closely involved in Labour's sudden defeat began to adopt a more historical perspective. In some part of themselves everyone had known that Britain is a basically conservative country. Labour only wins when the Tory vote goes Liberal or stays at home. However, if the polls could be believed at all, the more uncomfortable fact was that the Tories had started the campaign three points behind Labour. In the actual vote, they were six points ahead. If Major and his team *did* manage a nine-point shift, then perhaps there is some justification for calling their effort the most successful Conservative campaign ever.

After a month's breathing space, I began a series of interviews in which I spoke to some of the principal participants about why Labour lost. I started by meeting Julie Hall at the House of Commons. She had burnt her nose badly on holiday. It was hazy and she had not realized how hot the sun was. We took a pot of tea out on to the terrace.

DH: *When did Neil realize he'd lost?*
Julie Hall: I think he realized for definite over the last week. His instincts about how people are thinking are extraordinary. For a long time before the three-week campaign he didn't think the national mood for change was there. We hadn't succeeded in galvanizing that, although people never stopped despairing of the government. But it never stopped Neil giving his all, right up to the close of polls. He's a fighter, a natural leader. And he so wanted that change.
DH: *What do you think of the post-mortems you've read?*
Hall: Mixed. They fall into different categories. There were knee-jerk anonymous briefings by some, immediately in the wake of Labour's defeat, which were basically about positioning – various individuals trying to reassert themselves or their own agendas. Then there are the academic post-mortems which will take a long time. One lie I'd like to nail is that Labour lost because its packaging was too glitzy. It's so easy to blame glitz and packaging, but if you go down that road, you get into real trouble. You start saying our problem was we presented ourselves too well. Rubbish! It's the product, and by that I mean the policies, which ultimately lost Labour the election.

DH: *Forgive me, but in my view your real failure was to get Neil across. He's a very passionate and interesting man. Yet for four weeks it was as if he was holding himself in.*

Hall: I agree absolutely. Ever since I joined, that was my message. Be yourself. But there were also pressures on him not to be his natural self, to hold himself in. So we didn't get the real Neil across. And the fact is, the more people saw the real Neil – the more they got to know him – the more they liked him.

DH: *Why were some of the advisers so cautious?*

Hall: Because some of his colleagues appeared to believe the propaganda. They believed what they read in the Tory papers. Some appeared to accept the version of Neil presented in the tabloids, and this is terribly undermining, because you're then saying, play your personality down. Politics is about confidence, too. Neil, quite rightly, was always alert to his colleagues and their assessment of his performance. Of course you can say to someone, 'Look, you're being attacked because you're so good – after all, who wants to knock the bad apple off the tree? . . .' Nevertheless, if you're reading that stuff every day, or thinking about others reading it, it must get you down. And if it doesn't, then that's when you should really worry. The problem of course wasn't just in the last four weeks, it goes way back, right through the eight years. In my view, you're lucky once in a generation to get a man with Neil's qualities. To get a partnership like Neil and Glenys. And now we've lost him. What I most regret is that in those eight years we failed to counter the public perception of Neil and promote the man as he really is.

DH: *Why do you think you lost?*

Hall: It has to be the policies. Tax in particular. I don't think we should ever have got into an argument about what our tax policies were going to be, we should just have said, look what a disaster the last thirteen years have been, record unemployment, worst recession since the war, the poll tax fiasco. Come on now, it's got to be time to change. We should have said to govern is to choose; we know it'll be hard when we get in, but as soon as we do and as soon as we can, we will make our priorities social: industrial regeneration, education, health. Our message should have been, these are our priorities and, unlike the Conservatives, when elected we will work to deliver them. Instead of distinguishing between our priorities and theirs, we played the game in their half on tax, when we should have played it on their incompetence and the economy. We allowed ourselves to become defensive about our policies, instead of attacking the government for theirs.

Anyway, we failed to get a mood of change into the electorate. We looked defensive. It's always a problem with Labour, it's essentially a defensive movement.

DH: *What do you mean?*

Hall: Well, a lot of the time it's trying to hang on to things. Standards.

DH: *Yes, that's an irony of Thatcherism. She made conservatives of us all. We all found ourselves defending institutions which previously we would have had no time for, because those institutions were better than barbarism.*

Hall: We were up against Tories who were completely disciplined. Not over three weeks, and not always amongst themselves. But what always united them were their attacks on Labour. They never let a chance go by.

DH: *Kinnock says, 'We preach solidarity: they practise it.'*

Hall: Yes. They just banged on about three things: tax, extremists in the wings, and the deficiencies of Neil Kinnock. They gave the same answer regardless of the question. Whereas in the Labour Party we do still have some touching belief that elections should involve engaging in real debate.

DH: *If, as we say, Kinnock wasn't getting across, why didn't he just stop the campaign and rethink?*

Hall: He was locked into it. He couldn't stop. You've seen how hard he works.

DH: *But, hold on. John Major stopped his. Halfway through we know he decided he had a disaster on his hands and he over-ruled his advisers and changed direction. Why didn't Neil?*

Hall: Because he was tearing round the country, he was writing every word of his speeches. The time wasn't built in. If only he'd been at the strategy meetings every morning – because he is a brilliant strategist.

DH: *There is a strange parallel between Neil Kinnock and John Major. They both seem to stand on a platform of 'What you see is what you get'.*

Hall: But Major is a politician, first and foremost. I mean, some of the lines, like in that election broadcast – 'from Coldharbour Lane to Number Ten', when he's looking out for that house, and says 'Is it there? Is it there? It's there!' I mean, please! Neil would never allow that by. He wants to be more than a politician. He writes and writes. It's a mania. His attitude is: it's got to be me.

DH: *What do you think of the people who blame Sheffield for your defeat?*

Hall: What depresses me is not that the press misrepresented Sheffield, but that so many people in the Labour movement are now willing to buy the press's account of it.

DH: *Yes. The point of Sheffield was the audience. The disenfranchized. That's what made it so moving.*

Hall: Yes, exactly. In politics you have to remember what you're there for. To represent the people. Neil always did.

Neil Stewart

It was still difficult to get to see Neil Stewart. He postponed our meeting several times because he was still so busy trying to organize an orderly handover of power to John Smith. When we did finally meet in the tea-room at the House of Commons, he was feeling depressed. 'Delayed reaction, I suppose.'

Neil Stewart: I think we lost over a three-year period, from 1989. We never finished the other side of Meet the Challenge, Make the Change. That was when I joined Neil's office. Neil said his main assistant, Charles Clarke, was doing eleven things, and that he wanted me to do five of them: Liaison with the Labour Party, the Conference, the NEC; dealing with by-elections; and, lastly, trouble.

DH: *Meaning?*

Stewart: Reselections. I'm not just unpopular with the Left. A lot of the Right don't care much for me either. The Labour Party puts things to the vote. The Parliamentary Party is experienced enough to know that many votes resolve nothing and are meaningless and divisive. The NEC would vote on every leaflet. The CLPs and the conferences test their courage on votes. So that's where I come in. Persuasion, arm-twisting and so on – the black arts.

DH: *Why did you lose eventually?*

Stewart: Because the public finally didn't trust us with their money. And there were two reasons. Partly Neil's public image and partly the policies. Neil was in a very difficult position because he knew his image was part of the problem.

DH: *And why was that?*

Stewart: I don't recall hearing many of the politicians around him, except Hattersley, ever talk Neil's leadership up in public. Roy is an old fashioned Labour loyalist, disciplined to talk up and support the party Leader. He understood that you have to build the leadership. The others were too mean to do it.

DH: *Was that from a sense of intellectual superiority?*

Stewart: In some cases.

DH: *They accepted the media's version of him?*

Stewart: Accepted and fed it. There was always resentment that the leadership had jumped a generation. Neil had that resentment from the start.

DH: *Do you think that sort of thing is endemic to socialist politics?*

Stewart: We are instinctively anti-leadership. Labour is the dissident party and the activists are the deviants within that. The party has often had splits. Deference plays little part. But it was the lack of internal discipline which was fatal. Some of our people were exhausted after four weeks of campaigning! I wanted to say to them, Neil started eight years ago, he's been flat out for eight years of incredible physical effort. And it's because other people wouldn't make that kind of effort that now they're travelling on the red buses when they could be in nice red Rovers. Some have only themselves to blame.

DH: *Did you believe in Labour's industrial plan?*

Stewart: Absolutely. We would have encouraged investment. People say the City wouldn't work with us, but it's finally pragmatic, it makes things work when they have to. Certainly some fast money would have gone, but so what? A lot of it was gone already, a week earlier. The market would have had to cope. And the advantage of the ERM was that our allies in the EC are obliged to help. That strength would have given us protection.

DH: *But finally it looks as if yet again you lost the election on the question of tax.*

Stewart: That's right. People felt insecure about change. The campaign advisers had warned everyone they would. The politicians said, we don't want to get into the tax area, because we can't beat the Tories there. But we kept saying you have to change, or you are going to lose the bloody election. As one of those advisers I don't reproach myself. I don't lacerate myself about failure. We did what we could. We proposed changes, they were rejected, and we know exactly how we lost.

DH: *Are you saying defeat could have been avoided?*

Stewart: What happened was the Tories went after us last September on a sort of trial run. They hit us on two issues: tax and Kinnock. And we fought back. I think they were trying to kick the door open for a possible autumn election, and if Major had gone then, he could have got in with a much larger majority. But he lost his nerve. After that we argued that the economic team had to change its tax package. We talked a lot about presentation, and about green taxes, but Smith and Brown's advisers said green taxes would be inflationary, and the change would make us look slippery, so we chickened out. So we got all we could and Neil went on campaigning in London, the Midlands and the North-west from September on. And if you look, that's where we picked up almost all our extra seats.

DH: *So what went wrong?*

Stewart: The economic team needed to be out there selling the industrial policies with the same passion as Neil. Instead they spent too much time with the City. I've no doubt they had very civilized debates, but the City Tories aren't bloody civilized. They're not frightened to fight, and fight hard. And Tory backbenchers are the same. They interrupt Neil in the Chamber, howl him down every time he opens his mouth. Some of our backbenchers are great heroes in private, but when we send them into the Chamber, they fade in the face of the Tories.

DH: *If you knew the election was slipping away from you, why didn't you try and regroup?*

Stewart: We did, but without any great big crisis meetings. There's a myth that meetings solve problems. They don't resolve anything. Neil was getting constant feedback from Charles and me and others. We are purveyors of opinions, and as such are often deeply, deeply resented. But we do it accurately. So by Monday night, Neil knew it was slipping away. We knew the vote was weakening, so it was decided to keep banging away at our strengths – health and the economy. But for some reason the broadcast media had switched off and decided the election was over. So we got no real TV coverage. This was a disaster for us, because eleven million people were still undecided and the tabloids had gone on the attack.

DH: *Why did your campaign fizzle out in exactly the same way it did in 1987?*

Stewart: I don't think it was the same. This time our campaign wasn't reported. That weekend we seemed far ahead. Oh, people always say there's an ideal position, just behind and coming through like Sebastian Coe, but in fact in politics there's only one place to be. In front. All the time. That weekend the Tories concentrated on stopping the haemorrhage to the Liberals. And they did that by talking about money, and only money. But it wouldn't have succeeded if our appeal hadn't had an underlying weakness in the first place. Neil was seriously worried from Monday night on. He saw the tabloids and they were very hard-hitting. And we had nothing in reply, except the broadcast media, and they had given up reporting. They were taking the weekend's polls, which still had us ahead, and behaving like it was over. That's what did us. Not Sheffield or anything like that. What horrified me was a Tuesday night news story: a story about Major on his bus and what a nice man he was. It was just colour, it was a magazine piece, and it was appearing as news. Yet our press conferences, which were really good on health, were getting no real coverage at all.

DH: *Where were you on the day itself?*

Stewart: I was in London. I'd been preparing all week for what would happen with a hung Parliament, organizing to get the keys to Number Ten. I was setting up an office in the St James Hotel where we could be secure from the media circus while any constitutional discussion went on, if Major refused to move out, but still able to brief the press on our view. You see, I didn't think we'd lose absolutely. None of us ever thought we'd get 326. But I still thought 296. Even after the exit polls. Even at six o'clock that evening, they still showed a hung parliament. Our worst hours at the polls were between six and ten in the evening. That's when we really got clobbered.

DH: *Has Neil been depressed since?*

Stewart: No, he has kept us all going. He lets his emotions out. Sometimes it horrifies tight-arsed Scots like me. We're the ones who go along, never show a flicker of feeling, then drop down dead from a heart attack. Neil lets his feelings show. He has nothing to reproach himself with. He gave 100 per cent. He saved the careers of politicians all around him. A lot of people say he shouldn't have needed an office like us around to do the work, to compensate for Walworth Road. And of course they're right, but someone had to force the pace.

DH: *What will you do now?*

Stewart: I don't know. Remember, I was once an NUS president. It's the best training ground for rejection you'll ever get. Someone was saying to me the other day, 'Oh, I don't think I'll stand for election. I couldn't stand the rejection.' I wanted to say, I've had a political lifetime of rejection.

Neil Kinnock

I met Neil Kinnock for lunch with his wife, Glenys, in a friend's garden. It was the first warm day of spring, and we sat in shirtsleeves drinking good white wine, and letting the English sun reach us for the first time that year.

Kinnock: I was in a terrible situation for the full eight years I was Leader. For all the time, I was trying to get the party back to respectability. Now respectability is something that I think belongs somewhere in the fourth division of political virtues. It was totally ridiculous, but I had to make it an ideal. I was always frightened there would be a reversion to the old ways of the Labour Party, and sure enough, in the leadership election, there has been. I've heard each person put their own recipe and their own point of view, but not one of them has said, 'Vote for me because I can beat the Tories.' The Labour Party is full of superior people who can't be bothered to work out how to beat the Tories. Of course, once Smithy gets in it will be easier. Things won't be as hard. They'll never be as hard as they were.

DH: *I want to talk to you about how you seemed to be during the election.*

Kinnock: How did I seem to be?

DH: *Angry.*

Kinnock: That's right.

DH: *Do you remember one day you came in and said to me you wanted one of the splat guns the kids have in* Bugsy Malone?

Kinnock: (*Laughs*) Yes, I did.

DH: *Pow-pow to the whole room.*

Kinnock: That's right. And in the last few weeks, during this leadership contest, I've been angrier still. There's been one leadership candidate who has been sounding off about what went wrong with our election effort. But he doesn't dare to come out and put his criticisms to me in person. They're always scared to. They conduct all their campaigns through the press, that's what's so damaging . . .

DH: *This whole question of splits is so odd. Everything you do in Labour politics is to avoid seeming to be split.*

Kinnock: That's right, all the time, it's essential . . .

DH: *Yet the Tories were split on Europe throughout the election and they're allowed to get away with it.*

Kinnock: Yes, but the media in this country can basically be relied on to back them up in good times and not to make things bad when times get hard. I know people think it's weak to blame the media for everything, but they do determine the environment of politics. I know it seems like alibi hunting, but for the Labour Party all the trails trace back to the media, because at any point, if there is the slightest difference between any of us, they can point to the terrible damage of the past. The Labour movement has one basic fault. It denounces the capitalist press on one hand and yet on the other it accepts what it reads in it. This is a terrible self-inflicted weakness among us. That, and a great deal of vanity.

DH: *Presumably you'd thought there'd be a hung Parliament?*

Kinnock: We all did. But of course you don't win during the campaign itself. After all the years, after all my work, the fact is we were further behind than I thought. I'd always thought it would be a two-innings game. I was wrong. This is a three-innings match.

DH: *When did you first realize you were in trouble?*

Kinnock: I knew the Tuesday before that we were going to lose. The previous week I'd warned about something called the Brecon effect. You get too good an opinion poll lead and the people are suddenly scared you really are going to get in. The Wednesday before the last week we were seven points ahead. From then on I could feel the shift.

DH: *But your campaign problems started earlier?*

Kinnock: They started on the Monday we announced our tax proposals. The announcement happened, then the plan was we should push it like hell, Smithy doing his Scottish doctor act. By Wednesday I was alarmed because we did a good launch but he wasn't on TV every day really pushing it. I had a weekend meeting with him a week later and said, 'You've got to get out there.' But he didn't get the coverage.

DH: *Were you at odds about the actual tax policy?*

Kinnock: It was not so much the policy as how late it arrived – the week of the Budget – our deciding what it should be, whether to raise National Insurance and so on, and I was thinking, this is ridiculous, this election has been coming for a long time, it's not been suddenly sprung on us, and here we are deciding the policy at the last moment. On one or two occasions it was necessary to let my irritation show. Not enough of the bloody work had been done.

DH: *You'd set up the economic unit because after 1987 you'd presumably decided that tax was the most important thing for Labour . . .*

Kinnock: Absolutely. By all the indicators, Labour governments are more successful than Tory ones at what's called managing the economy. That's a fact. They have a much better record. But all the time you are fighting the impression that Labour government means fiscal blunders. So that's what I set out to counter this time.

DH: *Do you feel let down by the people around you? I mean the Shadow Cabinet . . .*

Kinnock: No, no, no, no, no, no . . .

DH: *Reading your speeches from those eight years, they climax in the mid- to late eighties, then in the last two years there's a bit of a rhetorical falling-off.*

Kinnock: Yes, the party thought it had reformed itself so I had to make a judgement, and I decided I couldn't go on chastizing them and chasing them, when they themselves felt they were a model of good behaviour. I was a bit lost for a message in those last two years because the reforms had put us ahead, the poll tax put us in a wonderful position and I tried to say, 'Don't take it for granted.' But of course, that's not a very powerful message.

DH: *You were constrained even then?*

Kinnock: I never was sure the whole party was with me. I was always dragging it inch by inch, advancing a little, fighting more, advancing. I had to choose my ground so carefully. The memories of the early eighties were so powerful. I had to face the fact I was dealing with a circumspect country. If I'd been more adventurous, I would have opened my flank. You see in a game, the flash of genius, the unprepared charge can do something. It can do something for a while. But in politics, conducted as Labour politics is in hostile territory, you never know when you'll hit mud, or a cliff-face. And dare just once to be brilliant and you may find you've failed and used your best shot. Unless you secure everyone's consent, you re-open the problems of the Left, and people say, 'Ah yes, the real Labour Party is coming through again.' You have only one chance to make one thrust. Lose once and I would have lost everything. I had to be careful all the time. People say, 'Well, you only ended up with 35 per cent of the vote – what did you have to lose?' My answer is: Some of that 35 per cent.

DH: *Do you feel at all let down by the voters?*

Kinnock: After thirty years in politics, I am shocked when I see a divergence between a politician's public image and his private face. And I hate it when politicians are cynical about the public.

DH: *But you must have mixed feelings about the people. After the last three results . . .*

Kinnock: The people let themselves down. They went into the polling booth and voted to stab their own grandparents and children in the chest. But I don't hate them for it. You'd go mad if you hated the public.

DH: *Do you recognize the charge that you got very isolated over the years? That your private office blocked you from access to people?*

Kinnock: I can't stand this idea that I was prisoner of a group. Any mistakes I made were mine and mine alone. It was said by some that I wasn't seeing enough people. It wasn't true. The door was always open. But MPs actually didn't want to see me because when they came with their complaints, I used to tell them to sod off. I'd tell them, if that's all you've got to cry about, then frankly you haven't got enough to do.

DH: *To MPs? You're hard on MPs.*

Kinnock: I think we should be. Nobody conscripted them, they get paid, they are there to be activists and to win. They have the right to complain of course. But not to whinge.

DH: *Why didn't the changes you made bear more fruit?*

Kinnock: Change is a risk. There are benefits from making changes but it's not all gain. It doesn't matter when non-politicians change their minds, but when politicians and parties do, it can have a credit or a debit effect. It's very dangerous, because to change is to invite the charge of inconsistency.

DH: *But this is at the centre of your problems, isn't it?*

Kinnock: Yes.

DH: *The public won't accept a public debate which is genuine. I mean, did you consider letting on to the public the true and disastrous state of the economy?*

Kinnock: We couldn't. Too risky, you see. First, I would have been accused of talking Britain down. Second, it would have made an already cautious electorate more cautious. 'Oh, if things are that bad,' they'd say, 'we can't risk Labour.' It would have rebounded. I can never, never use the word crisis. You see, in many ways the recession itself worked against us. It was in part our fault. We hadn't worked long enough. You mustn't just work hard in politics, you must work long as well.

DH: *It must be hard being back, having to live out these last weeks as Leader of the Opposition.*

Kinnock: The Tories have been so lucky, they can't believe their luck. I look at them and think, 'With luck like yours, there's nothing between you and eternity.'

OFF THE RECORD

Through the three months which followed the election, I became as fascinated as the participants themselves by all the extended post-mortems on why Labour lost. A number of people spoke to me with the most extraordinary freedom, and at the most extraordinary length, often spending hours trying out explanations on me which were sometimes economic, sometimes political, but most often psychological. People who had taken no notice of my presence during the campaign were now turning to me, as if somehow my jotted record of their deliberations might provide the clue they were missing to events they still could not understand. There was the usual evidence from private polling. Tory surveys, taken as people left the polling booths, showed that the two most popular reasons given for not voting Labour were the threat of tax-rises, and distrust of Neil Kinnock's personality. Yet for most of those who had taken part, these explanations did not seem enough. There were contradictions. Kinnock was apparently admired as a campaigner, liked as a man, but distrusted as a potential prime minister. Most people I interviewed were in a sort of grief. Few who had worked with him spoke of Kinnock without tears appearing in their eyes. The impact of his personal tragedy – which was, a year later, to turn him into a sort of national hero – mixed with an infuriating sense of lost opportunity.

Adviser: Nobody but us knows what a campaign is like. What you actually go through. God, nobody knows! It's unbelievable. You remember Black Friday?
DH: *The day Neil came storming in because the dossier had been released?*
Adviser: Yes. And Robin Cook wanted to apologize! Apologize, for Christ's sake! In an election campaign!
DH: *I know.*
Adviser: Why do you think that was?
DH: *Well, I've heard a theory that Cook was shaken after Monmouth . . .*
Adviser: That's right . . .
DH: *He'd taken so much abuse from the tabloids because he went to Monmouth and said the Tories were going to privatize the NHS.*
Adviser: It's true. What no one understands is, Robin was under terrible pressure because there had been a systematic campaign in the tabloids to destroy him. What no politician understands is how the press works. They think it has something to do with reality. And it doesn't. They put out a press release and it gets a good response in the press. Then they put out another and it gets a bad response. AND THEY ACTUALLY THINK IT HAS SOMETHING TO DO WITH THE PRESS RELEASE ITSELF!
DH: *I know.*
Adviser: They don't understand. The arguments against us were prepared in advance. They were ready. The Tories were prepared to attack Jennifer's Ear before it even went out. They would have said what they said, regardless. Yet our people persist in believing it's a reasoned reaction. It's chess, for God's sake. You move your

pieces, they move theirs. It isn't *sense*. We fatally let it slip because we backed off instead of advancing after Jennifer's Ear.

No two people I talked to had the same theories about what exactly had gone wrong. Most people involved, including the politicians themselves, were contemptuous of John Prescott's over-easy diagnosis that the public had been turned off by the packaging and the glitz. There was more substance to the charge that the politicians had too readily deferred to their unelected advisers. I had certainly watched over and over as politicians skulked in corners, drinking the poison of the opinion polls. But this was hardly the advisers' fault. If, as they afterwards claimed, the Labour candidates had ignored their own instincts about what attitudes they were meeting on the street, then the politicians had no one but themselves to blame. The idle assumption that public relations is of itself necessarily a bad thing seemed to offer too easy an alibi. The problem was the parcel, not the wrapping.

Nowhere was the role of advisers more contentious than in the decision to raise the issue of proportional representation in the last week. It was Patricia Hewitt who had argued most forcefully for sending out conciliatory signals about PR to voters who were thinking of choosing the Liberal Democrats, and it was she who was most bitterly attacked by insiders in the following months. PR had been picked up carelessly and far too late, not because the Party had a coherent commitment to it, but because it could, in the awful jargon of the day, 'soften its image to voters'. It had served as a disastrous distraction. While the headlines switched from the economy to PR, the Tories had made their famous late surge.

Of course, in private, a great many Labour supporters blamed an unbalanced and mendacious press for their downfall. Contemplating the tonnage of newspaper print produced about the election every morning, I had begun to conclude that after Mrs Thatcher's destruction of our manufacturing base, the only growth industry we had left in Britain was commentary. But, again, Labour's problems seemed to lie not with Labour's enemies, but with its own credulity.

DH: *Neil Kinnock says it is the Labour Party's greatest weakness that it secretly believes the Tory press.*

Second adviser: That is true. That is so true. Absolutely. Did Neil say that? That is absolutely . . . absolutely . . . absolutely true. He is absolutely right. It is not the press itself which is damaging. It is when your own party starts to believe what the press says.

DH: *But why did they?*

Second adviser: Because in many ways the party wasn't behind Neil.

DH: *Not just the party. I think one of the things that surprised and perhaps shocked me was that the Shadow Cabinet didn't seem to be putting as much into the election as Neil was.*

Second adviser: Looking back, the terrible thing is that everyone who fought this election has had their career advanced except Neil. Think of it in those terms. Labour people see their lives in terms of getting to the top of the Labour Party. Not government. Government's another world. And in those terms, everyone's done well. Whereas Conservatives have to be governing. There's no point for them unless they're in power. Our lot are as happy losing as winning.

DH: *You see, Kinnock's view is that the Party didn't really want to be modernized . . .*

Second adviser: That is so true. So true.

DH: *They did it reluctantly and gave him no credit for it.*

Second adviser: That's absolutely right. It's like when your wife's driving and she says, 'I'm going this way'. And you say, OK, I'll go along with it. But you know it won't work. But you agree to it. Just waiting for it to fuck up. The Labour Party supported change in the same way as I support Graham Taylor as manager of the England team. I don't believe in him, but I say, OK, OK for now. It's exactly the same! I go with it for now, but, my God, how great it will be when we lose!

DH: *But you're not blaming the Parliamentary Party for the defeat?*

Second adviser: No, no. In the last couple of years there was nothing to take the project forward. Thatcher goes, and we are reduced to tactically reacting. That's the problem. Labour loses its voice. From 1990 onwards, what's the message? Do you know? What does the Labour Party stand for? Do you have any idea? I keep asking round this time, 'Now come on, tell me, please, what message do we have?' People wanted to know how voting Labour would improve their lives. And we didn't tell them.

DH: *I suppose what's oddest to me is that after 1987 you knew the one thing you had to do was win the economic argument. You had to make people trust you with their money.*

Second adviser: I don't know we could have done anything. It should be enough to hold the lead in the polls. And we did. We planned all the time for our worst case. We tried to stop the women and the C2s going away. But the problem was, finally, the don't knows moved *en masse* to the Tories. There was a limit to what we could do. Given the cards we had, we made the best of them. We gave them all the encouragement they needed to vote Labour, and finally they didn't. They couldn't bring themselves to, because they believe Labour is outdated and doesn't understand modern aspirations. Are you a Labour supporter?

DH: *Yes.*

Second adviser: Well, I know it is very hard for supporters to understand that to many people the word 'Labour' appears to belong to the past.

Many questions about the campaign remained unresolved. But nothing puzzled me more than some of the questions about Kinnock's own behaviour. For myself, I had come to see him as an angry man who was not allowed to express himself. But one of his closest advisers challenged this idea.

Third adviser: Why do you think Neil was angry?

DH: *Because he was tied in. He couldn't be himself.*

Third adviser: Rubbish! Absolute rubbish! This is the great myth. The whole myth is that there was once a real Neil Kinnock. But Kinnock was always the most suburban man you will ever meet. He always was. He was always cautious. Being cautious is what suited him. The only reason he was angry was because he was fucking it up. No other reason. He hadn't smothered his own personality.

DH: *But surely he was angry because he couldn't say what he wanted. Say, on electoral reform.*

Third adviser: No, no, no, no. There is no *other* Neil Kinnock. There is only the one we have seen in the last few years. A Labour leader has to address three groups at once: the Party, the public, and the tabloid press. And that is an almost impossible balancing act. So he became very angry at his own failure. Many of us said to him, don't just stay there being angry. If you're angry, go.

DH: *You said that?*

Third adviser: Some people did. It's like at the moment, I'm angry that we lost. So I take it out on my wife. Every night. Yet I'm happy in my anger. I don't act on it. I don't think it through and think, OK, I'll leave her. I want the best of both worlds. Sit in the middle and be angry. It's not good. I've done a lot of transactional analysis, and we have here two games. Neil's game was IT'S A MESS: THEN DO SOMETHING OR GO: I WON'T. The Party's game was I WON'T GET RID OF HIM BUT I WON'T SUPPORT HIM. David, they are both losing games.

DH: *So you don't accept the idea he was trapped?*

Third adviser: The only thing that trapped Neil was Neil.

But whatever Kinnock's state of mind, one strategic decision in particular continued to bother me. Why, if Kinnock genuinely believed he was going to lose the election, did he not stop halfway through and conduct exactly the kind of reassessment of his own performance which appeared to bring John Major such improved results?

Fourth adviser: The problem of speeches really summed up Neil's difficulties. You must remember, Neil was a great orator, the best I've ever heard. When in 1983 he made the great 'I warn you' speech ('If Margaret Thatcher wins on Thursday, I warn you not to be ordinary; I warn you not to be young; I warn you not to fall ill; I warn you not to get old'), then I tell you, it raised the hairs on my neck. But he then had a problem. The Leader of the Labour Party has to make at least seven major speeches a year. And Neil was absolutely determined that every single word of them should be his own. Other people would do drafts for him, and he would be uncomfortable with the words he was given, he would at once want to rephrase them himself. And an absolutely disproportionate amount of his time as Leader would be spent writing speeches. We used to dread it. We used to think, oh God, there's another speech coming up. Because every time he was working on a speech, we couldn't get anything else done.

DH: *I see. And during the election . . .*

Fourth Adviser: Well, during the election, he actually made only five major speeches.

DH: *Why was that?*

Fourth adviser: I don't think he had a great deal left to say. That was the real thing. We'd been in opposition a terribly long time. That is a major factor. We had said all the things you can say in opposition. We couldn't really find any new ways to say them. There was a plan that he should go barnstorming round the country in the last week of the campaign. But he wouldn't do it. He said he was too tired. And it's true, his voice was going. Just physically, it would have been hard. But also – I don't know . . . the fact is, he was worded out.

DH: *That's very sad.*

Fourth adviser: Yes.

DH: *You see, I watched the campaign, and let's say, well, there were various obvious weaknesses of organization and of rhetoric. They were obvious. Perhaps, as you say, simply because you'd all been waiting so long. But I never for a second doubted that if you'd got into government, you would have been transformed. I felt all your weaknesses would have turned into strengths.*

Fourth adviser: Absolutely. That's right. And we were so close! On the Monday the Cabinet Secretary – Robin Butler – was so sure that we'd won that he approached Jo Richardson and told her where he was going to put our Ministry for Women.

DH: *Some people seem to think it's the word Labour which is outdated. That the word itself depresses people.*

Fourth adviser: Yes. Well, most of what we say, people agreed with. But they don't agree with it when it's us that says it.

The exasperatingly low self-esteem of this last remark perhaps typifies the tone Labour insiders favoured in reviewing their defeat in the 1992 election. It was a tone I grew used to. After four successive Conservative victories, it was all too understandable. And yet, for me – the man who had not been through it, the man who had simply sat and observed – I admit there was a different sadness, and one which, even a year later, still marks my memory of this period. I did find myself wishing, in the awful aftermath of those days, that Labour had done more to tell the truth.

I am not so naive as to imagine that bolder tactics would necessarily have brought victory. (No-one contemplating the avalanche of mealy-mouthed, foreign-financed, word-weaselling disinformation which passed for the overall Tory campaign could believe for a moment that truth-telling is, in itself, a guarantee of electoral prosperity.) But on the other hand, a party that has convinced itself it will seem unpatriotic and alarmist if it tells the public the true state of the economy – a party that believes it is *not in its own interests* to stress the gravity of the crisis the country is passing through – seems to me to be one which is not just having chronic problems of self-confidence, but one which has become hopelessly implicated in the shortcomings of the government it is there to oppose. Its leader had, on his own admission, made a pact with respectability. It had been, in its own way, a tragically necessary pact to make. Yet, at the end, he had felt cruelly defeated by the fact that he had got himself, on various issues, into a situation where he did not feel free to express his own point of view. It was not only the fear of being accused of 'talking Britain down' that hobbled his attacks on the Tory economy. When, in the last week, schoolchildren laughed at him on TV for refusing to say whether he personally did or didn't believe in Proportional Representation, then Kinnock himself knew that he had paid a terrible price for the pact he had made.

Last adviser: If Peter Mandelson had been there, we'd have got another point. Or two. But the key dynamic was, the better Labour did, the more reaction there was against them. But on the other hand, eight years ago, the party was unelectable. Now it is saved.

DH: *Do you think it'll win again?*

Last adviser: All over the world, Left parties don't do well. If you work on the Left, you lose. I'm thinking of going to Australia. We'll lose there. Very few elections does the Left win. In one part of yourself, you know that, but it doesn't help. I think about it all the time. Every day. I've known the overwhelming horror of defeat. I feel I can cope with anything. One percentage point. Getting Neil in would have been wonderful. It would have shaken the whole bloody country. Getting John Smith in won't be the same.

DH: *I don't know why you do it.*

Last adviser: Peter Mandelson managed to get out. He's an MP now. He's 36, so his turn will come. There will be one Labour government in the next twenty years and he will be in it.

DH: *Maybe. Maybe this Tory government will fuck up faster than you think.*

Last adviser: It's funny. If you add all this together, we could probably have got them out. A hung Parliament. If we had, it would have bucked history. People didn't want a Labour government, but they nearly got one.

Peter Mandelson's Party

21 July 1992

As summer came and I continued my interviews, John Smith duly succeeded to the Leadership of the Labour Party. I had arranged to meet Peter Mandelson in his house at the back of Sadler's Wells. In all the conversations I had had, both with politicians and with party workers, Mandelson had been spoken of as the missing element in the 1992 election effort. At some point, almost everyone I interviewed paused to regret his absence from this particular campaign and to attribute to him a strategic acumen which might just have made that vital difference.

It was the end of the parliamentary session, and as I arrived, Mandelson was making preparations for a last party before everyone scattered for the holidays. As the waiters set about putting up tables, we moved out to the park opposite, where we were joined by Sue Nye, who had been Neil Kinnock's political secretary and closest confidante for many years. By now, enough time had passed for them to settle into their new lives. Mandelson had become MP for Hartlepool. Sue Nye had cleared out the office in which she had worked for eight years and was considering a job organizing a big charity event.

As Mandelson sat giving me his version of the events of Neil Kinnock's leadership, he would occasionally get up, either to check whether the wine had arrived, or to go and supervise the decoration of the rooms. When he was gone, Sue Nye sat on the park bench beside me, chewing gum obsessively, often gazing into the distance in silence, still stung by the memory of the defeat.

Gradually, as we talked, politicians began to arrive, looking rather like the plain-clothes CID men I had seen in Clapham Police Station. Casually dressed, they looked curiously ill at ease. Tony Blair appeared, wearing tight black jeans and a cowboy shirt. Gordon Brown was in a conspicuously casual suit. One by one, nearly everyone with whom I had spent that extraordinary month began to assemble, but now in the company of their husbands or wives.

Inside, I was told that the guests of honour were the Kinnocks. Neil had given up the leadership the previous day, and it was Mandelson's generous instinct to assemble all his old friends to reassure Kinnock that even though he had left the office, their affection for the man himself remained.

But the atmosphere was sticky, formal, subdued. People were standing in uncomfortable knots, not able to get past the first cocktail stage. Having talked briefly about the latest political scandal – a Conservative minister and his girlfriend, as it happened – and told each other where we were going on our holidays, nobody seemed to be able to think of much to say.

Then from the doorway there came the sound of the Kinnocks arriving. You could hear the vitality from down the corridor. The man whom we were meant to be consoling was laughing, greeting us one by one, giving us the energy we were supposed to be giving him.

Neil and Glenys came in, the party warmed and a glow came over the room.

AFTERWORD

On any project of this scale, an author must accumulate debts of gratitude which cannot be properly repaid. My most heartfelt thanks must of course go to all those individuals who originally agreed either to be interviewed or to be observed at work for all three plays. Over and again, I was touched by the extraordinary generosity with which I was received.

After them, first among equals, comes the editor of this book, Lyn Haill, who with the help of Liz Curry has mastered and reduced the much larger amount of material from which this book is drawn. For each play I was helped by research assistants: Caroline Wilson for *Racing Demon*, Chrissy Skinns and Sophie Milton for *Murmuring Judges*, and Sue Powell for *The Absence of War*. I would not have had such free access to the Church without the help of its press officer, John Miles. During the writing of *Murmuring Judges*, Bernard Simons, Ben Hytner QC and Mary Tuck were a formidable team to deal with any question I had about the British Criminal Justice System. Bernie's death, just before the completion of this book, was a terrible sadness. The third play, *The Absence of War*, would not have been possible unless Neil Kinnock had been so trusting and open towards it. The book itself has been edited at Faber by Tracey Scoffield.

The realization of the trilogy at the National Theatre was in the hands of a team: Richard Eyre (Director), Bob Crowley (Designer), Mark Henderson (Lighting), Richard Hartley and George Fenton (Music) and Trish Montemuro (Stage Management). Mark Douet took the documentary photographs which were such a striking feature of the settings, and John Haynes took brilliant production photographs. Unusually, the production team met together so that the design and staging were integrated into my ideas before I even started writing. As I delivered each script, I relied heavily on the National Theatre's literary advisers, Giles Croft and, most especially, Nicholas Wright. Many of my friends who would be embarrassed to be named gave me their ideas on various drafts. I was also greatly helped by readings at the National's Studio.

The trilogy would have been impossible without the outstanding skill and encouragement of Richard Eyre. He has been its producer, its director, and its literary midwife. Its development over such a long period also depended on the loyalty and dedication of an outstanding team of actors. It was the memory of their excellence which at all times inspired me to keep writing.